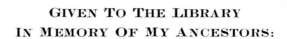

Given To The Library
In Memory Of My Ancestors:

George W. Moyer
1825-1900 LYKENS-VALLEY VIEW
AND HIS WIFE

Caroline Shade Moyer
1821-1881 GRATZ-VALLEY VIEW
AND THEIR SON

David Shade Moyer, M. D.
1852-1928 LYKENS-VALLEY VIEW-
FRIEDENSBURG-DONALDSON
AND HIS WIFE

Fietta Reed Moyer
1856-1944 HEGINS-VALLEY VIEW-
FRIEDENSBURG-DONALDSON

BY

David George Moyer
MOYER'S BOOK BARN
1419 VILLAGE ROAD
STRASBURG, PENNSYLVANIA 17579-9625

In Good Conscience

IN GOOD CONSCIENCE

Reason and Emotion
in Moral Decision Making

Sidney Callahan

HarperSanFrancisco
A Division of HarperCollins*Publishers*

FIRST EDITION

Library of Congress Cataloging-in-Publication Data

Callahan, Sidney.
    In good conscience : reason and emotion in moral decision making /
Sidney Callahan.—1st ed.
        p.   cm.
    Includes bibliographical references.
    ISBN 0-06-061292-4 (alk. paper)
    1. Conscience—Religious aspects—Catholic Church. 2. Catholic
Church—Doctrines. 3. Christian ethics—Catholic authors.
I. Title.
BJ1278.C66C35 1991
241'.1—dc20   89-46467
                                                  CIP

91   92   93   94   95   HAD   10 9 8 7 6 5 4 3 2 1

This edition is printed on acid-free paper that meets the American National Standards Institute Z39.48 Standard.

Contents

Introduction

Why Write About Conscience and Individual Moral Decision Making?

As the twenty-first century rolls in, our world is being turned upside down. The new era arrives full of surprises. After a series of revolutionary developments in Europe, the United States Congress was addressed by Vaclav Havel, the new playwright-president of Czechoslovakia. Having suffered for years in and out of prison because of his moral beliefs, Havel offered some wisdom learned from experience:

> The specific experience I'm talking about has given me one certainty: consciousness precedes being, and not the other way around, as the Marxists claim. For this reason the salvation of this human world lies nowhere else than in the human heart, in the human power to reflect, in human meekness and in human responsibility.[1]

This clear call for moral conversion comes with a general realization that, yes, a plethora of different developments is producing "the concurrent horror and excitement of geometrically accelerating culture."[2] Not only are political developments in both East and West provoking internal policy reassessments and realignments, but new understandings in science and technology are forcing us into new collective decisions. Even more challenging is the question of our moral readiness for the new era upon us. What is our current moral condition, or the state of that "consciousness which precedes being?" How fares "the human heart," or "the human power to reflect?" I write this book on conscience and moral decision making to begin to explore these questions.

A debate now rages over the moral state of our culture. Many observers see our society as rapidly slipping into moral decline, if not already entering terminal collapse in a new Dark Age. Book after book, on and off the best-seller lists, warns of our perilous moral state. The American mind is closing, or exists as a rootless, homeless mind. The family is disintegrating, men are infantile, women love too much and lead lesser lives—almost everyone is addicted, dysfunctional, and

1

codependent. More ominously, our children are unhealthy, ill-educated, morally unsocialized, and regularly abused as rampant narcissism deforms our habits of the heart.[3]

A bleak picture is drawn of a floundering society that is morally disintegrating. Evidence of the pervasive moral decay is found in the increase of drugs, violence, crime, sexual disease, divorce, abortion, and political corruption in the greedy pursuit of hedonistic goals. Our moral apathy and irresponsibility are seen to increase the probabilities of ecological and nuclear disasters. Whether we would call this a moral recession or a great depression, there is a widespread feeling that our culture has lost its moral backbone and is sinking into a moral slough of despond. Many perceive our society as rapidly depleting moral capital accrued by our more morally upright forebears.

Are these jeremiads true? Are we dooming ourselves by the general decay of conscience and moral character? I doubt the diagnosis. It is good to remember that decline-and-fall prophecies featuring moral collapse have been perennial standbys of popular cultural criticism. Such scenarios induce the same sensations that make disaster movies so appealing. The *Titanic* sinks, the towering inferno topples, the world ends with a bang or a whimper—while we who watch in safety simultaneously agonize and celebrate our exemption from the catastrophe. So it is with predictions of moral debacle; fear and trembling over the end of Western civilization as we know it arouses and invigorates us. We can feel morally superior to the barbarians at the gate, or to those already empowered within the establishment. Pessimistic moral critique certifies our membership in the saved remnant of civilized enclaves.

Other more-optimistic observers of the current scene refuse to be stampeded into moral despair. The same signs and portents can be read differently, especially when we grant that nostalgia for some better, more morally ideal period in the past is illusory. Women, children, blacks, Native Americans, and other members of historically submerged populations might see Western history as having suffered from one prolonged bout of chronic moral illness. The symptoms may change over the centuries; one war gives way to another, alternating with oppressive regimes. If there never were any good old days, then the present and the future at least offer hope for positive changes amidst the social ferment.

Optimists can also point to our society's recent surge of interest in morality and ethics. Within the last twenty years, we have witnessed what can only be called an ethics and virtue explosion. (Ironically, pessimists can read this as *proof* of how bad things are.) Sanguine observers see a rise in moral consciousness reflected in burgeoning public discussions of ethics, morality, moral development, and moral education.

The revival of interest in morality, justice, virtue, and moral codes of behavior has been present in all professions and disciplines. At the forefront of the movement, however, is the emergence of bioethics as a new discipline. The moral awareness of society has been changed by the advent of new ethical dilemmas over heart transplants, kidney dialysis, abortion, neonatology, surrogate motherhood, the definition of death, and informed consent. Ethical consciousness and questioning have spread—even to Congress and politics. By now, no science, profession, business, or institutional practice is exempt from ethical scrutiny or controversy, complete with media coverage. The public has been particularly aroused by public scandals in which highly trusted, highly intelligent persons have been seen to lie, deceive, and cheat—without a moral qualm or an ounce of remorse.

The Watergate and Irangate ethical disasters, combined with new ethical dilemmas and new concerns over crime, drugs, and violence in the streets, have produced ascending spirals of public interest in morality—or lack of morality. What has happened to moral character, to moral self-governance, to conscience in the professions, in institutions, and in the general population? Has there been some breakdown in traditional moral socialization, or are we facing particularly stressful environmental social challenges, not yet recognized and addressed?

Proposals are now being put forth to reevaluate and renew moral education in the public schools, in the same way ethics courses have gradually been introduced in the curricula of institutions of higher and professional education. A new wind is blowing when Harvard Business School receives $30 million to establish an ethics program. In the trickle-down theory of educational influence, we should see more and more new programs begin across the country. Sharp debates have already ensued over the appropriate goals, purposes, methods, personnel, credentials, and budgets for these projects.

One of the perennial conflicts encountered in moral and ethical education is whether the primary goal is a greater proficiency in identifying moral issues and using the analytic methods of philosophical ethics, or the moral formation of better persons—or some ideal combination of the two. People who provide hard money usually want to produce better people, while professionals in the field hope at most to induce more sophisticated analytic skills and increased moral and ethical sensitivity. Some ethicists resist the popular identification of the ethical with the moral, but maintaining a subtle distinction between the two concepts seems a losing battle. In this book, I too will employ the overlapping terms "moral" and "ethical" as loosely synonymous.

The provision of moral and ethical education in an ideal program for any age group would produce an increased body of moral knowledge leading to better moral decision making. Unfortunately, we know more about how to teach moral principles and academic ethical analytic skills than we do about the moral formation of a good conscience in a good person. The roots of moral and immoral behavior in the individual are an old and deeply puzzling problem.

The newest cycle of attempts at moral and ethical education inevitably returns to the oldest questions concerning moral behavior. Plato built his famous dialogue around Meno's question, "Tell me, Socrates, can virtue be learned or taught?" This crucial query is still debated, along with its underlying assumptions and corollary questions. In what does the excellence of virtue consist, and why and how do individuals become morally virtuous?

Even in our cynical times, in the midst of our moral confusions, few deny the reality of virtue and moral goodness. The best-sellers and TV documentaries, when not investigating scandals, regularly feature accounts of morally heroic and altruistic deeds. Headlines depict example after example of uprightness of conscience and moral courage. We recognize moral heroes, exemplary ethical resisters, moral freedom fighters, and even moral saints. Moral heroism and altruism intrigue us almost as much as moral decline and decadence. We may have difficulties defining moral virtue, or intellectually defending the possibility of altruism, but we know it when we see it.

Particularly impressive to those of us who live in comfortable, affluent democratic societies are the accounts of activists and prisoners of conscience who are persecuted and jailed in totalitarian regimes. If such prisoners would just "give in" and compromise the dictates of their consciences, they could be released and return to normal life. They must make the decision over and over to be faithful to their moral convictions, sometimes through years of suffering and deprivation. We read of Natan Sharansky's refusal to be broken by the Russian KGB, Nien Cheng's triumphant resistance to her Communist captors, and Mandela's fortitude and unwavering commitment.[4]

A stream of edifying accounts comes from South America, Cuba, Korea, Northern Ireland, and, to our shame, from imprisoned peace and justice activists in United States prisons. How does a person develop and maintain an adherence to conscience in the face of intense deprivation, psychological pressure, persecution, and outright torture?

In recent revolutions, we have seen persons courageously give their lives for their principles. Solitary figures challenge tanks in China, and in country after country, people die in the streets for the cause of democratic freedom.

Why do these encounters of a moral kind, these contacts with moral heroes, inspire us? Whether in the day's news or in history, religion, and literature, do these deeds grip us because such stories represent only dreams, impossibly beyond our ken? Or are we moved because we see reproduced on a large scale the moral struggles of our everyday lives? I take the latter explanation to be the case. As ordinary people, we play out our moral dramas of conscience on a smaller stage. As bit players, we resonate to the momentous moral struggles and performances of the stars; we are strengthened by their stories of conflict, commitment, perseverance, and hope.

If the proverbial alien, ET, were to come afresh to the human scene, one of the major facts to be explained would be the multitude of persons trying so hard to be good—in the absence of external coercion. As morally socialized creatures, we tend to take for granted the successful operations of conscience in everyday life. Along with the intelligentsia and news media, we attend more to instances of moral failure. Of course, the observant alien, ET, would also be intrigued by the glaring moral aberrations of earthlings. Do the individuals in this species fail morally through ignorance, or do they deliberately choose to counteract what they know to be morally right? Perhaps there are forms of weakness that keep human beings from doing what they believe they should? The famous confession of St. Paul's anguish has reverberated down the centuries: "That which I wish to do, I do not, and that which I wish not to do, I do. Who will deliver me from this condition of death?" Where and why does this perennial experience of inner division and lack of personal moral integration emerge?

Admittedly, I too am drawn to wrestle with the question of conscience because I have been challenged by my own moral failures. These troubles are often correlated with other difficulties in making personal moral decisions. I have found it difficult to fully understand my own personal moral processes before, during, and after they occur. How did I decide on my moral position on abortion? Or then stick to it despite opposition? How do other people arrive at their moral positions, and how do they govern their moral lives? As a practicing academic, much in the company of ethical and religious professionals, I have regularly observed ethicists at work. Often, I see "the name and the game" of ethics to differ. What is professionally prescribed and what appears to be done can be at odds. This conflict between theoretical accounts and actual observed behavior engenders still more curiosity about the internal, subjective processes at play. My earlier engagements with psychology and ethics, moral development and decision making, have further prepared the ground for my project.[5]

In this book, I attempt to formulate and present a picture of the operating processes of conscience and moral decision making with a particular agenda—a view that emphasizes the self as moral agent. I try to give a picture that takes into account new psychological understandings of self, emotion, reason, intuition, problem solving, and developmental change. In this attempted synthesis, I emphasize those aspects of personal moral activity that have heretofore been less explored and articulated.

In the metaphorical description of human beings as made up of heart and mind, I am concentrating more on the heart's contributions to the moral life. I give a great deal of attention to emotion and intuition, as well as to the ways emotion and intuition interact with processes of moral reasoning. I am trying to gain more insight into what might be called the foundations, architecture, and inner ecology of conscience; this effort can be as important for practical moral understanding and nurturing of moral development as study of the content of formal ethical systems.

Focus of the Book

If we want to fully understand individual moral functioning, we have to balance considerations of the person who chooses, and how the choices are made, with considerations of philosophical and rational moral justifications for moral choices. Psychology and philosophy must complement each other in the study of morality, for it is the whole person who reasons and accepts or rejects moral arguments. When psychology has wrongly ignored the real power of free, rational moral agency and the force of reasoning and philosophical justifications in decision making, it has misread human experience. Similarly, an exclusive focus upon analytic methods of rational moral decision making and the content of arguments wrongly ignores the self who is inevitably informed and shaped by emotions, tacit personal knowledge, intuition, imagery, developmental history, and group experience. Either way, grave distortions appear. Taking account of the full range of human capacities is necessary to adequately understand and map moral functioning.

In embarking on this compelling but formidable project, I must venture into interdisciplinary and generalized discussions. Investigating moral functioning, with all its complexities and ramifications, forces the breakdown of traditional disciplinary boundaries. This book joins the increasing number of works appearing as "blurred genres,"[6] in which social science and the humanities blend—and in which personal knowledge and private experience are explicitly called upon to contribute to the study.

But in order to set some limits, I have not ventured into the sea of theological argumentation underlying and surrounding the topic of morality. Religious perspectives on conscience arise from historical traditions that require distinct and full treatments, complete with expositions of the theological foundations and historical evolution of ideas. That is a massive scholarly task beyond me here. Mine is a psychological and philosophical approach to conscience and moral decision making as a general human phenomenon. When I use religious or scriptural references, or advert to the ideas of religious thinkers, I take them as recorded examples of inner human experience. Religious writings, like poetry, philosophy, and literature, are used here as expressions of self-conscious persons confronting the moral challenge of the human condition.

I am not attempting to produce a scholarly history of the secular debate over morality and conscience; nor for that matter can I hope to do justice to the full psychological and philosophical foundations undergirding my project. My aim and methods are not those of detailed technical analyses of various primary sources. I am trying, instead, to generally understand and give a holistic interpretation or "thick description"[7] of the subjective processes that can take place when we act in conscience. I see this effort as a personal critical reflection, using ordinary language and aimed at providing definitions and an overview created from an intelligent synthesis of ideas and experience. I use without apology, and with gratitude, the intellectual work others have done in diverse academic vineyards. My effort is to distill a new vintage consisting of both old and new wine.

I think we need to use old and new elements in taking on these questions of conscience and moral decision making. We cannot rely on either allegiance to past traditional wisdom or on faith in the future findings of psychology or neuroscience to explain human consciousness. Thinkers who put their trust in traditional wisdom are more often based in the humanities and will, like C. S. Lewis, appreciatively call the perennially recurring ideas about human nature the universal "natural law," or "the Tao."[8] For Lewis, traditional wisdom passed on in religion and literature manifests abiding moral truths; these truths are foundational moral axioms, which recur and persist in human thinking because they correspond to universally objective moral reality. These moral axioms undergirding human life cannot be proven, but they are open to discovery by the use of human reason. Those societies that stray from the traditional wisdom will pay a heavy price.

Indeed, it would seem an act of hubris not to appreciate the guidance and authoritative voice inherent in the common moral traditions of the past. But then one faces the problems of discriminating among, and choosing from, the incredible diversity of the past tradition, while trying not to simply baptize the inherited status quo. If there is to be change and growth in a living moral tradition, we have to be willing to question the moral pronouncements of our predecessors and make discriminating moral decisions about what should be kept and what discarded.

While the past contains treasures of moral wisdom, it also (looked at with a feminist eye instructed by mother wit) includes much dross and not a few moral atrocities. Progress in moral thinking has been aided by the incorporation of rational, scientific understanding of human functioning. (Illness is not divine punishment; madness is not caused by demons; women, blacks, and natives are not biologically inferior.) The problem for those living in the here and now is how to decide what of the past is worth keeping: which traditions will we willingly endorse?

On the other hand, some philosophical thinkers enamored with the future promise of neuroscience have labeled basic and perennial assumptions about human nature as "folk psychology."[9] Those who use that term usually have a strong commitment to leaving behind these primitive and confusing concepts of human psychology as soon as scientific understanding comes to the rescue. Those thinkers who put their faith in scientific progress trust scientific methods of investigation as more firmly grounded in reason than the humanities. Some fine day, rational, empirical investigations of the human mind/brain will displace our traditional notions of consciousness, free will, morality, and other basic assumptions of the traditional wisdom.

For these thinkers, "folk psychology" may be tolerated as a workable, commonsense tradition of popular theorizing that can serve us *until* a science of the human mind arrives with a more accurate and rationally based understanding and worldview. Come the revolution and future scientific breakthroughs in brain science, and we will have a totally new view of human mental functioning and thinking, complete with a new epistemology and understanding of thinking and the self. Obviously, such new understandings will have important repercussions for ideas about conscience and moral decision making.

To count on such a revolution seems misguided. After all, faith in science has no proven record in guiding practical human affairs. In my own approach to moral reflection, neither tradition nor new psychological findings can be automatically relied upon—or completely discounted. The arguments of those advocating the new and of traditionalists defending the authority of the past should, I think, remain in constant tension. Neither faith in tradition nor hope for future scientific and moral progress can stand alone. In the present, we have to sort out what new empirical scientific findings seem worthwhile and what of traditional experience seems important enough to integrate into our current maps of moral functioning. Today, moral reflection and deliberation take place on constantly rumbling scientific and philosophical ground; we can see ourselves as living atop the intellectual and scientific equivalent of the San Andreas Fault, subject to cracks and shifting movements underneath our feet. The explosion of scientific information and the shifting of paradigms make for a great deal of uncertainty. With the new physics and new biology, we can hardly understand matter, time, or life in the universe—much less the reasoning human mind or the nature of rationality. Philosophy and psychology are equally torn by opposing movements questioning fundamental premises. Perhaps the most instructive metaphor for the difficulty of all modern theorizing is an image presented by the eminent modern philosopher Willard Quine when he says: "Science is like a boat, which we rebuild plank by plank while staying afloat in it. The philosopher and the scientist are in the same boat."[10]

Attempting to understand conscience and moral action also involves staying afloat while continually rebuilding the ship. But there are some constancies that can be recognized. In the midst of our moral and intellectual voyage, we passengers retain the idea that we need to possess "a boat." We stay committed to the cooperative intellectual activity of rebuilding to stay afloat because we see and hear the ocean round about. If the ocean is seen as wave after wave of irrationality, chaos, and moral nihilism, we rightly fear death by drowning. Whether viewing the human intellectual predicament through a scientific, philosophical, or pragmatic lens, humanity has basically decided not to abandon ship.

Here, I also feel the need to defend my primary focus upon the individual self's moral functioning from the accusation of being one more fall into "the self-awareness trap," or flight into narcissism.[11]

American individualism and concern with the self and its psychological vicissitudes have been regularly deplored as sad symptoms of the "me generation." Again and again, we have heard the warnings against pseudo-self-analysis, against the triumph of the therapeutic, against the fall of the public person, and against the psychological retreat into self-manipulation.[12] Preoccupation with the inner life and self-consciousness has been seen as symptomatic of the self-indulgence accompanying the breakdown of culture.

But I maintain that to concentrate upon individual conscience and moral obligation is hardly to retreat into narcissism. In fact, an unrelieved concentration upon public morality, social justice, larger environmental forces, and civic morality can be a one-sided perspective. Slowly, society has begun to seek a balance between a concern for the individual's moral functioning and the group's moral functioning. I think this is happening because we have begun to regain our belief in the capacity of rational individuals to make a difference in their own lives and the lives of others. Consequently, we are witnessing a resurgence of interest in private consciousness and in the self—but this time it is the moral self, as free moral agent, which is the center of attention.

I concentrate on individual conscience, or individual moral decision making, not only because of my moral conviction that each individual is intrinsically valuable, but because I see the interrelationship of private and public goods. I am convinced that the larger community can only be as morally strong as the general moral functioning of its individual members. When a society is undergoing moral erosion and cultural strain, and when community supports weaken, there is an even greater need for individuals to stand morally firm. When things fall apart, an individual has a more pressing need for the moral self-guidance of conscience. It will not be enough to have a society that has created elaborate ethical guidelines or devised sophisticated theories of moral development if individuals are not themselves subjectively committed to moral action.

The individual is the fulcrum of moral decision making. A free moral agent can selectively process and reshape the social environment. I grant that scripted programs and intellectual competencies are prescribed by family, class, language, and culture, and exert potent force. And yes, the media, economics, technology, and other structural and environmental factors limit our thinking and behavior. But if "consciousness precedes being," then individuals shape the media and society, as well as the other way around. Collective forces and communities are constituted, maintained, and transformed by individual moral decisions.

Culturally enshrined concepts of the strict division between public and private morality have begun to be questioned as private moral decision making is seen to have costly social consequences. Perhaps some reevaluation is taking place because breakdowns of individual moral commitment now threaten the effectiveness of our vital socializing institutions such as the family and school. Ecological awareness and sensitivities are also escalating; they make us see that private morality is public. Persons become more alerted to the ways the general good is entwined with individual moral behavior. The moral decisions, for example, of one person who has AIDS, or access to a terrorist bomb, or a computer network, or a nuclear missile, or the helm of an oil tanker, become crucial for large numbers of other people. The growing awareness of interdependent systems and interlinking networks focuses attention on the power that a single person at any one particular point can exert upon the system as a whole.

We are ready to hear that, in the moral domain, it is also true that "for want of a nail a shoe was lost, for want of a shoe a horse was lost," and so on. Or better yet, for want of an individual's moral commitment to carrying out a job conscientiously, the nuclear reactor melted down, and the tristate region was lost. We are prepared to focus our thinking once more on the individual self, self-consciousness, conscience, and individual moral decision making—hence this book.

Chapter 1

What Is Conscience and How Does It Operate?

Few persons claim to be without conscience. Most people consider themselves to be moral and want to do the right thing. They worry about what they ought to do and feel guilty when they behave badly. Questions of morality regularly come up. How should we vote our conscience on abortion or take a stand on nuclear arms? Ought we to blow the whistle on a coworker who is incompetent, and should we join the fight against local environmental pollution? In our family and personal lives, we also worry over difficult moral decisions and ponder how to be a good spouse, parent, or friend. There are so many demands upon our time, energy, and money. It is not easy to decide our moral responsibilities to those we encounter, or to achieve a balance between our obligations to family, friends, and strangers. Are we once more going to walk around the homeless beggar in the railroad station or throw away the plea to send money to starving children?

Daily life echoes the testimony of literature, drama, opera, TV, and comic strips regarding moral deliberation and the challenges of conscience. Even lowly soap-opera plots appear as long-playing case studies in moral casuistry: Ought Jennifer to tell Scott about her previous affair with his father, or should Dawn, who feels guilty over betraying her sister in the past, now reveal her sister's dangerous drug addiction to her employer? Viewers of popular entertainment, which now includes most presentations of the news, cannot avoid a series of moral inquiries. Every murder case and horrific crime, every political scandal, provokes questions about the failure of conscience.

Everyone talks about conscience but few define the term. Our inchoate cultural awareness or assumption is not the same as a fully articulated understanding of what conscience is and how it operates. We

13

have been continuously instructed to "follow your conscience" and "let your conscience be your guide." But how do we go about putting these fundamental moral commands into practice?

What Is Conscience?

One way to handle a difficult definition is to first describe what a thing is not. Conscience is not a small, isolated voice emerging from a little man inside (the homunculus) or a Jimminy Cricket kind of guardian angel hovering over one's shoulder. Conscience is not located in some particular site in the body; it is not evident upon autopsy. Nor can the operation of a person's conscience be equated with some passing thought or emotion, some whim or impulsive act that may occur from time to time. Conscience cannot be reduced to an occasional pang of guilt, anxiety, or fear, or the idle memory of a maxim or moral rule wafting through one's consciousness.

Going to the dictionary, we can find conscience defined in ordinary language as "the inner sense of what is right or wrong in one's conduct or motives, impelling one toward right action."[1] This succinct definition not only sums up a great deal of human moral experience, but also endorses a broad, dynamic, and active view of conscience. My expanded definition of conscience would be similar: conscience is a personal, self-conscious activity, integrating reason, emotion, and will in self-committed decisions about right and wrong, good and evil. It is clear that there are several important converging characteristics that make conscience a unique human activity; there is something special going on within a person's consciousness, while at the same time there are special goals and standards motivating the process. Since all these characteristics of conscience are complex, I will take them up one by one.

Conscience Is Personal, Self-Conscious Activity

Conscience is a word describing an inner, self-conscious psychological activity that is not a visible, concrete thing. A language filled with nouns can mislead us into thinking that our names for dynamic, recurring patterns of activity are material objects. Conscience is not really an "it" that a person "has" in the same way that a person has a car or a telephone, or has a baby or a mother. Conscience can only be an unseen, inner, dynamic process of personal consciousness. Confusion arises because we use words to refer to recurring patterns of activity in a person, which we then say a person "has"; we actually mean that, over time, a person has built up predispositions for potential patterns of characteristic activity. So a person has a personality, or has writing talent, or has athletic skill, or has a temper, and so on. In this sense, a person has a conscience because he or she has repeatedly engaged in past acts of conscience that predispose him or her toward characteristic acts in the present. Having a conscience is a shorthand description of a built-up potential for a kind of act or activity; conscience is used to describe the specific activity and the general pattern or potential for the activity.

Obviously too, conscience as a personal, self-conscious activity means that one has to be awake, aware, and acting with conscious awareness of self and the environment. We would not say that conscience operates in a hypnotized, drugged, or sleeping state. Psychologically, we now understand that persons cycle through an ever-changing flow of different levels of consciousness and arousal, and experience various states of awareness. Conscience requires self-consciousness and attention to what one is doing—as well as something more.

Conscience Is Holistic, Self-Integrated Activity

Conscience is awake, aware, self-conscious activity, but this hardly makes it unique. Conscience is also an activity in which there is a unified integration of thinking, feeling, and willingness to act; it refers to those acts of a whole person who is simultaneously thinking, feeling, and willing. Other personal activities may not be so unified or integrated.

Human psychological consciousness is complex and multidimensioned, with varied capacities, functions, and partial systems, which can operate semi-independently. Even when one is awake and conscious, there can be a lack of inner, integrated focus. A person can be absorbed in abstract thinking about a logical problem ("with his head in the clouds"), be emotionally enthralled, or be caught up in some intense physical sensation or overwhelmingly stressful ordeal. The personal stream of consciousness is often one-sided, not broadly engaged, or focused as a whole.

At times, a person is "not really all there" and "doesn't have it together." Conscience operates as a fully integrated, fully together, self-conscious activity in which no one capacity of a person acts in isolation. But this integration still does not guarantee uniqueness. Because holistically unified consciousness can also be found in other human activities. Sex and work, as well as war and emergencies, can integrate and unify consciousness. The fact that one will be hanged on the morrow concentrates the mind wonderfully, but this concentration is not necessarily an activity of conscience.

Conscience Is Self-Committed

Conscience is integrated, aware, self-conscious activity that is also self-avowed and self-committed. Commitment occurs when the self acts as agent, and simultaneously mobilizes one's inner personal capacities to support and infuse the action with personal emotive force. Self-consciousness in a committed act is self-consciousness squared, or self-multiplied; we reflexively muster our selves and our inner resources as guarantee in self-authorization. Because we are self-conscious, we can be self-consciously self-directing, and produce inner mobilizations of self-binding, self-warranting, self-authorizing acts. We can knowingly will to will our actions; we can desire to desire in the deepest core of our fully self-engaged consciousness. We can commit ourselves in deeply self-invested actions that make our other one-dimensional plans, preferences, or intentions seem like simple, thin, and superficial acts. With self-commitment, we put ourselves on the line, we commit ourselves to carrying through, we stand upon our actions.

It is important to see that the definition of an act should be broadened beyond motor or muscular movements that others can observe; personal acts that are voluntary can also include bringing into consciousness words, thoughts, images, feelings, and other mental operations as we deliberately hold and fix our attention and consent. Voluntary acts are decisive, personal focusings of attention, or as one psychologist put it, "Choice is a fixing of attention within a specific framework to which one is committed."[2] We can act not only by moving through space and speaking sentences, but by privately thinking and feeling in self-directed ways.

When I speak of personal decisions, I include voluntary acts of many different kinds. Thus we are acting when we struggle to solve a logical problem, deliberately imagine something, or induce an emotion—as well as when we speak, gesture, or perform observable public acts. We decide and act when we "make up our minds." Even paying attention to others—focusing upon them, listening to them, or watching and waiting with them—can be as exhausting as heavy physical work. The free deployment and focusing of attention produces voluntary, decisive acts.

However, not all personally avowed, self-committed, integrated acts are activities of conscience. Acts of conscience are further distinguished because they are oriented to moral values and standards of worth; they have as their goal effecting the right and the good, and avoiding wrong-doing and evil. A person can make promises, self-commitments, or vows that are not directed to moral ends. Indeed, persons can self-consciously fully commit themselves to carrying out what they recognize as evil, such as pursuing revenge and murder out of envy, or engaging in the obsessive pursuit of a blood feud.

Conscience Is Oriented to Moral Values and Goodness

Conscience is integrated, self-committed, conscious activity oriented to moral values and moral standards of the right and the good. Our personal, self-committed acts of conscience are pursuing the right and good thing to do—what we morally ought to do and what morally ought to be. Such acts cannot be equated with knowing or deciding upon the facts of a case, the most efficient or profitable solution to a problem, or even some aesthetic valuation of beauty. We cannot decide how we morally ought to act by appealing to science, economics, biology, aesthetics, etiquette, custom, law, or existing social conventions. Many kinds of active inquiry and pursuits of knowledge and facts may help us to morally decide, but they cannot finally settle a moral question of conscience. Presented with convention or customary rules as preferred solutions to moral quests, we can always ask whether these laws or customary rules of the game are the morally right ones. Ought we to endorse these as the right ones?

When I become engaged in "ought" questions of right and wrong, I feel morally responsible to actively decide on the good and right action—or at least the better, or least wrong, action. An inner dialogue and a complex process may then begin. Moral inquiry presupposes human self-consciousness with a capacity for inner self-self confrontations and deliberations leading to self-committed decisions. When we make personal moral decisions, we must stand upon them or avow them to ourselves. The very word conscience, or con-science, means "with knowledge" or "knowledge with," so that something more than deciding upon facts is involved. The additional dimension, I hold, is integrated, personal self-commitment to action on behalf of the good and the right.

I think the self-committed moral decision of conscience implies following through; it is prescriptive, not just descriptive. Personal,

committed moral decisions of conscience are not made with such isolated detachment that we then must make other moral decisions about
whether we are willing to enact or further what we first decided ought
to be. Further decisions on appropriate methods or means may be necessary, but not affect an original commitment.

The Scope of Conscience

Since we live in linear time, freely observing and engaging ourselves, others, and the world, the direction and scope of conscience can
range widely. We can make moral decisions about our selves in the
past, present, and future. What ought we to have done or left undone
in the past? What ought we to do right now, and in the immediate and
distant future? Traditionally, when conscience was directed to behavior
already in effect, it was labeled "juridical conscience," and when directed to what should be done in the present and future, it was called
"antecedent" or "legislative conscience."[3] Obviously, there is an overlap
here, since what we think we ought to have done will affect what we
think we should do, and vice versa.

There are some differences in decisions about what has already
taken place in the past and decisions about the present and the future,
but it is the same person's conscience that is operating. In reference to
things irrevocably over and done with, we can exert little retroactive,
overt control, but we may change our minds and attitudes in significant
ways.[4] There are also many differences in the degree of difficulty and
challenge in various decisions of conscience; sometimes the uncertainties and unknown risks of the future make a decision more problematic.
More deliberation and struggle may ensue than when a challenge to
conscience is a familiar, simple one. But difficult and unfamiliar or not,
we cannot restrict our self-committed decisions of conscience to backward, after-the-fact decisions. After all, our decisions of conscience
about the present and the future are creating our pasts, minute by
minute. The concept of conscience is sadly truncated if it is defined
as operating only in the past, and is not understood as proactively
directed to the future.

It seems equally misguided to confine conscience solely to personal,
private behaviors over which we can exert complete control.[5] Conscience, like all human thinking, can not only move back and forth in
time perspective, but also be vicarious and broad ranging in focus. We
inevitably make self-committed moral decisions about the behavior of
others and about moral issues in the world at large—even though we

cannot dominate or control outcomes. We can each morally decide and be morally self-committed to standards of worth that other individuals ought to meet. We cannot simply mind our own moral business and ignore others in our common moral community. Our individual consciences can compel us to intervene in child abuse, engage in whistle-blowing at work, stop thieves, lay down our lives to fight Nazis, persuade, admonish, remonstrate, demonstrate, petition, organize, vote, boycott, disobey the law, and so on.

Our self-commitments of conscience may take different forms in different decisions, just as they can when past, present, or future time frames are at issue. We may not have as much direct influence or control over circumstances in effecting some decisions of conscience as we do in others. Although our direct influence may be limited, once convinced in conscience, if we could, we would effect the right action or goods to which we morally commit ourselves. Of course, when it comes to questions of influence and control of self and others, we make other important corollary decisions of conscience about what means or methods are morally right to use. Few persons of developed conscience will be morally indifferent to the morality of means and methods. As Gandhi so wisely said, "Means are ends in the making."[6] But personal consciences can hardly be confined to private, personal behaviors when we constantly interact with others in a common life.

Certainly the great moral heroes and exemplars of conscience have committed themselves to moral decisions about the behavior of others— either about their moral actions as individuals, or their behavior as members of institutions responsible for political and legal decisions. Gandhi and Martin Luther King, Jr., for instance, were impelled by their consciences to intervene with others to effect political, social, and institutional changes. They definitely attempted to shape the moral decisions and conscience commitments of others according to their own visions and convictions about right action and the moral good. I think that great harm is done when conscience, with its qualities of self-commitment and self-engagement, is seen as different and disconnected from other kinds of moral decision making. Such a view implies that in narrow, very private domains, self-committed conscience can be active, but in interpersonal, social, and other moral questions, the same conscience must somehow disconnect from moral self-commitment and always be confined to operating in some self-absent, value-free mode.

Boundaries to conscience do exist, but they are not boundaries of time or space. The boundaries, often fuzzy and difficult to discern, are between an analytic, inquiring, imaginative, tentative, exploratory mode of consciousness and a personally self-invested, emotionally self-committed mode of rational conviction and assent. There is a difference between moral analysis and a committed moral decision. Moral inquiry and deliberation must often precede difficult decisions of conscience. Before personally deciding or fully investing ourselves in commitments, we may first seek facts, investigate circumstances, seek diverse opinions, think about relevant principles and the testimony of different moral traditions. We reflect and deliberate by asking ourselves many questions, thinking through various answers, critiquing and appraising the different findings in our search, and weighing other ideas, intuitions, or emotions that come spontaneously into consciousness.

In the process of moral decision making, we can, through critical self-reflection, assess our reasons and intuitions, our own past and present actions, our personal emotions, our motives, our aspirations, our remembered images, our mentors and teachers, and so on. Many have noted that the inner self-self moral dialogue is to a great extent based upon past experiences of interpersonal dialogues, from either actual experience or vicarious experiences through literature, Scripture, or cultural stories.[7] The inner, self-assessing dialogue can be engaged in, not only to work things out for ourselves, but also to prepare us to morally justify to others what, why, and how we are deciding. If we are going to stand upon our own decisions, we must convince ourselves and be prepared to convince others if challenged.

Search and Reflection

Before we commit ourselves—give our consent or morally decide in conscience—a long or short period of search and reflection may intervene. Every decision has the temporal, structured components of notice, engagement, hesitation, oscillating attention, deliberation, and choice.[8] The time period may vary from less than a second to a decade or more. During the hesitation period, we may engage in much thinking, feeling, imagining or, information seeking, which serves the purpose of deciding but is not yet deciding. In other words, while hesitating, we may attend to a variety of modes of consciousness with different content before we fix our attention, give our consent, and finally decide.

The phrase traditionally used to describe this seeking and inquiring about the right thing to do has been "to inform one's conscience." Before acting or deciding, a person can also be said to have "an unsettled [or undecided or unconvinced] conscience." This hesitation is different from a situation in which we have morally decided in conscience but, through weakness or inner division, fail to behave in the prescribed way. When we hesitate because we are still undecided, we don't yet know what we ought to do or what we think ought to be done in a specific situation.

Should all the preliminary self-self dialogue and searching to inform conscience before self-commitment be counted as part of the operation of conscience? This approach would make informing conscience, moral analysis, and moral deliberation an operation of conscience.[9] I do not think this a wise move. The preliminary preparations for decision and the actual decision are different; the preparations can be detached, unfocused, tentative, fragmentary, and ambivalent, while the decision is self-committed, integrated, focused, and fixed. To ignore the differences and equate the various modes of consciousness makes the definition of an act of conscience too broad, inclusive of everything passing through consciousness that is vaguely related to a moral concern.

Admittedly, in real life, it often can be difficult to tell where seeking and searching end, and finding and deciding begin. Discriminations become difficult because in decision making, a person's stream of consciousness oscillates, ranging here and there, performing different kinds of operations at different conscious levels, processing at different speeds. The actions of consciousness involved in deciding can be so dynamic, circular, and complexly blended and blurred that it can be hard to disentangle boundaries or fix upon a discrete moment of decision.

In order to initiate moral inquiries and persevere in the serious effort to find out what we ought to do, we must have already developed operating consciences able to make decisions to actively pursue truth and the right thing to do. We must, at some moment, apprehend that there are moral challenges before us. Only past decisions of conscience will have given us the moral sensibility to recognize the need for a committed moral decision in a new set of circumstances. We are also enabled by previous moral decisions of conscience to understand that we are morally obligated to inform our consciences and make adequately grounded decisions.

Once we are morally aware, engaged, or hooked, we may have to make repeated commitments of conscience to keep the process of inquiry going. In the midst of distracting or stressful events, it is always tempting to give up a moral quest and take the easiest, quickest way out that presents itself, or as the saying goes, "to turn a deaf ear to conscience." It takes energy to keep attention deployed and directed in a search for relevant moral considerations. In ongoing, problematic decision-making processes, we may have to keep making brief personal commitments of conscience in order to refocus and to reenergize the search. The exploratory inquiry continues with preliminary fact-finding, analysis, scenario building, assessments of consequences, and so on, but may be punctuated with acts of conscience recommitting us to the obligation of properly informing conscience. When a committed decision is made, we say that one's conscience is settled, convinced, resolved, fixed—and this condition is different from the preceding condition of hesitation, inquiry, analysis, and reflection.

Moral Analyses Without Moral Decisions

A distinction between exploratory moral inquiry and committed conscience recognizes the fact that moral analysis can exist without personal moral commitments of conscience. Such thinking, and analysis of the thinking, is the basis for the formal academic disciplines of ethics, moral philosophy, and moral theology, and the new disciplines of bioethics and professional ethics. Philosophers, ethicists, and theologians do research, write, and think about morals and ethics as their profession. Today, scholarly expertise in ethical analysis may lead to professional practice as an ethical consultant for institutions outside academia. Ethics consultants may, for instance, be hired by a hospital or research center, which faces many morally complex issues in health care.

A professional consultation or an academic article may involve analyses of the moral issues involved in a dilemma, case, or policy option, but an explication is not the same as a personal moral self-commitment. Persons educated in professional ethics can provide an ethical critique of a problem and set forth relevant ethical and moral arguments from different points of view. They can demonstrate how different principles and ethical approaches may apply to a particular case. Philosophically trained ethicists or moralists can also critique the quality of various moral decisions, and give an account of the foundations for different ethical principles. While these analyses of moral principles and methods may be examples of moral reasoning, and sometimes include abstract moral judgments, they are not personal moral decisions of conscience. Such decisions do not take place unless the professionals personally commit themselves to a decision about what ought to be done. An analysis that can serve as a guideline to action is not the same as an act of personal moral commitment.

In an election, for example, a political analysis of the issues presented is different from one's decision when confronting the choices in the voting booth. They are certainly related but not the same thing. Another example is making a move in a game of chess. First, one has to learn the rules and gain practical experience from instructors. Then, before making a move in a real game, a player must think through the many options—using intelligence and energy to determine the best move in the circumstances. If playing by mail, one would have time to consult with experts and fellow players, study past games and an opponent's style, and review the various scenarios arising from different strategies. These processes of reflection or inquiry finally end, however, when one must move the chess piece in a decisive act.

I see the study of ethics and morality and ethical consultation not as acts of conscience, but as predecisional moral inquiries similar to a chess player's search for the best move. Skilled chess players, after many moves in many games, can look at a chessboard and immediately grasp the probable course of potential game plans. They are intuitively drawn to a selected array of the best moves and strategies. In the same way, morally developed persons build upon previous moral acts that have produced a store of personal resources that affect each new decision of conscience. They see more and interpret what they see in more morally sophisticated ways. Those who are, in addition, ethically educated may call upon more explicitly articulated intellectual arguments before making their moves. But in the end, an ethical analysis is different from actually making a moral decision of conscience.

Conscience is that personal activity that is uniquely characterized by going beyond analysis and exploration to morally committing ourselves to what we avow we ought to do, or what we avow ought to be done. Our reasoned, conscious decisions are infused with wholehearted self-investment. The decisive bid is constituted by the extra ante of self thrown into the pot. And as always, when the self becomes fully engaged, the stakes become serious. Since conscience consists of self-committed moral action, it has always been recognized as having an overriding, imperative force.[10] But little agreement has been achieved about what produces this demanding sense of moral obligation.

What Impels Us to Morally Right Actions of Conscience?

Whence comes the imperative, prescriptive force of conscience—its obligating, overriding quality? Many experience the impelling moral force of conscience as similar to pure necessity. Here I stand; I can do no other. Innumerable individuals have endured incredible tortures, persecutions, imprisonments, and death on behalf of personal

conscience; moral self-commitment is stronger than the desire for physical survival or relief from suffering.

The question of why moral motivation can be so potent goes to the
heart of the debates over the nature of human beings and the nature of
ultimate reality. Human nature and ultimate reality are far too much to
take on here, though a few comments are in order in regard to moral
imperatives. Explanations of the moral sense tend to point in two different directions. One position sees the human individual as a rational
animal, intelligent enough to create powerful moral illusions and
myths, which are then accorded belief and obeyed as though they were
real. Another interpretation claims, by contrast, that individual conscience is an appropriate responsiveness to *actual* moral realities that
exert real force.

Skeptical naturalists reduce the moral imperative to some ingenious,
collective confabulation of the human mind, which flies in the face of facts
but helps shore up psychological defenses and maintain social order. Moral realists disagree, and see human moral consciousness as responding
and resonating to moral realities operating dialectically, or simultaneously
from within and beyond human beings. Despite the arguments over the
origin and function of the moral sense, all would agree that potent moral
motivation comes in both a negative and positive form: there is a fear of
future self-punishment from bad conscience and a positive attraction toward ideals of goodness and good conscience.

Self-Punishment of Bad Conscience

A negative moral self-judgment is much dreaded, as both modern
and ancient testimony readily reveal. Self-conscious human beings can
observe the self as others would, could, or will—but also have more
inside evidence from introspection. Awareness of one's moral acts
emerges before a self-observing eye, or "I." When one morally decides,
often after some inner dialogue, one is standing before the court of
one's own self-governing, self-judging observer. One's moral acts, during, before, and after the fact, can be appraised, approved, or con-
demned by one's self-conscious self, acting as juridical conscience.

The self-punitive force of moral self-reproach appears in Old Testament imagery in which David and other wrongdoers proclaim that
they are being smitten or reproached by their hearts. The heart has
been so often associated with conscience because it aptly symbolizes
the holistic, emotionally fused reasoning and commitment characteristic
of conscience.[11] A member of a western Kenya tribal culture describes
the powerful emotional feeling of a rational decision of conscience:

You remain unhappy because you have something in your heart that will draw you to a shadow of being afraid of something that you have done to someone else. Because you will charge yourself according to your heart that you were not right at that time.[12]

Accounts of inner psychological castigation and inner torture over moral wrongdoing have been features of myth, drama, literature, Scripture, and philosophy. Plutarch described the remorse over having done a dreadful deed as "like an ulcer in the flesh" in which regret "ever continues to wound and prick."[13] Since one is being stung and chastised by one's own feelings and inner reasoning processes, there is no escape. In other of life's misfortunes—those caused by external circumstances or other persons—there is hope that one's power of reasoning, resignation, or stoic detachment may provide strength and comfort; in other kinds of pain, one can engage in reasoned strategies of relief, but not when one's own reason is the accuser.

In Old English, conscience was fittingly called "the agenbite of inwit," a wonderful phrase picked up by James Joyce for the description of bad conscience.[14] "Inwit" is an incisively precise term for our inner sense of decisive knowing, and "again biting" ("agenbite") describes the nagging, repeated puncturing of self-condemnation as consciousness repeatedly brings up the painful memory of moral failure. The seventeenth-century English poet George Herbert describes his nagging painful conscience as armed with "a tooth or nail to scratch."[15]

It is this fear of future self-reproach to which Shakespeare refers when he writes that "conscience doth make cowards of us all." Like Hamlet, we hesitate and struggle to avoid wrongdoing because we want to be sure that we will not look back in guilty shame and sorrow. We know that our self-consciousness is always with us, sees all, and can decisively judge all. Little chance exists for escaping the self-conscious burden of moral responsibility when we are fully conscious, hence the perpetual appeal of the dimming and numbing effects of drugs, drink, frenzied pleasure, fatiguing work, or aggression turned against others. The existence of subtle evasive strategies to avoid bad conscience leads to intriguing questions of self-deception, which will be taken up in the chapter on moral failure.

Attraction to Good Conscience

There is also abundant testimony to the attractive force of the good and of moral ideals. There has always existed "that endless aspiration to perfection which is characteristic of moral activity," as the philosopher Iris

Murdoch expresses it.[16] Goodness and perfection as infinite universals will obviously be more difficult to define than specific evils and wrongdoing; peace is harder to define than war, joy is more elusive than sorrow. But humans, from childhood on, do seem to have some sense of moral goodness, and personal efforts to be good can continue throughout life. Can this perceived attraction to moral goodness be an illusion?

Unfortunately, many recent psychological explanations of moral motivation have been fairly reductionistic, denying the reality of moral value. In the familiar behaviorist model, all internal moral self-processes spring only from past learning and conditioning from the environment. Punishments and rewards by parents and others in society can produce patterns of moral anxiety and habits of approach and avoidance in an individual. A human being can also be conditioned vicariously, displaying the same thinking patterns as nurturing or punitive models. Eventually, a person can take over the self-reinforcing or self-punishing moral socializing, or covert self-talk, which has been reinforced by the social environment.[17]

The Freudian explanation is more complex, much too complex to give here in detail.[18] But essentially the psyche in the young child incorporates into the developing self-structure parental authorities and other regulating cultural norms. Positive ideals of perfection are induced by somewhat different processes. Unconsciously, in the matrix of early nurturing, environmental and instinctual forces become internalized as a superego and an ego ideal in the mind. Through self-directed, instinctual forces of love and fear, a conscience is formed that exerts psychological moral pressures to abjure wrongdoing and seek moral perfection. Operations of conscience are really complex, internalized moral legacies from an individual's unconscious past experiences as a child. Human beings begin as instinctual animals but can become partially controlled by civilization, despite its discontents. Persons may rationally modify their original unconscious moral legacy somewhat, but the force of conscience is rooted in irrational, instinctual, and infantile inevitabilities.

For many reductionist natural skeptics, the human species is basically determined by biology and the vicissitudes of early social environment, despite the fact that as adults we may think we are making free rational decisions and moral self-commitments to the good. The reality of moral values is besides the point, for humans are only an accidentally evolved species in a vast universe devoid of value and any final purpose. Perhaps this bleak view was best summed up by the pessimistic scientist Jacques Monod when he said: "Any mingling of knowledge with values is unlawful, forbidden . . . man knows at last that he is alone in the universe's unfeeling immensity, out of which he emerged only by chance."[19]

Other scientists consider this opinion an unwarranted, foreclosed ideology, having more to do with nineteenth-century mechanistic determinist models of science than with twentieth-century scientific explosions of knowledge. Freeman Dyson argues that "the idea of chance is itself a cover for our ignorance," and that in our current state of knowledge, we can not rule out more optimistic views of the relationship of human mind and consciousness to the universe.[20] He thinks modern physics can support the assumption that human consciousness is integral to ultimate reality and may play an active role in shaping reality. The ancient covenant between nature and humanity is not broken, for as he says,

> I do not feel like an alien in this universe . . . I think our consciousness is not just a passive epiphenomenon carried along by the chemical events in our brains, but is an active agent forcing the molecular complexes to make choices between one quantum state and another.[21]

Those scientists who emphasize harmony between human intelligence, consciousness, and the cosmos have less difficulty seeing human thinking as being able to penetrate, rationally discern, and resonate with universal realities. Originating in the universe as we have, made up literally of stardust, we are not, as George Wald says, "looking into the universe from outside. We are looking at it from inside. Its history is our history; its stuff, our stuff. From that realization we can take some assurance that what we see is real."[22] Realists in science think that the rational quest of human minds successfully approximates more and more adequate understandings of reality—which itself is so rationally ordered that there is a natural fit between the reasoning brain and the rationally structured universe. Thus scientists create hypotheses and theories that work. I think those scientists and others arguing for a new and more-open vision of reality as rational and not alien to human consciousness are winning the day.

It is a long leap from scientific theories to the philosophy of science, to disputes over the reality of the moral imperative experienced in human consciousness.[23] But in our world, reigning approaches of science pervade our imagery and thinking to such a degree that the validation of human reasoning and human consciousness in a more-open, nonmechanistic science would be influential in moral philosophy. These new scientific movements of thought can challenge reductionistic models of human nature and give indirect support to moral realists who claim that moral intuitions or moral truths and goods are not illusory projections. Moral reasoning can be seen as successfully discerning, resonating to, and approximating moral truths—just as scientific reasoning can penetrate unseen realities and produce new visions of order.

Apprehending something as rationally true and real, one submits, assents, accepts its necessity, and is sure that it cannot be willed otherwise. Reality can be loosely defined as something that is not the product of one's own cognitive functioning—something that exists beyond one's ken or say-so. Obviously, different individuals at different times and places, with better or worse resources at their command, can do better or worse at apprehending realities. But for moral realists, moral obligations and the overridingness of the moral imperative are real and dialectically related to truths and values that are not autistic, defensive projections.

Reason operates in us and connects us to realities beyond our selves. We must submit to the imperative command of reason if we choose to be consistent with our rationally functioning selves; to deny reason is to deny our nature. An observation on this is Heidegger's reported comment on the moral law that "in subjecting myself to the law, I subject myself to myself as pure reason. . . ."[24] If reason and rationality are a real way to truth, then we participate in something real beyond our selves when we feel obligated by our moral reasoning. Many thinkers have agreed that one source of the imperative quality of morality consists of the capacity of human moral reasoning to reach a rational reality. Through reasoning, a rational mind can reach an impartial, universal moral truth, which logically must be the same for anyone in the same situation. We see it and cannot deny it, and this rational necessity provides the force of the moral imperative.

Others would also stress the reality of the potent attraction of goodness and value. Values are real, attract us, and permeate our consciousness of existence. Our desires for goodness are central to the operation of conscience. Our innate response to the attractiveness of real goods is not illusion but real participation in a universal good.[25] Transcendent goodness permeates nature, human nature, and other real values such as beauty and excellence. When an act participates in the good, then the attractive force of the good not only impels us, but confirms us.

In this view, human beings innately seek the good and resonate to all those real goods they apprehend, including moral goods. These essential moral goods can be as self-evident as rational, logical truths. We are intuitively drawn to appreciate the excellence of virtue and, through moral aspirations, are drawn toward moral decisions of conscience to serve the good. Our ability to love and appreciate the goodness and beauty of reality is a central factor in the genesis and development of conscience and moral aspiration. Many would also claim that goodness is unified, so particular goods and values are related.[26] Often, aesthetics and morality are not strictly differentiated in this approach; beauty, truth, and goodness are seen ultimately as one reality. Beauty is truth, truth beauty, and so on.

Whatever the ultimate metaphysical truths may be, I am convinced that both moral ideals of goodness and rational understanding powerfully motivate the activity of conscience. Rational human beings seek consistency, and do not wish to be seen to be incoherent or lacking integrity. Thus in contemplating a choice to be made, we are morally impelled by our positive ideals for ourselves. (Since motivation is often mixed and complex, we may or may not also be partially motivated by fear or love of some external authority, by thoughts of the pain of future guilt or shame, or by thoughts of other future consequences.) If morally guilty, we will be sorry about external negative consequences and also about the betrayal of our selves and those positive moral ideals we hold. Thus we submit to what we perceive to be morally right and good. Conscience is not alien to us, for moral obligation can seem the innermost personal act, and yet at the same time, a response to a compelling reality beyond ourselves. Moral stuff is our stuff, and we are moral insiders responding to something real in us and beyond us.

The idea of a moral dialectic between inner human consciousness and some larger moral ideal and reality beyond the self has emerged in many forms. Western religion has seen a personal Creator as the source of this inner dialectic. Other spiritual traditions posit other transcendent ideals permeating the perceived world: an idea of the Good as Platonic form, the existence of a world soul, or some pantheistic concept of divine eternal consciousness that is immanent in all of nature. Indeed, Eastern and ancient ideas of the perennial philosophy, often fused with Jungian psychology, are rapidly penetrating Western thought.[27]

If we do not perceive that compelling outer and inner moral force as emanating from God or some other spiritual reality, we may interpret it as a collective cultural consciousness by which historical societies constitute themselves and the individuals born into the community. Collective social reality can be as real and as potent as any other force in creating moral obligations. Seeing the moral rule and sense of morality as coming from society, the sociologist Emile Durkheim explains his version of how an external reality is also within:

> Because society is beyond us, it commands us; on the other
> hand, being superior to everything in us, it permeates us. Because it

constitutes part of us, it draws us with the special attraction that inspires us toward moral ends.[28]

In a secular recasting of spiritual visions, Durkheim sees that an impetus toward duty and an impetus toward love of the ideal can fuse and permeate the inner person; a person is attracted to society because, being prior and more extensive than the individual, it creates individuals and imprints them with its sense of moral ideals. Clearly the integrated fusion of reason and love will generate energy, but this psychological force will be magnified when a reality beyond us is perceived as permeating our consciousness.

I am convinced that in many psychological experiences of felt moral obligation, our integrated self-commitment is perceived as responding to a fused, unified moral reality; the good and the right, the true and the real are apprehended as one and the same.

Philosophers use language more carefully, and many philosophers follow long traditions that make distinctions between the right and the good, and between different levels and kinds of truth and reality. But other philosophers and many ordinary persons do not differentiate the moral appeal in an argument such as "Come on, you know it's really true; this is the good thing to do; let's do the right thing." There is a felt sense that the true, the right, the good, and the real are one and must of necessity be one.[29]

For those living in a post-Christian culture, this sense of unified reality may be a legacy from monotheistic affirmations of the reality of the one true, good God, who creates and sustains a real, unified universe. Or it may be a secondary faith derived from science's implicit assumption of a unified reality that must be coherent. In any event, the perceptual conviction that there is an underlying synthesis of truth, reality, and goodness can generate intense forces of moral attraction and inner compulsion.

The sense of a unified reality that morally compels us from beyond can resonate with the unified, integrated action of conscience. We simultaneously know, feel, and will what we avow in conscience ought to be. When this integrated self-authorization is felt as participating in a unified ultimate reality, then the authority and compelling force of conscience is intensified from within and without. I ought to, I must, because I am reflecting the true, resonating with the good, confirmed by the real—and thereby compelled and empowered to obey the moral mandate. Refusing and betraying the moral self-imperatives is felt as a betrayal of self and ultimate reality.

I am compelled by a sense that the dictate of conscience is real, as real as things can get for me. I cannot deny this moral truth without denying all my ability to rationally understand things or my wholehearted allegiance to the good. Reality, truth, and the good seem to be one, and my movement toward the good implies my allegiance to truth and truth's hold upon me. The fused force of the real and the good—the attraction of truth and goodness combined—impels me, calls me, commands me.

Many observers and thinkers do not agree with the view I offer here of the operation of conscience and the moral imperative. I think human beings can rationally and emotionally penetrate a reality that exists beyond ourselves; this mysterious reality in which we swim permeates our beings and is not alien, irrational, or value-free. This conviction leads to the further belief that the succession of subjective psychological constructions or approximations of reality we create in our innate human desire to understand can be tested over time and shown to be either adequate or misguided.

However, while not all would agree that there is a moral reality informing human thinking, most of those who take the rational moral enterprise seriously agree upon some things. Clearly, conscience and the moral imperative can never simply be reduced to whatever we choose to be the case, or to whatever may give us comfort, or to whatever will ward off the threatening and unpleasant aspects of our individual lives. All moralists and all the wise and good of the world remain firmly committed to some form of the reality principle, whatever their view of ultimate reality. No matter what our theory of number is, we know that wishing that two times two could equal five can never make it so. Even those who think that the best human thought can do is to construct a morally coherent account of things rationally resist settling for illusions or intellectual magic tricks. Just as few would be willing to settle for hallucinations in their perceptions of the external world, so they reject a cynical acceptance of wish fulfillment as an answer to the moral quest.

No one confuses the search for right action with the effort to rationalize an acceptable confabulation. Sincere seekers in the moral quest, whatever their differences, do not resign themselves to being morally self-deceived. Certainly when we admire moral persons of good conscience, we are not admiring the creativity of their self-deceptive strategies. We admire their integrity, their willingness to make self-commitments—including that most important of all moral commitments, to undertake a continuing, critical search for truth and goodness. While a multitude of philosophical and psychological questions remain unresolved, I do think

it is safe to say that most of those who think about moral decision making
agree that human beings can fruitfully engage in rational moral reflection
and thereby make better moral choices.

Individually and collectively, we experience ourselves as able to exercise self-direction in pursuit of moral aims and agree that it is better
to try harder to do better. Accepting this theoretical minimum seems
necessary if we are going to spend time and energy trying to engage in
moral reflection to determine what is, or is not, the better moral decision. If we are without conscience and incapable of moral decisions, if
we are completely environmentally determined—truly beyond freedom
and dignity—why waste time and energy on an illusion?

Among all moralists, religious and secular, one can see a basic consensus: self-conscious persons exist, and moral decisions can be oriented to doing good and avoiding evil. All persons ought to do what
they ought to do, or in its more psychologically subtle variant, persons
ought to do what they believe they ought to do. Those who hold to
this moral universal commandment, and consider moral self-direction
an operation of conscience, are heirs to a long history of the concept in
Western culture, well worth a brief account.

Some Background on the Western Idea of Conscience

One prominent scholar of conscience, Eric D'Arcy, claims that the
concept of the directive function of conscience, or moral authority to
legislate or decide future behavior, is, in Western culture, a Christian
innovation first appearing in St. Paul's letters.[30] Classical Roman thinkers such as Seneca and Cicero recognize the moral self-judgment of
judicial conscience, but Paul is credited with the innovation of taking
over the Greek word for self-consciousness and creatively forging a new
dimension to the usual meaning. In Paul's new usage, conscience is
more than simple self-consciousness; it is also used to mean morally
obligatory self-direction.

In his discussions of conscience, Paul also puts forth the view that
there is an innate conscience or moral guide in all people everywhere—
even the pagans have the moral law written upon their hearts.[31] In other
interesting uses of the concept, Paul implies that a person's operating
conscience can be weak, uneasy, or doubtful—indeed, even be incorrect
through ignorance or immaturity. Obviously, the implication is that one
person can have a more-developed and appropriately operating conscience than another, although the more-mature person must respect

the weaker consciences of others. But whatever the adequacy of a person's moral self-guidance or decisions of conscience, an individual must always follow his or her conscience. These early Christian ideas of personal conscience initiated centuries of theoretical and conceptual developments and disputes over the idea of conscience that continue today.

The Pauline idea of conscience, which has shaped our own religious and secular tradition of moral decision making, seems firmly based upon an assumption that a human person has the potential to be psychologically self-conscious, and that a person's inner self-consciousness can be differentiated from the body or bodily acts. In a more concrete, holistic view of human beings, words such as "heart," "loins," and "bowels" are used in the Old Testament to refer to an individual's inner moral sense.[32] There was no Hebrew word for "conscience," but "knowing in one's heart" seems to be the moral equivalent. When God is recorded as adopting the Israelites, Yahweh says, "I will place my law within them, and write it upon their hearts," and a later prophet sees God promising "I will give you a new heart . . . taking from your bodies your stony hearts and giving you natural hearts. . . ."[33] We also have the cry of Job asserting his moral innocence by saying that his heart does not reproach him.

This use of the heart to signify the inner moral self continues into the New Testament. Authentic, personally owned moral acts come from the heart or from inner motivation and are not performed for external motivations such as display or pride—"for with the heart man believeth unto righteousness."[34] This body imagery conveys a sense of the integrated unity of thinking and feeling in self-committed moral decision making, which unfortunately was often lost in later conceptualizations of conscience and the nature of the person.

When one traces the developments in the idea of conscience over the centuries, the varied concepts can be seen to change along with changing ideas of human nature. As with Paul, there is always an implicit psychology in formulations of conscience. A certain view of the self and its capacity for self-consciousness and self-regulation is a necessary foundation for the Christian and post-Christian secular views of conscience as a form of moral agency. To agree that conscience "impels us to right action"—to do good and avoid evil—implies an acceptance of the existence of a self that can discern, deliberate, and decide between good and evil.

Accepting the traditional idea that individuals who are moral agents can be impelled, but not coerced or determined, to choose right action implies a belief that human beings are free. They are at least free enough and capable of enough self-regulation to choose between competing desires and options. One strong statement of this enduring Western view of the self-direction of conscience is the famous definition given by Bishop Butler in the eighteenth century. Building on St. Paul's words, Butler, who was a shrewd observer of persons and a subtle thinker, says in his discourse on human nature that human beings have natural dispositions to be social and to do good, but at the same time, they have equally natural dispositions toward private interests and disordered, selfish passions.

Humans would not be able to discriminate and tell the difference.

> but there is a superior principle of reflection or conscience in every man, which distinguishes between the internal principles of his heart, as well as his external actions: which passes judgment upon himself and them; . . . It is by this faculty, natural to man, that he is a moral agent, that he is a law to himself . . . .[35]

For Butler, conscience is an authoritative, superior principle of self-conscious reflection; it is an active, deeply personal capacity that, as in Paul's vision, is natural to all human beings everywhere, whatever their culture or religion.

Those in the Christian theological tradition that preceded Butler and followed after him would affirm, as he did, that conscience as a natural human phenomenon has been provided by the Creator to creatures made in God's image. We have been so created that we can govern ourselves and make good moral decisions for our own good, our ultimate happiness, and the good of the whole creation. This idea of the innate naturalness and exalted role of conscience stretches from Paul to the church fathers to St. Thomas, through the reformers, to Kierkegaard, to Newman's "sacred and sovereign monitor," and on to modern theological thinkers and statements of official church teachings on the freedom and sacredness of conscience.[36]

In this continuing Christian theological tradition, there is a conviction that one's conscience is the divine inner light or voice of God immanent within the depths of the whole person (not a small, separate voice), and the inner light of conscience was often identified both with reason and with the operation of the Holy Spirit. In the Christian theological tradition, conscience is a sacred, sovereign authority that must be engaged, consulted, and obeyed as one would obey God. But this consensus that conscience is a divinely given inner capacity natural to all humans has not stemmed the centuries of debate and theological argument over exactly *how* conscience operates in the divine dispensation. Is conscience identified with the power of human reason? In what way does conscience manifest itself in the consciousness of the individual believer? Can it be suppressed, seriously distorted, corrupted, denied, or in error?

Everyone from Paul to all present observers has recognized the obvious fact that individual consciences differ; some of us are morally immature and err in our behavior, according to the judgment of the larger moral community. Even so, Paul and most theologians have concluded that we still have a moral obligation to follow our consciences because we cannot know any better and must be guided by the moral truth we do know. But there has been little agreement over what should happen when there are serious conflicts of conscience within a group. The problem of conflicts of conscience within the Church, within the state, and between Church and state, have been topics of continuous moral and philosophical dispute.

The theoretical, philosophical, and theological difficulties have given rise to pragmatic pastoral difficulties in guiding other persons in their spiritual and moral journeys. Coping with these practical personal problems involving conscience has been called the activity of moral discernment, or discernment of spirits—no small challenge for individuals, groups, and their pastoral advisors. The virtue of prudence has been seen as the necessary requirement for good moral decision making.

In Western culture's parallel development of secular moral philosophy, which increased as the ages of faith receded, philosophers and those interested in conscience and moral agency eliminated the moral relevance of a Creator and the moral authority of revelation through Scripture, discounted belief in the Holy Spirit immanent in the Church or the individual person, and did not equate conscience with the divine inner light or voice of God within. In removing the theological, transcendent superstructure and Holy Spirit within each person, secular philosophical approaches to moral functioning focused solely upon the processes of human reasoning, the presence of moral feelings and moral intuitions, and the moral values and moral principles that may be known solely through reflection upon human experience.[37]

In the course of the secularization of concerns with conscience or moral decision making, many different approaches to human moral capacities developed in many different directions. If today we inherit a confused, fragmented moral consciousness, it is partly because philosophy, theology, psychology, law, and the behavioral sciences pursued diverging paths and different goals in their treatment of morality.

Behavioral sciences, like sociology, social psychology, and anthropology, approach moral standards and socialization practices as components of existing cultural systems. Most social scientists are not trained to employ moral reasoning to find out what people ought to do, or to examine the normative nature of morality. They describe moral activity or mores as embedded in larger social and symbolic systems and competencies; social science usually aims to be descriptive and interpretative rather than prescriptive.

But moral philosophers in applied ethics—and to a lesser extent, those in the law, policy studies, and psychology—still work at moral guidance, prescribing what counts as an acceptable level of moral development or moral responsibility in different circumstances. Moral theologians and religious ethicists continue to address applied ethical problems. The ideas of secular and religious thinkers dealing with moral questions often converge.

Debates continue to rage over what rationality is, over what human reason can or cannot achieve, or ever hope to achieve, particularly in the moral domain. Today, the most problematic questions about the operations of human reason are focused upon the nature of the self, the capacities of human consciousness, and the functioning of the mind/brain/body unit. Philosophy and moral philosophy must come to terms with increasing progress in psychology, neuroscience, and investigations of cognitive science. When conscience is seen as an operation of self-consciousness, we need to understand what self-consciousness means. Since such issues are vital to the understanding of conscience and moral decision making, we need to ask some crucial questions: Who or what is the self? What is self-consciousness? Who can act in conscience?

Chapter 2

Who Has a Conscience?
The Self and Self-Consciousness

Who can make moral decisions of conscience? What does it take to engage in the subtle and complicated psychological processes of moral self-direction? Throughout history, many personal acts of conscience have been described. Take for example the comments of two "prisoners of conscience" living in different eras, of different religions, different genders, and different cultures. Natan Sharansky, a prisoner of the KGB in modern Russia, refused to falsely confess his guilt in order to be released, and reflected upon his ordeal in these words:

> On that occasion, when I was stripped and searched, I decided it was best to treat my captors like the weather. A storm can cause you problems, and sometimes those problems can be humiliating. But the storm itself doesn't humiliate you. Once I understood this I realized that nothing they did could humiliate me. I could only humiliate myself—by doing something I might later be ashamed of. . . . *Nothing they do can humiliate me. I alone can humiliate myself.*[1] [emphasis in original]

Many centuries earlier, an illiterate peasant girl called Joan of Arc expressed her remorse over her earlier confession of guilt with a similar account: "What I said, I said for fear of the fire . . . I did a very wicked thing in confessing that what I had done was not well done. . . . *I was damning myself to save my life.*"[2] [emphasis mine]

Such self-reflections demonstrate how complex an understanding of self, moral acts, and moral assessment can be. The self can be judged by the self, an "I" whose approval is valued more than bodily existence. These persons, as conscious moral agents, appear to fear the loss of their inner moral integrity more than their lives. But they also recognize that the self can be inwardly torn, divided, and inconsistent; some actions or words performed in fear or under stress may later be repudiated as morally unworthy.

They assume further that as free persons they have the power to observe their own behavior, to learn from failures, and then to guide future courses of moral action by better moral standards. Subtle self-observations and discriminations are made of personal weaknesses and temptations under pressure, and new strategies of moral self-direction are devised in order not to repeat moral lapses. The focus of consciousness moves both backward and forward in time.

Again and again, similar accounts of inner decisions of conscience and moral deliberation have appeared in historical records, as well as in biographies, drama, literature, and confessional religious writings. It would be an intriguing exercise to collect a number of instances of different kinds of crises. There are many moving inner soliloquies in which persons struggle toward moral self-governance or labor to make worthy moral decisions. These struggles of conscience and cries from the heart echo down the ages and across cultures—from Job to Thomas More to the latest political prisoners.

Such testimonies reveal a picture of human beings possessing an inner self with amazing capacities of awareness and self-consciousness. In the preceding chapter, I simply assumed the traditional claims for moral agency to be true, and spoke of adult persons making self-committed moral decisions. But such claims have been disputed. Behavioral scientists, among others, have vigorously denied that human organisms can be self-conscious, self-directing moral agents. The moral claim to conscience has often been denied on rational, scientific grounds.[3] Is this still the case? Or can modern science and psychology present evidence to support the presumption that humans are truly doing what it appears that they are doing when they give accounts of self-conscious inner moral struggles of conscience? If we are "the self-interpreting animal," does the moral interpretation have validity?[4]

Psychological Prerequisites of Conscience

To have a conscience (as defined in chapter 1), a being must have self-awareness, a sense of self-identity, an ability for self-regulation and self-direction, a capacity for self-evaluation, and an affective desire, or caring commitment, to measure up and act according to some perceived standards of moral worth. Such qualities require highly complicated mental, emotional, and social abilities.

Obviously an animal or an infant cannot think in such complicated ways. Computers may or may not be able to think in their fashion, but can machines ever self-consciously know and observe themselves or care enough to have emotional commitments to moral standards of worth?[5] It is most unlikely.

The key to conscience and moral decisions appears to reside in self-consciousness. Self-consciousness implies the owning or possessive appropriation of a self-aware, self-recording, continuous identity through time and across situations. More than ad hoc information processing or instinctual reflexes geared to specific goals are necessary. Through the centuries, philosophers and others who have considered morality have focused upon human self-consciousness as the most important requirement for human identity: "I think therefore I am." If we can be aware of our inner selves, processing information, images, feelings, plans, interpersonal reactions, and so forth, then we can be also aware of other persons, things, and relationships in the world.

As we wake up and "come to" each morning, the apprehension of the world and others comes into consciousness and assumes reality. Self-consciousness may be the first indisputable experiential ground of all that we apprehend, but it also seems the most mysterious and puzzling phenomenon in existence.[6] How is it that we should now be awake and aware of ourselves as ourselves within a world that appears to be real? This basic question of consciousness stretches human thinking to its limits and beyond—before one even enters the more complex questions of moral decision making.[7]

Despite the lack of final answers about consciousness, the consensus in the Western moral tradition has held that self-consciousness is necessary for conscience.[8] An individual needs a highly developed degree of continuous self-consciousness, along with the freedom and ability to choose between possible options. If one is held responsible as a moral agent after a choice, one must be the same person before and after the fact, and at the moment of choosing, be able to think about different possible behaviors and their future consequences. To be a moral agent, one must also be able to direct one's acts to one's self-chosen purposes. Then one is morally responsible, or response-able, for acts initiated, consent given, or responses made.

Control

Acts or responses that are beyond the self's control cannot be considered within the realm of personal moral responsibility. They are, as

Sharansky says, like storms in nature, or like other brute facts beyond human causation. We may be able to control our responses to, or attitudes toward, uncontrollable events in the environment, but not initiate, control, or affect the events themselves. We also cannot control or change many things that happen within our bodies; we will have to sleep, eat, suffer illness and gradually decline and die. It also seems the case that if you torture persons in certain sadistic and clever psychological ways for long enough, even the strongest may eventually be broken.[9]

The existing boundaries between controllable and uncontrollable events or actions may be extremely difficult to discern in any given situation. But in our moral tradition, we have recognized that there are limits to human agency and moral responsibility. Recognizing these limits as real, we have rationally agreed that in moral self-direction, "ought" must imply "can." It is contradictory and irrational to order the self (or others) to do that which it is impossible to do.

The distorted patterns of thinking in mental illness manifest themselves in contradictory demands, impossible expectations, or illogical goals that cannot be met in the real world. In a rational moral tradition and in definitions of normal, mature mental functioning, self-commands, or demands for committed moral decisions, must be reasonable, noncontradictory, and in accord with known reality. To be able to think logically is a psychological prerequisite for a well-functioning conscience.

The "I" who morally decides must also be integrated and unified. One must be sufficiently unified as a whole organism, with all the different dimensions of self in gear, to be able to act upon one's purposes. There are different subsystems within a personality, sometimes alluded to as the existence of multiple selves,[10] but they must all report to the same executive commander and operate under orders as a unit. To be a moral agent, one can have neither paralysis nor chaotic disorganization within.

Yet paradoxically, one can best operate as a unitary being by having complex inner subsystems, functional specializations, and inner divisions. This diversity enables a person to process information from different sources, select from diverse engendered possibilities, and then choose and stand upon one's choices as one executes planned strategies. To choose, one must know that one can act in different ways as one self-consciously surveys oneself and the environmental circumstances. The more one can be conscious of oneself as a subjectively functioning individual—stand back and observe oneself—the more objective one can be about one's situation.

Observing one's self thinking and feeling gives distance from automatic responses. Abstract thinking, or the ability to have experience vicariously, gives space and time to choose; it opens up different perspectives, and different perspectives encourage the realization of different options that can be taken. Instinctual reflexive behavior, mindless behavior, or coerced behavior cannot be fully owned and free, because such acts are not chosen or owned by the self. The most fully human acts are those done intentionally while fully awake and aware. Morality and conscience is best understood as a self-reflexive enterprise.

Awareness

Self-consciousness in a moral decision of conscience has to operate in a complex double-directed way. There must be an awareness or connectedness with the real outer environment at the same time as an awareness of the inner environment of the self as self. Moral action requires both consciousness of self and consciousness of a reality or standards beyond the self. If someone is sleepwalking, hypnotized, brainwashed, brain injured, or drugged, she or he may be conscious enough of the external environment to function but not conscious of the inner self, i.e., not fully self-aware. When hallucinating, subject to schizophrenic thought disorders or delusions, or under intense shock or stress, a person may be out of touch with the real external environment, as well as unaware of her or his own distorted perceptions and functioning.

Mentally retarded, mentally ill, or brain-diseased persons can lack sufficient consciousness of self and their environment to make moral decisions. The brain diseases or injuries that take away self-awareness and the memory necessary for continuous identity are destructive to moral functioning. Other pathological conditions in which emotions are blunted and normal interpersonal responses affected are also morally deforming. The caring or emotional investment necessary for relating or committing one's self to standards in the environment can disappear.

There are some criminal psychopaths and other brain-damaged persons who, while retaining information-processing skills, seem to lack normal emotional responses. The writer-physician Oliver Sacks has observed that when some brain-damaged persons become emotionless—equally indifferent, and flat in responding to all things—they seem to truly "lose their humanity or souls."[11] They may, like a psychopathic criminal, be highly intelligent, indeed be able to recount moral rules and moral knowledge, but not seem able to emotionally care about them. They do not care about self, others, the good, future consequences, or anything else. They simultaneously lose their inner emotional self-investment and the impetus to care about doing good and avoiding evil, about moral self-respect, or about evaluating their moral functioning.

Moral functioning, then, requires not only a high degree of self-consciousness and awareness of self, the environment, and standards, but also a self-commitment or emotional response toward self, other persons, ideals, ideas, and standards. Once the self's subjective participation and motivation is granted as crucially important, then judgments on the moral worth of a human act cannot be made solely by assessing its external consequences without regard for the human agent's intention. Only in amoral systems are self-conscious intentions or motivations of a human agent disregarded, and punishments meted out for bad outcomes, innocent errors, or failures. No account is taken of whether bad acts are motivated by guilty minds or not.[12]

While proponents of the Western tradition have agreed on the psychological prerequisites of highly developed self-consciousness for the operation of conscience, they have not agreed on how widespread the necessary attributes are in the general population. An optimistic assessment would see the necessary criteria as normally present in most adults. As the philosopher C. D. Broad says in his treatment of conscience, ". . . the vast majority of sane adult human beings are capable of ostensibly moral cognition, of morally directed emotion, and of moral motivation. Now every such person is also capable of *reflexive* cognition, i.e., of contemplating himself, his experiences, dispositions, intentions, motives, and actions, from various points of view."[13] In other words the ordinary person can reflect upon their past and future actions and appraise them as right or wrong.

Broad is also true to the fullest understanding of conscience in emphasizing that emotional, self-invested feeling and caring about moral standards is necessary. He points out that in addition to the intellectual powers required, one must have and exercise "the emotional disposition to feel certain peculiar emotions," such as remorse, guilt, approval, and so on, in response to the moral characteristics one believes one's acts and dispositions to have.[14] In other words, one must be emotionally responding to one's self, through observation and moral evaluation. Finally to "have a conscience" in Broad's sense, the person must be seeking "to do what he believes to be right and avoid what he believes to be wrong."[15] Other thinkers have called this basic commitment to be good "the fundamental option" toward goodness and the moral life.[16]

A person's specific moral decisions are grounded on a prior, general, foundational decision to seek the good and avoid evil.

In each of the human dimensions of thinking, feeling, and willingness to act, an individual must meet certain criteria or have developed to a certain capacity in order to be able to operate morally. Achieving the necessary capacity and potential does not mean that individuals will automatically hold to the same definitions or beliefs about right or wrong—or act accordingly. Persons may have very different ways of finding out what they ought to do, or ought to avoid. They may think the problem through in different ways, have access to different bodies of knowledge, have different emotional allegiances, and reach different conclusions with varying degrees of ability to act effectively; but the person with an operating conscience will have achieved a certain level of self-conscious thinking and awareness, and have certain kinds of emotional commitments.

Other optimistic thinkers are also sure that free moral agents can develop beyond the moral minimum. Persons can observe and morally judge their own present desires and emotions—and want to want more.[17] One can obtain enough distance from oneself to judge and evaluate one's own desires, and desire to be more ardent about more important things—or realize that one has become hardened and should be more emotionally disturbed by one's moral failings. Instead of simple here-and-now choices between this and that action, human beings can choose moral aspirations and life goals concerning what sort of persons they wish to try and become.[18] This ability implies that humans can go beyond the present self in active pursuit of growing and changing for the better. Persons can make complex self-evaluations of their own standards of worth. At the highest levels of development, persons can morally appraise themselves and others by judging how strongly they seek more-noble desires and more-worthy moral standards.

The question next arises whether this traditional depiction of human beings as free, self-directing selves with moral consciousness and moral aspirations is a realistic account of the human condition. Many have denied it.

Skeptics and a Response to Skepticism

There have always been challenges to the belief that human beings can be self-conscious or free enough to act as moral agents. The challenges have come from those thinkers who believe in great overarching, determinist forces complete with immutable laws that govern a universe, which surely could never be affected by the acts of individual human beings. Human assertions of, or beliefs in, self-consciousness and freedom have been thought to be beside the point in the "real" world. The determinist laws and systems that have been proposed as "really" governing the universe include the biologically evolutionary, the socioeconomic and historical, and the physically ma-terialistic—or some combination of these. A basic skepticism holds that all talk of free, self-conscious moral choices is an illusion of one kind or another. Self-consciousness and a sense of self-direction are, at best, an epiphenomena, or verbal phenomena, which rationalize after the fact those events that happen from other causes.

After all, if human life truly is nasty, brutish, and short, with a rigidly determined biological war of all against all for survival, who can countenance the effects of supposedly free moral deliberations? If we are clever animals strictly programmed by selfish genes, or manipulated by deep, unconscious, instinctual forces of sex and aggression, or sim-ply blindly responsive to environmental conditioning, then the pros-pects for free, rational moral self-direction, or true altruism, are dim. Skeptics assert that all determining influences upon the human orga-nism must arise from unconscious programs, biological systems, or en-vironmental conditions. The true causes of behavior are from the bottom up, and the outside in—despite our comforting illusions of being inner selves with freedom to choose.

If self-consciousness is at best an epiphenomenon that provides confabulated illusions of personhood, while the really important mech-anisms of the brain and environment whir along on their determined course, then moral inquiry or moral choice is more or less beside the point. The neuroscientist William T. Powers describes scientific deter-minist thinking in a witty passage detailing what he thinks most of his fellow behavioral scientists assume when confronting questions of hu-man nature and consciousness. Their unspoken consensus, he claims, would run as follows:

> Sometimes it seems that organisms seek goals, want things, decide things, and act spontaneously. But you and I know that such appear-ances are illusions, because we know that natural laws of physics and chemistry are behind all such appearances. In ordinary affairs, we use ordinary language for convenience, but when we want to speak as scientists, we have to put metaphysical nonsense aside. If laymen criticize our scientific descriptions, that is only because of leftover

superstitions, beliefs, and sloppy habits of thought from their primitive past. We scientists do not have any superstitions, beliefs, or sloppy habits of thought, especially since such things do not really exist in the first place. And if you won't call attention to my consciousness, I won't call attention to yours.[19]

With those last words, Powers calls attention to the built-in contradictions of a scientific dismissal of free, rational consciousness—the fact that scientists themselves have conscious selves that appear to freely reason their way to new and creative discoveries. Powers goes on to discuss his own research on the brain's processes, which led him to change his mind about minds. He concludes that human minds have the capacity to exercise control of the organism. Powers reports that there are an increasing number of researchers who have begun to affirm the brain/mind's powers to direct attention and consciousness; they provide new evidence for "top down" controls in the human organism, as well as "bottom up" bodily mechanisms. In interpreting his research findings, Powers breaks the older unwritten scientific consensus, and challenges the dismissals of consciousness as epiphenomenon.

Changes in Scientific Thinking

Powers affirms that the most recent scientific work on control systems and the brain's control hierarchies forces open the scientific blinders to the existence of self-conscious self-regulation. Today, the chasm dividing the subjective experience of consciousness and the scientific study of brain, behavior, and experience is being bridged. New technologically sophisticated investigations of the brain, combined with the parallel development of information and computer sciences, are producing a new era of scientific exploration of the human brain's abilities. A scientific shift called the cognitive, or consciousness, revolution has taken place in the last decade. Articles, books, and research reports pour forth, all devoted to the new cognitive sciences and new efforts to correlate the workings of the brain with human experiences of self-consciousness.

Articles such as Karl Pribram's "The Cognitive Revolution and Mind/ Brain Issues" describe what another prominent scientist, Roger Sperry, has called the "scientific turnabout on consciousness."[20] The turnabout, or major new claim, is that at the top of the brain's hierarchies and systems, there is something, or someone, that can make decisions and exert a great deal of decisive control over subsequent human functioning. Sperry describes the consciousness revolution of the 1970s: "The new outlook puts subjective mental forces near the top of the brain's causal control hierarchy and gives them primacy in determining what a person is and does."[21] The subjective conscious self reappears in science as an agent, or as one bemused commentator has colorfully expressed it, "The soul . . . is making a sly return by the back door of science."[22]

Previous scientific approaches understood that information and environmental stimuli go up the brain's control hierarchy and affect thinking and feeling; it has been known since the nineteenth century that a brain injury, such as an iron bar staved through a person's forehead, affects the intellectual and emotional functioning of the unfortunate victim. Medicine has always granted that individual consciousness changes through organic insults, illnesses, and the intrusion of lesions, tumors, intoxicants, poisons, infections, and so on; all kinds of internal and external accidents to the brain can impair mental functioning.[23] Reading the various works of Oliver Sacks can be frightening proof of the damage that can be wrought upon the personality and higher mental functions from brain disease and brain damage.[24]

But what is now newly granted and appreciated is "the principle of control from above downward, referred to as downward causation."[25] In other words, higher subjective mental functions can control and direct lower systems of the organism. Causal factors can go down from higher emergent properties of mind, as well as up from below; that is, "The control from below upward is retained but is claimed to not furnish the whole story. The full explanation requires that one also take into account new, previously nonexistent, emergent properties, including the mental, that interact causally at their own higher level and also exert causal control from above downward."[26] An individual's mind or mental states, known as "macro" or "molar" or "emergent properties," can exert control over the brain and body. A common analogy used is the TV set (brain) with its electronic receivers being subject to the incoming programs (mind). A crashing blow or a blowout of some electronic part can interfere with the program, but no examination of the mechanisms of the box can explain or predict the incoming programming of news, soap operas, or documentaries.

Another intriguing information-based model of emergent self-consciousness is provided by the physiological psychologist E. Roy John. His thesis, similar to those of other scientists working in the new mode, is that consciousness, subjective experience, the self, and self-awareness are constituted by an "emergent property of sufficiently complex and appropriately organized matter."[27] At certain levels, "a system transcends a simple summation of the elementary properties of the constituent parts."[28] A whole is more than the sum of its parts, as the Gestalt psychologists would say, and this applies to the brain and the neuronal activities that, at a sufficient level of complex organization, emerge as a self-conscious, self-programming mind.

At different levels of information transmission, different properties emerge. The concept of a hierarchy of capacities for consciousness is important for understanding other forms of life. Also, it helps in understanding how complex a human organism can be, since humans normally develop through all the levels to become the most complete information-processing entities ever known. In John's scheme, a first order of incoming information produces *sensations* or *irritability* of living matter that people and protozoans share.[29] If an organism can interpret the meaning of sensations with stored information about previous experiences, *perceptions,* or a second order of information, emerge. These low levels of organization John considers to be preconscious or unfelt categories of information processing. *Consciousness* emerges at a more complex third order of information processing and, with more complex reflexive processing, can progress to a fourth, a fifth, and a sixth order of information processing, which, at the very apex of the ladder, emerges as subjective *self-awareness.*

Consciousness that emerges at the third order of information is described as a unified, multidimensional representation or reading of the state of the system and its environment, which can be integrated with other information from memory and present needs of the organism. Consciousness generates emotional reactions and programs of behavior to adjust the organism to its environment. It is ongoing and complex enough to have many levels and different kinds of content with different constellations. Information comes up from preconscious sensations and perceptions, but reorganizing programs can go back down the hierarchies, as well.

But it takes a fourth-order transformation of information to produce *subjective experience,* or a process that reorganizes the sequential series of events of consciousness into a single experiential *episode.* As episodes are extended through time and an individual personal history is produced, one finally sees the emergence of a self. The *self* is a fifth order of information transformation, or an individual historical record in memory of subjective experiences or episodes. At the top of this hierarchy, one sees that *self-awareness* emerges as a sixth level of information transformation. This means that the individual can interpret present subjective experiences in the light of patterns of previous subjective experiences.[30]

Most importantly, for a view of the self as conscious agent, or potential moral agent, this theory admits that information and organizing

programs that arise from subjective self-awareness can be sent back down
the hierarchy to control and effectly reorganize behaviors at lower levels.
The other important feature of this approach that impinges upon considerations of moral agency is the assertion that a great deal of information
processing takes place at preconscious or nonconscious lower levels. It
now seems clear that within the human organism there are different levels
of information processing and levels of consciousness.[31] There exists what
has been called a "continuum of consciousness."[32] As we shall see in future chapters devoted to reason, intuition, and emotion, the idea that only
a certain amount of information reaches consciousness or is accessible to
full self-awareness is an important fact to take into account when assessing
the processes of moral decision making.

But again, the important point to be emphasized here is that when
adult human beings as subjective selves consciously think in the self-
aware, self-directing way the unimpaired human brain can, the higher
processes of thinking can influence the lower processes. John nicely
defines cognition or thinking as "the ability to have subjective experience vicariously."[33] If one can abstract and imagine routines without
carrying them out directly or having the stimuli physically present,
then choices and alternative programs can be envisioned and enacted.
Thinking humans can also directly activate their stored information in
an arbitrarily organized way for some new purpose or goal.

Human minds are not strictly programmed or confined to reflex responses to the perceived environment; humans are free to manipulate,
recombine, and reorganize accumulated stores of experiences so that "the
self is continuously in the process of modification and of analysis of its
own experience."[34] In other word, in self-aware consciousness, there is a
continuous, dynamic processing of external and internal incoming information, along with constant self-reorganization of internal experiences. In
this testimony from neuropsychology, we see the kind of consciously reflexive self that has been traditionally seen as the necessary prerequisite
for the moral enterprise and the operation of conscience.

New Theories

Self-Organization

The physics of consciousness in the brain has been speculated upon
as well. One daring new approach sees the key to consciousness in
quantum mechanics. In a provocative book called *The Quantum Self*, an
author trained in physics claims that consciousness is an emergent

property of complex matter and that the top-down influences of human consciousness will be explained by new understandings of matter given us by quantum mechanics.[35] This effort is another return to the mind/body problem that tries at the microlevel of wave/particle events to overturn older deterministic models of human beings. Here again, the self and human free self-consciousness make an appearance in another part of the new science.

If these new theories of actively self-organizing human consciousness are correct, and it seems that they are as scientific evidence accrues, those thinkers who have maintained that consciousness is at most a meaningless epiphenomenon of brain function will be refuted. If self-consciousness could not, in fact, initiate control of the lower hierarchies of the organism, then it would always be reduced to some after-the-fact constructed narrative—a creative confabulation to rationalize and explain the really decisive operations going on at the organism's lower levels of organization. Such confabulations have been observed in posthypnotic subjects, but whether this is a special case is the crux of the question.[36] If there is "downward causation," then the claim can be made that the self-aware consciousness of a normal adult can integrate, organize, and control many of the systems of the organism to a greater or lesser degree.

Volition

Other exciting, new experimental efforts in mainstream psychology that aim to show the free action of human volition are also pointing toward the existence and effectiveness of free, conscious decisions. Experimental psychologists are exploring new evidence and publishing articles in professional journals with titles such as "Of Course There Can Be an Empirical Science of Volitional Action," "The Next Steps Toward a Science of Agency," and "Whither Volition?"[37] The old determinist paradigm is not yet dead, of course; some still resist the idea of free, conscious self-regulation.[38] But it can be said that free will is slipping back into the scientific picture of human nature, following the consciousness revolution.

Evolution

Other more evolutionary-minded scientists take the existence of consciousness as a given, but are more interested in the question of how human consciousness evolved. Why and how did consciousness appear over the eons of recorded life on the planet? One emerging explanatory hypothesis is that consciousness developed in the evolution of life as a selectively advantageous response to the need for mobile organisms to get around and survive in a changing and challenging environment.[39] Focusing upon the organism's need to adapt to the environment helps explain the objective orientation of consciousness—why we are usually conscious *of* something, or focus upon objects outside of ourselves. Plants, which are stationary, do not need an ongoing recording system to adapt and survive. Organisms in water also do not face as demanding an environment as those on dry land. Getting around on land is a tougher challenge for an animal than floating in the ocean (thus the failure of dolphins to develop further?). Outwitting the predators on the savannas takes a more alert recording consciousness than surviving in the treetops.

Brains and consciousness increase in capacity among survivors who figure out and master the ups and downs of a hard, increasingly complex environment. In his emphasis upon the functional goal directedness of consciousness—defined as "life made aware of itself"—the distinguished Soviet psychologist A. R. Luria says, "Consciousness is ability to assess sensory information, to respond to it with critical thoughts and actions, and to retain memory traces in order that past traces or actions may be used in the future."[40] Consciousness is so often focused upon the environment, "out there," and upon discrepancies and problems, because mind evolved as a coping and problem-solving device.

Conscious attention or conscious awareness can be likened to a searchlight constantly scanning the environment in order to increase operating abilities. Turning the light inward and becoming consciously self-aware may be a unique, late-appearing, complex development in the evolution of consciousness and in the development of the individual. But since we are a socially bonding species, self-consciousness has its important uses. When an individual must deal with other individuals in social matrices—be they nurturing bonds, mutual dependencies, cooperation, or competition—then self-consciousness becomes adaptive as a way to understand and cope with others.

The theorist Nicholas Humphrey sees consciousness to have evolved not so much to cope with the material environment as to cope with other humans and the social group.[41] Nothing in the natural environment can provide as complex a challenge as coping with our ever-changing, active fellow members of the social group, who are as intelligent as we and must be handled carefully. We are able to read each other's emotions and intentions from facial and bodily signals by inference from our own inner experiences. Sensitivity to the inner self helps with reading the cues of others, who exist as inner selves in their own subjective centers.

As the brain and human powers increased in complexity over the eons of selective development, human beings became organisms with diverse hierarchies of structured control systems, adapted to making the whole human being function more efficiently. The complexity of the brain and the multidimensionality of our human interacting systems have been seen as an adaptive advantage—if one system fails, another may provide resources to cope. Redundancy and variety of functioning components in any system is a safeguard and an advantage. Of course, the complexity and interactions of a system with so many parts also mean that more breakdowns and malfunctions are possible. But normally, the intertwining and fusing of the subparts into a whole produces prodigies of holistic efficiency.

Subsystems

One helpful approach to the human organism sees the individual as constituted of several main functioning subsystems, which interact and overlap as they use the same final pathways of brain and body.[42] These subsystems can be differentiated as physiological-homeostatic, motor-active, drive (thirst, hunger, elimination, and so on), cognitive-informational, and affective-emotional.

The physiological-homeostatic system keeps the body regulated and functioning. Most of these operations are completely unconscious, unless something goes wrong and pain signals, spasms, or fever intrudes into consciousness.

Then there is a drive system that controls hunger, thirst, elimination, and, to some degree, sex; this system registers consciously in recurrent cycles and can even dominate consciousness when deprivation is severe.

A motor muscular system enacts movement and action, often in the service of the drive system, and it too is partly conscious and partly unconscious in operation. When first learning a new motor skill, such as tying shoelaces or driving a car, every move is a conscious effort, but with mastery, habituation takes over, and the movements become unconscious and automatic. It makes sense that consciousness and attention are limited and must be efficiently deployed; what no longer needs self-directed effort recedes from focus.

Of course, the most intriguing subsystems, almost always in focus, are those at the core of human self-consciousness: the affective-emotional system and the information-processing, or cognitive-perceptual, system. These operations constitute self-consciousness in an awake human being; they provide our experiences of perceiving, thinking, imagining, remembering, and responding emotionally. But as we have seen from the new neuropsychology, these systems, too, emerge from lower-level preconscious systems of analysis, hierarchical selection, and information processing. Again, a limited consciousness could not attend to the prodigies of work involved, even, for instance, in perceiving and recognizing a visual image. Much processing and filtering of inner and outer stimuli is performed outside of conscious awareness.[43]

While we now know that we have bottom-up and top-down processing, no theoretical model of the mind's structure or processing has gained the adherence of all researchers. The awesome complexity of the brain and body's interacting systems remains a challenge. The newest scientific frontiers consist of finding out and mapping how the organism's subsystems are activated in the brain. Global divisions into left-brain and right-brain functioning or the tripartite mapping of reptilian, mammal, and human brains seems much too simple an approach. The organizational structure of the brain may have many modular parts and identifiable components that contribute to the final products of awareness.[44]

Each subsystem of the main human systems can be separately analyzed into smaller and smaller components, but at the same time, all the systems interact and function as a whole, often supplementing one another. Take memory, for instance. At this moment, if asked, we can consciously call to mind the name of our fourth-grade teacher, or some other bit of personal knowledge, but we are not conscious where it is when we are not thinking about it, or how we are able to call it to mind. At other moments, things from memory just come into consciousness, often in accord with emotional states. Obviously, we could spend a lifetime studying memory alone—iconic memory, episodic memory, long-term memory, semantic memory, implicit memory, declarative memory, forgetting, decay, interference, and so on—and memory is just one subpart of the cognitive perceptual system interacting with all the others.[45]

In human consciousness, the cognitive and affective emotional systems are intertwined and interactive in a multitude of ways. Some theorists emphasize the separate parallel operations of the systems; others emphasize the interaction and near fusion of the two. But every theorist recognizes the fact that the cognitive and affective systems regularly interact and overlap, producing structures that are partly conceptual and partly affective—and probably stored in memory in both ways. To make it all the more complex, the emotive-conceptual structures can instantaneously interact with the other subsystems of a human being. A thought can make one laugh, blush, or lose one's appetite, and a perception of an opportunity or danger can produce an instant action or reaction, complete with future plans and strategies. The moral relevance of these interactions will be discussed at greater length in the following chapters.

Today, studies of the complexities of consciousness and thinking make use of new technologies for recording and providing images of the interactions of brain, biochemical, and muscular activity.[46] We can see shadows and images of thinking and feeling with new empirical recordings and imaging of the brain at work. While consciousness remains invisible to the eye, its diverse activities or its absence, as in brain death, can be newly detected within the organism.

It seems reasonable to conclude that the progress of science has been such that subjective self-consciousness can now be recognized and properly valued as more than metaphysical nonsense or superstition. While there is more unknown than known, at least the cognitive and consciousness revolution has newly grounded inquiries into the subjective nature of the self and the psychology of moral agency.

Psychological Inquiries into Subjective Self-Consciousness

In its beginnings, psychology took the self and subjective consciousness as a primary domain of exploration. Then the study of the self and consciousness suffered a partial eclipse during the supremacy of the behaviorists. They affirmed materialism and hard scientific determinism, posited the concept of "the empty self," and proclaimed the irrelevance of the epiphenomenon of consciousness.[47]

But in the last decades, as a corollary of the cognitive and consciousness revolution referred to earlier, there has been a resurgence of research on the self, self-consciousness, self-concepts, self-attributions, self-esteem, self-efficacy, self-disclosure, self-presentation, self-regulation, and so on.[48] Even some of the most committed behaviorists accepted the findings of human cognition and became convinced that it makes sense to at least follow a model of the brain provided by computers. One can conceptualize the self minimally as an executive program for the rest of the brain's information-processing systems.[49]

Other psychological researchers built upon the earlier foundations of psychology's explorations of the self and self-consciousness. If one were to try to sum up the general shape of today's inquiries into the self, one could see a focus on two arenas: one on the structure and content of the self, and the other on the active processes of subjective consciousness and information processing. Naturally, the domains are interrelated, since the various structures or dimensions of the self are built up through the active operating processes of consciousness over time. But the inquiries can be separated and explored by different research strategies.[50] The structures or contents of the adult self involve the answers to the direct question, Who am I?

When persons turn inward and try to observe the structure and content of the self, there is some rough consensus that approximates the original formulations of William James. For James, the observed self could be experienced as having different dimensions consisting in three main divisions: a material me, a social me, a spiritual me.[51] He discussed these dimensions at great length. The material me includes the body and can also be extended to those objects, possessions, or beloved persons that become extensions of myself. The social me consists of all the different social roles one plays with a variety of others in different groups. Then beyond the material and social me's, James discerned a spiritual me that includes all the internal, private higher faculties of thinking, willing, and feeling.

James noted that usually there is a hierarchy of value among these three dimensions, going from material through social to the highest and most valued spiritual. In a crude way, we can still validate this today, since most of us would far rather lose a limb or be stripped of a professional role than lose our mental abilities of thinking or remembering. Our bodies are certainly us, but our private thoughts and feelings seem more intimately us—at least when our bodies are healthy and not suffering the narrowing of consciousness brought on by excruciating pain.

Gordon Allport, the noted psychologist, building upon the work of James, called the self "the proprium," in order to emphasize the mineness—the owner-invested, warm, or self-appropriated quality—that distinguishes the self from other phenomena in my experience.[52] For Allport, there are also many parts within the individual organism or personality that are not felt as intimately owned dimensions of the self because they are not perceived as mine or charged with warmth or personal investment. My spleen or reflexes, for instance, are not particularly mine, nor is my ability to discriminate shapes or other automatic, impersonal perceptual skills.

Allport also differentiates in the self, or proprium, components that can be roughly classed as material, social, or mental dimensions of me, but he has more categories. He sees the owned self as made up of a bodily sense, a continuous identity through time, a drive toward self-seeking assertiveness, a social extension outward with identification with loved ones and abstract groups, a rational problem-solving agent, a self-concept or image, and a set of unique, idealized, appropriate goals or aspirations for one's life course.

Most important, both James and Allport discern within the self an "I" or a knower, who knows the other components. The self is seen as dipolar, with a knower or an "I" fused with a "me" that is known in different dimensions. With self-consciousness, our own functioning structures can be observed while remaining part of consciousness. The experience is one of being, at one and the same time, a knower and a known, a subject and an object. When we massage our cheeks with our palms, we are both masseur and massaged. We can also turn the metaphorical eye or light of our conscious attention back on our bodily sense, or on our conscious mental processes, and observe the thoughts and feelings we experience in consciousness. We know that we feel sad, or angry; we can evaluate the social roles we are playing, or we can see that our thinking ability is having difficulty figuring out a puzzling problem as we apply different logical rules. The many facets of our selves and the operations of the selves can be known in acts of self-reflection.

Given the multiple dimensions of self and dynamic consciousness, each with a unique developmental history, it becomes obvious that within a range of common experience, there is room for distinct variations. Individuals will evolve different configurations and patterns of self over time. While large developmental stages may be common to all human beings, there are also singular combinations and recombinations, beginning with a unique genetic inheritance, that produce the self identity of each person. Different cultures and contexts may also encourage different aspects of the self more than others.

All the dimensions of self need recognition—those related to the body, to the mind, and to social roles with other persons. They all exist and can be observed in ordinary experience, as well as in the converging findings of the research programs of different investigators. Many self-theorists only emphasize the social self and slight the other internal dimensions. The social self has been given all the game by those who, following the great sociologist George Mead, think the self to be created and maintained mostly by consciousness of being observed by the "generalized other."[53] These theorists believe the self is dependent upon continuous social interactions and has a need for strategic self-presentation while playing different roles in the ongoing scripted social dramas of life.[54]

A more balanced approach, which parallels the James-Allport dimensions of self, appears in the work of infancy researcher Daniel
Stern, who is also a psychoanalyst. From the evidence of his experimental infancy research, he has produced a model in which different
dimensions of self regularly emerge in the first two years and then
continue throughout the life span.[55] According to Stern, the infant is
born with an innately programmed, primordial "emerging self" that
strives for expression, fulfillment, growth, and rationality. This process
of coming into consciousness remains throughout life as the preconscious reservoir of thought and creativity. Then there develops a core
self, or agent self, aware of an active body that can do things in the
world and cause effects in time and space.

After this, at around eight months of age, a great leap forward is
taken by the development of inner subjectivity and a conscious self
shared with other human beings—a psychological inner self strength-
ened through shared emotions and social experience. This interpersonal subjective self, along with the core self, also continues throughout
life. This emotional extension into "we" feelings is somewhat similar to
James's social self. Finally, by age two and with the acquisition of language, a symbolic linguistic conception of self appears in which an
infant can verbalize consciousness and refer to self as "I" and "me."
The linguistic self-concept and relatedness can then develop apace, but
the other dimensions of self continue throughout the life span as parallel senses of self-consciousness.

The existence of parallel, preverbal, emotional, interpersonal senses
has been increasingly validated by the latest round of sophisticated
research.[56] The linguistic, articulated conceptual self is not the whole
story of our experience of self-consciousness. We have a consciousness
also of emotional, bodily, core senses of self. The fact that linguistic
concepts of self develop later than a core or social self may also account
for the fact that certain cultures and languages define the self somewhat
differently from our Western individualistic tradition. Languages can
name or describe the self differently, but there can be other common
experiences arising from preverbal developments of self. Awareness of
the diverse components and dimensions of the self can emerge and
disappear in the flow of consciousness.

Stream of Consciousness

James invented the label "stream of consciousness" to describe that
continuous, dynamic processing through time that forms the sense
of human self-awareness.[57] Thoughts, feelings, images, and various

sensations and impressions ebb and flow into consciousness continually. But the flow of consciousness has many different characteristics as a process, and these have been the object of exploration and inquiry.[58] These differences in processing are crucial for theories of moral agency, as we have seen in the discussion of prerequisites for an operating conscience.

Some of the emerging content of consciousness appears spontaneously in daydreams, fantasies, intuitions, or sudden reactions to pain or other internal or environmental stimuli. Consciousness can be seen as a passive recording of experience that reactively serves coping and adaptation. The more crucial claim, however, is that a self can also be active and initiate processes that are not simply responsive and reactive. Our claim to human freedom and self-direction rests on the observation that the self in active processes of consciousness can focus, initiate, and control mental acts.[59] Directed thinking and problem solving consist of focusing attention, calling up past stores of information, and activating and evaluating skilled mental routines and programs. Other possible directed acts of consciousness involve imagining, remembering, and creating fantasies. We can also enact emotions and, indeed, create on purpose fully scripted plans or images for the future. We as humans can have abstracted vicarious experience by actively directing ourselves to do so.[60]

We can subjectively experience top-down, self-directed experiences as well as bottom-up, spontaneous reactions. I can sometimes experience myself drifting along in disconnected fantasies and diffuse associations, and at other times I can be highly attentive and so actively focused in concentrated consciousness that I lose touch with my immediate surroundings. And every state of arousal between the poles of high arousal and near unconsciousness can be experienced. Most often, persons seem to alternate between focused, effortful attention and a more relaxed, loosely controlled scanning, wandering, or mindlessness.[61]

The dynamic movements in a stream of consciousness have been portrayed in literary masterpieces by James Joyce and Virginia Woolf and in earlier soliloquies from drama and confessional literature. Artists predated psychological research into consciousness and even the early psychoanalytic case histories described free association. The varied processes of consciousness cycle through time and are experienced as either self-directed or spontaneous, as well as qualitatively different. They range from hyperalert states, to calm cruising, to more relaxed, meandering, and drowsy processing in states bordering upon sleep.

Today, this range of various and alternate states of consciousness is called the "continuum of consciousness."[62] Studies examine alternate states of consciousness—hypnosis, meditation, panic attacks,

dissociation, multiple personalities, stages of sleep and psychosis—
using new, sophisticated research technologies. Self-consciousness in a
normal, sane, wide-awake adult appears to have certain characteristics.
Not accidentally, these characteristics meet the prerequisites of moral
agency and the operation of conscience described previously. The self,
as an awake "I" fused with "me," experiences continuous identity, internal uniqueness, self-agency, and self-reflectiveness. In moderate
states of arousal, a person experiences a coherent self that owns or
appropriates its individual conscious stream or propriate self. My
stream of consciousness is mine and ordinarily confined within me; it
is often imagined as being centered somewhere behind the eyes, giving
rise to the metaphor of the third eye.[63]

Occasionally, in ecstatic or other unusual group situations, the "I"
of consciousness feels more merged with a group, or partially deindi-
viduated.[64] Drugs, intoxicants, hypnosis, and intense stress may produce states in which ordinary consciousness is altered.[65] But those not
ill, traumatized, or mentally impaired experience a conscious self as a
continuous unity over time. As we go to sleep or lose consciousness,
we lose our sense of coherence, but when we wake up, we wake up as
the same self who went to sleep. Yes, there is a continuum of different
kinds of consciousness discernible in our many-faceted selves, but
while awake and sane, we are convinced that the multiple states
through time, place, and social situation all are ours.

We retain subjectively the same internal consciousness while
awake, when we are in different settings or in different states of
mind. Each of us remains the same self over the passing of years.
We may feel inwardly identical with our earlier selves remembered
from age ten or twenty. This inner identity over time creates a slight
shock when we look in mirrors and see our aging bodies. Eastern sages
or learned philosophers who try to tell us that our sense of self-identity
through time and varying circumstance is an illusion never make
much headway.[66]

Only in severe disorders does the "I" of the self lose its sense of
ownership and unity with body, actions, emotions, thoughts, or past
memories. Normally, we live continuously and coherently into our fu-
tures, secure in the feeling that we will remain the same persons no
matter how much we learn or change or expand our consciousness
through new experiences. There is an interesting paradox in self-
identity: we desire to grow and change for the better but not to lose
our integrity, stability, and unique boundaries. As the clever quip goes,
"Persons may desire to be immortal but not to be ubiquitous."

Free Will

The desire to change and grow as a unique self has been deemed by most self-theorists to be an innate characteristic of the self. Self-realization—becoming, growing, emerging—has been seen as an essential characteristic of the human being. This dynamic characteristic is clearly evident in children, but perhaps less universally manifest in adults, who frequently exhibit stasis, stagnation, and regression.

But there is still enough evidence of adult development to decide that the optimists are more probably correct. For Allport and other humanistic psychologists, the self is seen to have an inner dynamism that innately, positively strives to grow and become more fully self-realized, effective, and complete.[67] Striving for ever-more expansion within a coherent integrated whole can be seen as the ruling characteristic of developing human self-consciousness. These views on intrinsic motivation challenge the more pessimistic theories of human nature, in which motivation for change can only be reactive, defensive, or externally conditioned. The theory of human motivation adopted affects one's subsequent perspective on moral development and moral agency.

Both James and Allport, along with other self-theorists, see the self as having the freedom to initiate movement, to grow, and to transform one's own self-identity. There can be a top-down self-regulation of self-consciousness. The self or proprium directs, executes, and actively selects and creates experience in the inner and outer environment, as well as responding to stimuli. This ability to self-direct, to select behavior, is popularly called free will and is the foundation of moral agency.

Whether it is called volition, self-efficacy, or free will, the freedom of the self to initiate and exercise self-control is increasingly accepted in psychology.[68] The basic idea is as ancient as the idea of moral reflection: we feel ourselves to be free agents, able to select among various options. What we choose, we feel responsible for; what we select makes a difference. What we do and become is partially up to us, and not solely the result of the genetic throw, environmental conditioning, or what happens to happen to us.

James described free will as the ability to keep an idea uppermost in attention despite distractions.[69] If attention is free and mobile and can freely select that which it attends to, then self-control of consciousness and behavior is possible. By focusing our attention, we can shape present responses, what goes into our memories, and our future selves, which are being built up in our historical consciousness. We partially create ourselves through our active self-consciousness.

The James-Allport model of the free self is similar to, but also different from, theories of the Freudian ego, the self of Harry Stack Sullivan, Hans Kohut, and other psychoanalytic schools of thought.[70] The model of a self that emphasizes freedom and consciousness is also different from Jungian ideas of the self as an unconscious archetype striving to balance conscious and unconscious elements in dynamic equilibrium.[71]

I think the self is best defined as constituted of consciousness and all that can be brought into personal consciousness. To posit an unconscious self leads to confusion over what would count as evidence for a self, since the unconscious is by definition inaccessible to direct personal experience. For most self-theorists of the Allport type, a self may strive to bring into consciousness and appropriate more and more unknown operations of the personality or organism, but until that happens, this nonconscious material remains beyond the self's appropriation and ownership.

Given the limited nature of consciousness and memory, there will always exist unconscious processes that are unknown to us or other alien intrusions into consciousness that we do not wish to own. Some characteristics and habits we may either not know about or, even when aware of them, be unable to freely exercise or inhibit them. The lament over our lack of ownership over forces within is an ancient cry. Efforts to achieve the fullest integration of the self have been seen in the wisdom literature of many cultures.

Ancient wisdom and modern psychology affirm that the self is not only cognitive, an intellectual concept, or an executive program. As all the previous arguments imply, the self and its processes of consciousness are invested with emotion. The self, in all its dynamic fusions of diversities of content and processes, is more than an abstract idea. The self is an idea we can have that is infused with our emotions and other nonlinguistic awareness. The emotional warmth accorded to our selves manifests our caring and investment—whether in positive or negative evaluative reactions.

While a person's self or identity is dynamic and multidimensional, certain dimensions of ourselves will be more central and important to us than others. We each have different hierarchies and rankings of our own self-characteristics.[72] If spatial imagery is used to describe the psychological consciousness of a person, some things are nearer or closer to the central core of self than others—and these patterns may change over time.[73] Since self-consciousness is a dynamic inner picture, patterns of self-investments of emotion and value can constantly shift. We each differ over time, and we differ from one another in our inner processes and configurations of self. Some of us are much more inconsistent than others, but we have little trouble recognizing the unique individuality of persons when we see patterns repeated through time.

Moral concerns over being a good, worthwhile, competent person are normally very close to a person's core self-concept. Self-esteem or self-respect—the positive image a person holds of his or her own self—has been appraised as all-important in both mental and moral functioning.[74] It seems built in to us to evaluate ourselves according to standards of moral goodness and excellence. And these evaluations are important for ongoing behavior. The self-image can control incoming information; negative self-concepts, as in depressed persons, bias what is accepted as reality.[75] When I despise myself or cannot accept my characteristics, the resulting incoherence and disorganization can produce maladaptive behavior.[76]

Most efforts at moral instruction, as well as remedial psychotherapies, take into account the need to establish integration and consistency of all the functioning dimensions of the self.[77] Our multiple senses of self must get themselves together. The dynamic processes of the stream of consciousness must be responsive to the direction of the conscious self. I am a moral agent.

However, when we make moral decisions of conscience, we are operating within our own dynamic flow of consciousness and have to deal with all the complexities of our multidimensioned selves. How do we make specific moral decisions? How should we direct our thinking and integrate other elements and operations of consciousness? What part do reason and intuition play in moral decision making?

Chapter 3

Reason and Intuition

After the questions "What is conscience?" and "Who can have a conscience?" it is appropriate to ask "How does one go about moral decision making?" In other words, how exactly should we let our consciences be our guide?

Different kinds of rational thinking and consciousness operate in various ways in moral decision making. Directed rational thinking and intuitive thinking can be integrated in the process. First, explicit problem-solving techniques of consciously directed thinking may apply to moral decision making. Second, I believe that moral intuitions—those thoughts and ideas that come spontaneously to mind—are important, although not infallible, in the decision-making process. There are strategies for using reason and intuition in the moral decision making of conscience.

A Challenge

At a conference on medical ethics, a mature physician of European background told me her method for making difficult moral decisions of conscience. When presented with a troubling moral dilemma in her medical practice in which she has to make a decision, she spends a day gathering all the relevant facts and pertinent information she can find. At night, she assembles all this material, reads it over, and then goes to sleep. When she wakes up, and returns to her problem of conscience, she reports that she immediately sees what she ought to do. Her problem is solved. She claimed that this method of sleeping on it has never failed her, and what did I, as the visiting ethical expert, think of her approach? I was nonplussed, sympathetic, and rather evasive at the time of this encounter, answering very little one way or another. But her challenge was not forgotten; it confirmed my determination—as one convinced of the value of directed reasoning and the scientific method—to wrestle with the question of intuition and the nonconscious mind in moral decision making.

My first positive assumption is to assert that, yes, a problem of conscience in which one does not know what one ought to do must be like other problems to be rationally resolved. Moral questions come into the conscious mind and must be processed through the psychological operations available to human beings. I affirm that the best moral solution must, among other things, be a rational, reasoned solution in which I, as a thinking human being, proceed to think as hard and as well as I can in the time available. I also have learned from the new cognitive science that human beings are constantly thinking, assessing, and actively processing information to solve a variety of problems presented by the outer and internal environments.[1] Problems and decisions in the course of coping with life can range from instantaneous microdecisions that one hardly notices, to the most global and abstract problems that can absorb the mind, emotions, and will for a long period of time.[2]

Even our perceptions are now viewed as dynamic processes in which a series of decisions are made at different processing levels of the sensory system and mind.[3] One may be engaged in deciding what an ambivalent perception in the distance actually is. (Raccoon or cat? A fluffy tail, stripes, and a fat body help me decide that I see a raccoon, and so on.) What do we see or hear, and is it real or a figment of imagination? We perceive what best organizes and fits the arrays of signals using the categories, expectations, and mental schemata we possess. If I am a New Guinea native, with no contact with outsiders, viewing my first helicopter, I may see a huge, noisy new kind of bird. The use of hypotheses, expectancies, and mental sets means that the mind is constantly active in constructing and assimilating the world.

We find our rational nature almost inescapable; rational, directed problem solving to obtain goals seems strongly programmed by evolution into the structure and operations of the human brain. I think most humans try to decide important issues rationally, most of the time, because we are innate problem solvers. In infancy, we began as small scientists in the crib attuning ourselves to reality and trying to make sense of the world.[4] Children learn gradually how to tell "reality" from the movies, TV, or nightmares they experience. All through life, we face constant rational problem-solving and decision processes, from the simplest to the most complex level. We continue to be committed to thinking and common sense because it helps us function, gets us what we want, and ensures our survival and well-being. Only under unusual conditions, while motivated by some defensive reasons, can we manage to avoid thinking about pressing problems. It takes special effort to employ distraction or denials and to withdraw from active problem solving.

It seems that even those who espouse "irrational" methods for making decisions, including moral decisions, usually do so for some reason. Maybe the decision is too trivial to care about, or there is no real difference between the goods of the different alternatives available. But when someone resorts to auguries, omens, signs, a toss of a coin, chance openings upon scriptural verses, or the I Ching to make a serious decision, it often means the person believes in some larger order or purposes that govern random occurrences. This belief may be judged irrational in our commonly accepted worldview, but make sense in another system. One may believe in God's providence, fate, karma, guardian spirits, or ancestor ghosts that manifest themselves through "chance" occurrences.

If one pays attention to dreams or intuitions, it is usually because of some implicit theory about what such messages portend. One believes in the wisdom of the unconscious, or that this is the way collective archetypes communicate to the mind, or that God sends important messages through dreams. Even if persons claim to dedicate themselves to irrationality and propose to decide issues by spontaneous, random whim, they must, in their rebellion, recognize the ground of order and rational purpose against which they protest. Only the most sophisticated, decadent, or despairing human beings can truly pledge themselves to irrationality—and even they find it almost impossible to be consistent. Some things will always seem to be more important and preferable, or less repugnant or disgusting, than other options.

Fortunately, in our Western tradition, we have more often accepted and proclaimed the powers of reasoning and developed and refined rational problem-solving techniques. These are major resources for moral decision making. These methods begin, as did the inquiring physician I met, with the collection of information and the gathering and perusal of relevant facts.

Problem-Solving Techniques and Decision Making

Today we have become self-conscious in developing explicit methods for reasoning and problem solving. The newest findings about the mind's workings and computer and information science have influenced an emerging field devoted to self-conscious thinking—the application of rational problem-solving methods to decision making.[5] In many different professions, decision analysis and other problem-solving techniques are propounded as the most effective ways to crystallize and reap the proven benefits of the scientific method.[6] Some of these formal techniques employ statistics and mathematics, some do not, but rational methods of problem solving are duly taught to aspiring professionals, managers, and other would-be rational decision-makers faced with various dilemmas. Similar rational moral and ethical decision-making procedures have been proposed for ethical decisions.[7]

These rational problem-solving methods are familiar to us because they parallel the scientific method and common sense. In fact, the scientific method can be seen as common sense plus—common sense that is focused, organized, thorough, efficient, and error corrected. Science has been defined as "trying not to fool ourselves," and since there are so many ways to be fooled, rational, scientific methods of decision making have been devised to outwit the foibles and weaknesses of human observers. Our disadvantages in operating with limited intelligence, partial viewpoints, and incomplete evidence have to be overcome as best they can, whether it be in morality or other fields. Scientists use the controls of testing, skepticism, impartial public inspection, and replication to avoid falling into error.

In order to solve a problem, be it in ethics or engineering, one explores and resolves doubts by devising different hypotheses, collecting evidence, scanning for alternatives, and controlling for biases. During this process, the problem-solver must direct and order his or her thinking processes. Directed thinking makes use of the human ability to have vicarious experience by activating stored memories and perceptions, and by reflecting upon prior knowledge and experiences as one collects new data. The intelligent thinker can arbitrarily organize thoughts toward a goal, rather than letting them randomly proliferate or rigidly repeat old routines. With the ability to gather, manipulate, recombine, and reorganize information in abstract, symbolic form, one can learn, generalize, and constantly reinterpret one's own thinking.

Reproducing certain successful aspects of human abstract thinking has greatly advanced computer science and artificial intelligence. Once an explicit step-by-step procedure or algorithm is produced for some type of problem solving, it can be reproduced in a computer program. So computers now play chess and do other amazing feats of calculation and problem solving—once they have been programmed to do so by intelligent humans. The challenge for those interested in artificial intelligence (AI) has been to devise programs that can be both global and specific, that can reproduce more and more closely the flexibility, efficiency, and adaptiveness of the human mind.

One exciting new discovery in information processing is that the brain employs parallel distributed processes (PDP) in which many microprocesses aggregate and achieve resolution when a system achieves equilibrium or relaxes.[8] Operating all at once, these distributed microprocesses do not have to go through a central processor or executive, so they are incredibly speedy. They can process faster than the central executive method, and so the effort now is to produce computers with these kinds of routines as well as the older programs. It appears that human minds apparently have bottom-up techniques of problem solving as well as top-down centralized executive routines. The interesting question is whether one can ever be conscious of the parallel distributed processes, or are consciousness and awareness restricted to the slower central processes of taking up one alternative at a time?[9]

A perennial question is how human minds, while less efficient than computers in certain feats of calculation and routine processing, are yet amazingly more complex and effectively superior in other ways. If we describe this superiority in imagery taken from computers, we would say that human thinkers can imagine, initiate, and create many programs at once, follow the appropriate programs when it is efficient to do so, and yet constantly change, rewrite, exchange, and modify programs when needed. Human minds can also take shortcuts and be galvanized by emotional energy. (Unfortunately, unlike computers, we can often turn ourselves off, unplug the energy sources, wreck the circuits, and arbitrarily blow out the brain's hardware.)

But while operating, adult humans of normal intelligence can be flexible in using many different strategies and capacities to solve problems. Intelligent human problem-solvers can monitor and modify their operations as they progress; they can step in and out of the system and observe how things are going, and then procede to jump in and out of various routines at will. If one tactic isn't working, they can try another that they think is better. One of the most effective strategies, of course, is to backtrack and see whether the problem one is trying to solve should be redefined and restructured. What, after all, makes a problem a problem in morality or other activities?

A problem fulfills three minimal conditions: (1) the problem presently inheres in some configuration; (2) the configuration is unsatisfactory—a change to another state is desired; (3) it is not directly obvious how to effect a change.[10] By definition, a problem must be brought to one's attention by some obstacle, question, discrepancy, conflict, or interruption in the smooth flow of functioning. Consciousness becomes engaged when it is necessary to pay attention to make things work.

Defining the problem—in morality or other areas—is the first step in all rational decision making and problem-solving techniques. Some students of productive thinking believe it is the most important step, since all else follows from the original definition. When a problem (or the first version of it) has been defined, then the search for relevant information, the devising of alternatives, the selection of testing methods, and a host of strategies are employed.[11] Heuristics, rules of thumb, and simple strategies such as trial and error, rote memory, or different kinds of searches may all be used. The problem may be divided up into parts and partial results used to get more results. As feedback accumulates and information recycles, it becomes obvious that solving a complex problem is a flexible, dynamic, and recursive operation.

Human problem solvers operate in complex, fluid ways that prescribed flowcharts and decision trees can only partially capture. There are complicated backward and forward operations from goals to means, to what information one has, to what information one still needs. Inferences, deductions, analogies, inductions, analyses, manipulations, operations, and transformations of information—these all take place as one uses what one knows in order to go further. Moral thinking follows these same processes. Impasses are reached, and attention is focused upon the part of the problem that presents an obstacle. New plans and tests are devised as parts of new subroutines.

Every step forward is critically evaluated and questioned. Perhaps the original definition of the problem must be restructured and redefined again and again. Some of the greatest creative breakthroughs in science and other intellectual fields, including ethics, have come from restructuring the original problem, or reenvisioning the whole so that known parts fit together in new ways. When all the hard work applied in one direction fails to produce results, the good thinker does not give up but starts over.

Rational problem solving and goal-directed thinking are hard because it takes energy to focus and maintain attention.[12] And thinking about moral questions, with all the personal ramifications involved, may be the hardest of all. Overcoming frustrations and returning to a mental task takes what we rightly call the hardwork of mental discipline. As one good quip goes, some mistakes could have been avoided by two minutes of thought, but then two minutes of hard, sustained thinking is a long time.

Directed thinking consumes energy partly from the effort needed to maintain attention on the big picture and one's final goal while working on particular points or the specific subroutines needed to gather information, test it, and categorize it. Some of the most acute descriptions of intelligence at work emphasize how important it is to be able to judge the relevant importance of different parts to the whole.[13] In moral thinking, this is no less a difficulty. Expert thinkers in a field are expert because they pay no attention to irrelevancies or the wrong moves, but focus at once on the relevant evidence needed for a correct discrimination or decision. Experts also have learned global ways to see patterns in arrays of information that beginners cannot.[14] They solve problems faster because they do not have to go through the step-by-step solutions that a beginner may require.

Recognizing Solutions

But how does one know when one has solved a problem? Does a correct solution come with built-in credentials? In the end, evaluating a solution may be as difficult as defining a problem and working on it. Statistics and the laws of probability have often been employed as aids to reasoning; they prevent misdirection by chance results or immediate appearances that look convincing. But intellectual, political, and moral problems are subtle, complex, more abstract, and not easily and immediately confirmed or falsified by a pattern of factual observations. If in engineering you arrive at the wrong solution, the building falls down, or in motorcycle maintenance, if you make an error, the motorcycle will not start.[15] In morality, the errors may be devastating in the long run, as in Nazi Germany, but it usually takes longer to see the resulting disasters.

One has to be able to assess whether one has a solution in hand or not, and then judge the adequacy of the solution. How does one know when reason has done its work? This question goes to the heart of reason and intelligence, and has been hotly debated in philosophy, theology, and philosophy of science. How do we know that we know, what warrant or justifications will serve as criteria? Contesting theories may all be rational, but which rationality should be accepted as valid?[16] The usual criteria for judging theories employ the traditional criteria used for assessing rationality: completeness, adequacy; logic; congruence and coherence within, and ecological congruence with, all other accepted theories and known facts.[17] In addition, in science, the more parsimonious solution is thought better, and a theory is considered superior that can be fruitful in stimulating new successful experiments, which both confirm the old theory and extend its power. When theories change and paradigms shift, a new map and ways of drawing a map must be adopted by the thinkers involved.[18] Large paradigm shifts in ethics or science, while rational, are never simple, but then neither are other lesser challenges to decision making.

The Whole Picture

From the subjective point of view of the person struggling to think through a problem, working it through and accepting a solution are complicated. Sometimes, the best rational solution to a problem may be instantly recognized. At other times, a slower, more subtle process is necessary. Historians and philosophers of science are quite sure that facts alone can never provide self-evident certainty—even successful predictions do not always decide a case.[19] What is true in science is even truer in ethics. There are endless potential facts in the universe; judgment and interpretation of the significance of facts, along with creativity in putting all the facts together meaningfully, are what count. One usually decides upon a solution to a problem after dynamic dialectical movements from specifics to the bigger pictures, to everything else one knows, back to specific facts, arguments, interpretations, and detailed evidence again.

This ongoing recursive problem-solving process is well described by the anthropologist Clifford Geertz as he explains how he tries to decide upon the nature of a newly encountered culture.[20] I think his account applies to moral decision making as well. Geertz compares the solving of an anthropological problem to a foreigner trying to understand baseball. One has to know what bats, bases, and balls are to understand the game, but if one doesn't understand what a game is, or a team, or a score, one won't understand the point of getting runs by batting balls and running around bases. In other words, to grasp something complex with a great deal of confusing factual evidence, one must go in circles, from larger global concepts or principles to specifics, and back again—back and forth, back and forth, and around and about. You finally begin to "get it" when order, structure, and the significance of parts as they relate to wholes begin to emerge.[21]

Seeing the whole picture in problem solving is more like getting a joke or reading and understanding a text than adding up a column of numbers or following a set of directions. One has to understand how the big picture and all the parts relate to one another before one can make some sense of the problem. Wrong moves or mistaken hypotheses have to be excised as the right and relevant internal and external relations fit together. Along the way, many subroutines are undertaken, and evidence is built up that can be put together and give the solution. Eventually, one may experience either a sudden "Aha, I've got it!" insight, or a slower sense of achieved resolution. Moral decisions are similar.

One image often used for being rationally convinced of a problem's solution is the creation of a rope from strands of hemp. Ropes are made of many separate threads. No strand alone would give much support, but when all the strands are tightly interwoven, the whole is dependable and can bear a heavy weight. These strands can be seen as metaphors for the many separate rational processes that the mind goes through. With enough interwoven strands, a new whole is created, a decision that we consider reliable—in morality, a moral conviction. We forge the results of a multitude of mental operations into a judgment.

John Henry Newman was interested in the processes of assent and in the subtleties of the operation of reasoning. He described the processes of building up rational convictions and problem solving in this way: "It is by the strength, variety, or multiplicity of premises, which are only probable, not by invincible syllogisms—by objections overcome, by adverse theories neutralized, by difficulties gradually clearing up, by exceptions proving the rule, by unlooked for correlations found with received truths, by suspense and delay in the process issuing in triumphant reaction—by all these ways and many others."[22] Moral reasoning proceeds in this way.

A rational problem-solving process can be so intricate, fast, and filled with different dynamic moves that it is almost impossible to recapitulate for others. Obviously, reasoning well to solve dilemmas is not as simple as employing clear-cut, formal, linear sequences of stepwise logical deductions. Therefore, I doubt that highly formal methods of problem solving, in morality or anything else, can ever be more than the most general of guidelines. Certainly in morals and decisions of conscience, the step-by-step programs proposed can only be minimally helpful. Yes, one can follow certain general outlines—define the problem, gather information, generate alternatives, test and retest, and so on. But at the same time, in and around the large steps, from beginning to end, other rational operations involving many subtle assessments will be taking place in circular fashion. From defining the problem to recognizing a solution, one will perform a diversity of testing and suboperations while jumping back and forth from one system or mode of thinking to another. There seems to be no substitute for the complexity of dynamic judgments that an individual thinker must make.

Complications

Formal systems that employ quantitative methods may appear superficially more rational than other general guidelines, but have more weaknesses. As one philosopher of science, David Braybrooke, rightly observes in his criticism of the flights of decision theorists laying out their quantifiable programs, "Such theorists forget that many of those quantities will turn up missing in real-life choice situations. They delude themselves and others into thinking that the prescriptions of the theory can be carried out or approximated when more often than not they cannot be."[23] Unfortunately, it is often the missing data, the yet-unknown information, which will make the crucial difference in a judgment. Moreover, in order to devise quantities to plug into one's formal system, one first has to make a multitude of microjudgments that may distort or prematurely decide the final outcome. Ironically, if a presenting situation or problem is definite enough, or familiar enough to provide known consequences that can be accurately quantified in a formal routine solution, then it may no longer be a significant problem worth our conscious attention.[24]

The complexity of reasoning and judgment needed to address difficult problems, especially in the moral domain, helps explain why intelligent, sincere persons so often disagree. Intelligent people seeking rational solutions to a new and complex problem can differ because they perform a multitude of complicated, dynamic microprocesses differently, with different resources and capacities at their command. The multiple mental operations and microdecisions necessary during the thinking process may affect the final outcome. Even experts in the same field often disagree in hard cases, because they estimate and weigh the evidence differently, or see it organized in different patterns against different interpretations of the context or environment.[25]

Another complication in problem solving arises when contexts and conditions differ. An intelligent thinker may be more competent in one mode of thinking than in another. The chess master who can outwit a computer because she can see global patterns and strategies better than the calculating chess-playing program can may not be adept at other kinds of problem solving. As Robert Sternberg, one astute researcher in the problems of defining intelligence, has summed it up, "Everyone knows people who perform well on tests but who seem to perform rather poorly in their everyday lives."[26] It is not so easy to assess what is missing when a person who can think well in one context cannot do so in another. (Indeed, the lack of moral intelligence in otherwise highly intelligent people has always been troubling.)

Sternberg defines intelligence as a form of "mental self-governance" that can be "purposively employed for purposes of adaptation to and shaping and selection of real world environments."[27] The intelligent person solves problems within and without, and there may be different ways of being smart. Some theorists of the mind such as Howard Gardner have thought that there may be seven different kinds of human intelligence, or frames of mind, which have evolved through biological selection.[28] Others divide up the various components of effective mental capacity differently. If the existence of multiple intelligences is correct, then some of the disagreements we see among rational, intelligent people may partly arise from the ways they are combining their different intelligences in their problem solving.

If, for instance, mathematical intelligence is different from linguistic, spatial, or interpersonal social intelligence, how do these different rational abilities relate in a decision-making process? This problem of combining intelligences may account for the unsatisfactoriness of using mathematical statistics and probability calculations for making practical decisions, particularly in deciding on public risk-taking policies.[29] Statistical probabilities and political and social realities may be at odds in an actual situation. The logical or statistical form of rational thinking may only be effective when it is appropriately deployed by a person in possession of other kinds of intelligence. A problem solver must have the social knowledge or personal tacit knowledge that will indicate when to apply or eschew mathematical strategies, as well as good judgment about how statistical results should be interpreted.[30]

Such problems of when and how to use which of our many different rational capacities have led other observers back to thinking that there must be an underlying ability or general intelligence that functions above and beyond, around, or through the different specific rational capacities. This generalist approach sees intelligent reasoning as operating within all the different intelligences, regardless of content. Optimists in this camp go so far as to maintain that this general ability to reason well and think critically can be explicitly taught.[31] I, too, think it makes sense to see that we have both general and specific rational capacities, and that general reasoning can be taught. However, when it comes to actual performance, particularly in moral thinking, I am convinced that there is still more to the story of successful problem solving.

The whole person, complete with emotions and past personal histories, will affect the ways that intelligence is used. Like other people, experts are subjective persons, who can suffer from mistakes or premature closure of the mind for reasons unrelated to the problem at hand. Experts can be so certain that they must be right that they refuse to think in a new way and miss moving on to a problem's solution. Many other factors in the distortion of intelligence and problem solving are due to other personality characteristics.

General Criteria

Some general criteria for distortion and failures of reasoning have been tested and stood up over time. Despite the existence of different theoretical frameworks, different paradigms, or conflicting theological models that govern larger philosophical and theoretical conclusions, criteria for assessing adequate rational thinking have garnered a consensus. Many people who do not agree on what intelligence is, or what philosophy or morality is, will agree that it is possible to recognize a failure or distortion of rational thinking when they see it.

Aided by logic and mathematics and validated by the triumphs of rationality, formalized in the scientific method, certain criteria for valid reasoning have been generally accepted. I think these criteria should guide us in our moral decision making. These criteria, like the criteria for scientific theories, have been articulated as consistency, logic, rules of evidence, appropriateness, coherence, clarity, completeness, and congruence with reality or known evidence. In Western culture, common sense operates with the same rough, inarticulated criteria because experience with the environment confirms the value of rationality.

Here I return to an affirmation of the innate rationality and problem-solving capacities of the human species. Those who look at the achievements of science have been led to think it probable that in a universe that seems amazingly correlated with mathematical and rational formulations, human rationality and even mathematical intelligence may have been imprinted in the mind over the eons of evolution. Other kinds of human intelligence seem innately preprogrammed as well. Evolved human consciousness and intelligence have a long track record of solving new problems arising from novel conditions.

In any event, intelligent human beings assess failures of rational thinking with some consensus. Serious inadequacies in adult thinking have been found in conditions characterized as mental retardation, psychosis, dementia, or brain injury and disease.[32] Less serious distortions in rational thinking have been assessed by consensus as neurotic, foolish, stupid, superstitious, fallacious, biased, or infantile. The characteristics of inadequate thinking fail to meet the criteria of rationality. Irrational thinking is inconsistent, illogical, incomplete, incoherent, biased, based on insufficient evidence, and incongruent with other known facts and realities.

The opposite of common sense, distorted thinking is autistic and not in accord with the commonly accepted canons of reasonableness used by the reasonable. Irrational thinkers are often trapped in incomplete processes of problem solving. They may be able to see only one point of view or be stalled in one perspective adopted at one moment in time. Irrational thinkers often cannot focus or successfully direct their thinking at will.[33] They are either rigid and inflexible or scattering blindly and wildly all over the place.

We diagnose distorted, out-of-control thinking with labels such as neurotic, psychotic, or demented—depending on the severity of the distortions or thought disorders. Since inconsistency and logical contradictions exist in what has been called primary thinking (the thinking of dreams and wish fulfillment), the thinker will be relying on incomplete evidence or distorted pictures of reality.[34] Real consequences in the environment cannot be accurately assessed. Persons who cannot reason well cannot protect themselves, much less flourish. So too, when flawed reasoning or distorted thinking is used to solve questions of moral self-guidance, it can produce primitive moral decision making. Mature, rational reasoning or mental self-governance is necessary to cope with the external environment, as well as to guide the self morally.

But are irrationality and distorted thinking to be equated with all nonconscious processes of the mind? I do not think so.

Nonconscious Mental Processes and Intuition

It is becoming increasingly certain that much rational thinking and cognitive processing of information is nonconscious, that is, the processes are unavailable to, or unnoticed or unappreciated by, our conscious phenomenological awareness.[35] Immediate consciousness always operates in the psychological present; we are aware of things moment by passing moment as we monitor ourselves in the environment and voluntarily control our thinking and behavior. But where does the content of consciousness come from, and how do nonconscious processes affect consciousness?

Our most rational conscious thinking processes appear to be directed, dynamic, and recursive, but also include intuitive processes. Many have noted that logical analysis, which is supposedly rationally self-evident, is in fact self-evident because analysis is in a sense immediately and intuitively clear.[36] We do not consciously deliberate about whether opposing contradictory claims can both be true—we just immediately apprehend that it is impossible; we do not deliberate or explicitly reason our way to many rational conclusions or deductions in logic that are immediately grasped as true.

Intuition is sometimes defined as "the ability of persons to be influenced and informed by considerations that are not explicitly represented in conscious awareness."[37] When intuition is correct, it is a nonconscious apprehension of implicit order or structure not yet evident to awareness. Another way of saying this is that correct intuition is the possibility of being tacitly informed without knowing why. While some theorists have stressed how nonconscious implicit factors can mislead thinking, because people are not consciously aware of factors influencing their thoughts, there exists a positive side to nonconscious mental operations.[38] In addition to the self-evident logical analyses mentioned earlier, intuition (ideas that just come to us) plays an effective role in directed thinking.

An intuition can set off an inquiry, or shape the direction of rational arguments. New creative ideas may suddenly emerge in the middle of an investigation. Intuition can also play a part in assessing the outcomes or achieved solutions. Our convictions of certainty about the solution to a problem may be partially intuitive. Intuition often aids the rational problem-solving process at the beginning, in the middle, and at the end. The question is, from whence do these ideas come? And further, can we consciously make use of our intuition?

The human mind has been poetically described by philosopher Amelie Rorty as like a rationally planned modern city imposed upon an earlier medieval city that just grew up over the ages.[39] The broad boulevards of the rationally accessible city run straight to design, overlaying and intersecting with intricate mazes of crooked streets and twisting alleys in the older neighborhoods. If we take this metaphor further, we could say that earlier generations may have been content to stride down the boulevards and ignore the rest of the city, but today, we have begun to feel that this is a misguided approach to city living. Understanding our less-accessible mental functions may be extremely valuable in finding our way around.

We are beginning to recognize that we are constantly shaped and influenced by mental processes of which we are unaware and do not yet fully comprehend. But once they are recognized and understood, it may be possible to use and shape our newly discovered resources—or at least not be so easily misled by them. As rational thinkers, we are faced with the intriguing question of how we should respond to the rationally convincing scientific evidence that there is a nonconscious mind, busily processing information outside of our awareness. To paraphrase Pascal, there seem to be sound indications that while the heart may have its reasons that reason cannot know, there are also reasons that reason cannot know.

Moral intuitions and "intuitionists" have been discussed and critically evaluated in philosophical investigations for many years. But where intuitions come from, how they arise, and what role they serve in thinking and problem solving have not been the focus of enough attention. How does the existence of nonconscious reasoning fit into the picture of myself as a rational decision maker? Or moral agent? Am I responsible for my nonconscious mind, or my preconscious processes? Can I do anything about directing them? Can I use these processes as resources in my life, and if so, how can they be integrated with my other capacities to reason and think?

That part of the mind that is nonconscious, unavailable, unnoticed is uncharted territory. What is the nonconscious mind like? At this point, while the theorists are fighting it out, the one thing all agree upon is that a very complicated picture is emerging. The new cognitive psychologies that study the way the nonconscious mind works have moved well beyond the approaches of older psychoanalytic giants like Freud and Jung. But the psychoanalytic movement is given a great deal of credit for sustaining interest in the mind and nonconscious processing during the long reign of behaviorists, who denied the importance of human consciousness, rational thinking, and the inner self.

New evidence for nonconscious mental processing has gradually accumulated from many sources. Freud's original insights about dreaming, meaningful mistakes, hypnosis, memory, and forgetting have been reinterpreted and given a more cognitive information-processing emphasis. The nonconscious looks far more rationally oriented now than it did when it was seen more exclusively as the repository of the repressed and voracious instincts of sex, death, and aggression.

New experimental research with normal subjects has supplemented inferences gained from clinical therapy with troubled patients giving retrospective accounts. While different models of how the nonconscious mind works are proposed and there is yet no complete consensus, some very tentative conjectures can be made.[40] In some of the newest rough-drawn maps of the mind's working outside of consciousness, there seem to be different levels and functions discerned. Some cognitive operations will be totally outside awareness, and can never be known or retrieved by directed attention. These processes, which can only be inferred, may include the innate hard wiring of initial perceptual processes and some procedural processes of information storage and retrieval.

We may never be aware of how our mind selects and processes perceptual stimuli. Nor will we be conscious of how we specifically encode information in the mind or carry out searches to retrieve the different kinds of knowledge we possess, whether it be knowledge of skills or facts. In the same way, we may have deeply inaccessible, nonconscious underpinnings to the other systems that make up a human being. Who can be conscious of the operation of one's liver or spleen, or of the myriad calculations necessary to move one's body about in the world?

At the opposite extreme, some nonconscious mental operations are easily available to consciousness and awareness by instantaneous acts of attention. We can easily call to mind in the present huge stores of available facts and procedural knowledge that we are not thinking of at that moment. I can immediately imagine my sister's face or tell someone how to apply for a driver's license, how to calculate a mean, or that George Washington was the first president. These easily available nonconscious functions and content have been called the preconscious because they are so easily made conscious, either by a self-initiated act of attention or in response to some environmental challenge. If a ball or unexpected question is suddenly thrown my way, I can either catch it and return it, or expertly duck and dodge the missile. Other easily available information, images, and emotions stream into my mind spontaneously. As we learn more things and store them in memory, we have more and more knowledge and skills easily available to consciousness.

Some things much less easily available may still be accessible if certain techniques or conditions activate them enough to call them to mind. They are not completely irretrievable to awareness, but neither are they as easily accessible as other things that seem to crowd in on the top of the mind or to be instantly available at will. It may take some doing to recall a whole host of things. Sometimes I can have something on the tip of my tongue and can describe the ghostly form of what I am looking for: It's an Irish name with three vowels, no *O'*, three syllables and it's not Harrigan—of course, I've got it, it's Callahan. Or in reply to a query, my initial blank responses may change as my mind warms up. If it's Roman history that is wanted, as I talk and think, I may recall more and more of the course I took on the subject thirty years ago and the subsequent books read and almost forgotten since then.

In autobiographical memory, a snapshot of some long-ago group event may prime me to remember people and events that I have not thought about for decades. Certain music, smells, emotions, or combinations of events, places, and objects perceived may make accessible something that is not easily available. Hypnosis, suggestion, and free association may enable me to remember or reconstruct other dim memories.

Moreover, there are intriguing conditions encountered in clinical practice in which people operate as conscious and awake, then temporarily forget their actions later. Some conditions of full consciousness appear to get separated, isolated, or disassociated from ordinary personal memories of self, from the dominant self's remembered sense of continuous identity. These conscious experiences are often connected with unpleasant, traumatic, or threatening events. Sometimes these experiences of dissociated consciousness are called the subconscious, as opposed to the unavailable unconscious and the easily available preconscious.[41]

Dissociated experiences may have been experienced in unusual situations—such as hypnosis, shock, trauma, fatigue, illness, or stress—and then not been integrated into the person's ongoing, easily available store of consciousness. While persons are in a disconnected or dissociated state, they often retain unimpaired abilities to learn and remember factual knowledge about the world and how to function consciously, but their experiences are not integrated with their autobiographical episodic memory or their usual sense of personal identity. Clinicians and therapists help persons recall and reclaim these separated states so they can be available, easily retrieved, and integrated into the conscious self.

It appears that in the complex, complicated mind, there are different cognitive subsystems operating outside of the everyday consciousness that we experience. The crucial question is, how do these nonconscious cognitive experiences affect us in normal everyday life? Obviously, one absolutely common experience is that while we are awake, without any effort on our part, we are aware of a flow of spontaneously emerging ideas, emotions, and images in various combinations. This stream of material simply comes into consciousness without our summoning it by a direct act of attention. Two questions intrigue us about this spontaneous flow. Why is *this* thought, or whatever, spontaneously coming into my consciousness *now*? What things might now be being kept out of my awareness and why?[42]

While it may be hard to find what we are filtering out, rapidly forgetting, or selectively not noticing, we do have some firsthand experience of what streams into consciousness. Musing and daydreaming are constant in human life, and all sorts of things seem to "pop" into our heads. As noted earlier, some of these spontaneous thoughts turn out to be rational insights and solutions to problems. Some ideas or images seem new and creative, but others seem irrational and fantastic. These musing daydreams appear much different from our experiences of active, directive thinking and problem solving. While consciousness seems unified and mine most of the time, there is a great deal of variety in its flow.

As we have noted, the direct deployment of attention and concentrated rational thinking takes energy and is experienced as hard mental work. When we relax from the effort, more-spontaneous, free-floating elements stream through consciousness unless checked and controlled by the redeployment of attention. There seem to be many different degrees of awareness in consciousness, ranging from hypervigilance to alert problem solving, to musing and daydreaming, to near-sleep or the dreaming states of sleep. Awake, rational ordering of conscious operations emerges from, and is imposed upon, spontaneous flows of consciousness, and then consciousness cycles back and forth between different states. William James described our flow of consciousness as often like the flights and perchings of a bird—a bird that flies round in circles we should add. Rational, directed thinking is defined by its contrast to the irrational, disorganized flow, or vice versa. The ability to focus attention demonstrates how one can freely choose from a progression of unfocused, drifting mental states crowded with ideas, images, facts, feelings, memories, and so on. One can also actively call things to mind or direct thinking in new ways.

The variety of our conscious states, or the crooked streets of the old city, points to the mind and brain's many different ways of processing information, and encoding knowledge and processes in memory and then retrieving them. Some of the crude first cuts of mental categorizations of operations into left- and right-brain processing for different kinds of information do not do justice to the incredibly involved picture that is emerging of mental functioning. It may be that there are large divisions into linear logical processes and more holistic parallel processes, digital and analogue processing, different kinds of memory organizations, top-down and bottom-up information processes, conceptual and narrative approaches to organizing information—and who knows what else is a heritage from the evolutionary development of the organic living brain.[43] The picture is still unclear. However, the mental system is so complex and normally functions so early in life with such superb results, as in language learning, that innate hard wiring from evolution must be a factor, and much mental processing must be nonconscious.

It appears that some innate operations outside of conscious aware-ness must select, categorize, and filter the overwhelming amount of information and stimuli with which a person is bombarded from inside and outside.[44] A person's aware consciousness could not possibly vol-untarily direct all the information processing that humans must do in order to function in the environment. Our conscious attention is lim-ited, and if we had to consciously process and voluntarily govern all the organism's operations, our efficiency would be severely curtailed. In fact, we find that once we learn to do something, like type or drive a car, the knowledge then becomes automatic and recedes from con-scious awareness—unless there is some problem or obstacle that needs attention. Having conscious operations become automatic is a boon for efficient functioning—and may be a large part of the moral life as well. It appears that conscious awareness remains at the top of the chain of information processing, ready and available for its monitoring and con-trolling functions in the service of problem solving and creative inquiry.

What we are not sure of is how much and at how high a level all the rest of our nonconscious thinking operates. Is the filtering system that determines spontaneous awareness a complicated, rational one? Can my nonconscious mind make plans, have goals, or solve problems when I am not attending to the process? It now appears that the mind can think and decide outside of awareness in very complicated ways.[45] The final answers to these questions will make a difference in how much attention and weight we should grant our intuitions. At this point, more and more experiments give evidence of automatic pro-cesses, subliminal perception, implicit memory, hypnotic amnesias, and analgesias that point to the existence of high levels of thinking and organizing of behavior outside of conscious awareness. Something or somebody pretty surely selects and filters what gets through to our awareness. Many models of the mind claim that it is the individual's long-term memory, along with innate selective mechanisms for envi-ronmental emergencies, which filter what will enter spontaneously the stream of conscious awareness.[46]

The idea that our long-term memory selects and filters the sponta-neous flow of consciousness is an interesting and important idea with many moral ramifications. If it is our memory that is selecting and filtering, then we can have some control over what is being selected, albeit outside of present awareness, because we have partially created and controlled what constitutes our long-term memory. Moment by moment, we choose to attend to a variety of things and thereby store them in memory. In other words, the deployment of present attention and conscious awareness will create the memory system that operates the filtering system for the future; in the future, what we have freely put into the memory partially selects and determines what comes into conscious awareness. An intuition entering consciousness can be seen as a message selected and sent into our immediate awareness by our dynamically active long-term memory.

Intuition and Creativity

This theory about where some of our unbidden ideas come from is corroborated by the fact that so many things that come into the mind without effort are things that we have previously paid attention to. We often relive aspects of our past in the present, finishing up some business begun earlier. Images of last night's movie recur, along with bits and pieces of conversations we particularly savor or would like to replay. Worries and problems that have engrossed us keep popping up again and again. In a positive way, many persons report that after sustained efforts to solve some problem, a creative new solution emerges into consciousness. This spontaneous, intuitive new idea comes to mind without trying. Either suddenly or after a time, we just see the solution to some problem we have been mulling over. It seems to come to us "out of the blue," as though the nonconscious mind and memory had been working away on the problem and devised a new combination of elements not thought of when we were struggling with the problem within the directed, conscious problem-solving process. It appears that as we struggled within the boundaries of our set idea of where the solution should be, we could not hear or see a newer, better way of solving the problem.

Many creative scientists and artists have experienced creative insights and solutions as coming to them spontaneously. Retrospectively oriented solutions of problems come, but so do hunches and intuitions about new ways to proceed. Some of the greatest scientific discoveries have been made by people following their intuitions about where they should go next to look for evidence—similar to sleepwalkers avoiding obstacles without being awake. The value of intuition in science is so well known that scientists can talk about building intuition. One immerses oneself in a problem by hard, focused mental work. Then one switches gears and spends periods of time puttering around in unfocused ways or working on different things. Intuitions, solutions, and new insights often come during the relaxed, unfocused times. Roger Penrose reports creative solutions that came to him while shaving and while walking along talking to a friend about other matters.[47] As a mathematician, Penrose is also quite sure that his most innovative thinking is often spatial and geometric in its form, not linguistic. I think he is correct in pointing out that thinking and language are not identical. We can think and be intelligent in different modes. Penrose reports that after thinking hard mathematically for a period of time, he often has difficulty replying to someone who speaks to him; it is momentarily hard for him to shift back to the world of language and linguistic thinking. He also has to translate his mathematical spatial insights into language so that they can be communicated to others.

Penrose also claims that his intuitions and solutions to problems that come to mind arrive with different degrees of confidence in their correctness.[48] I think this is a general characteristic of intuitions, including moral intuitions. Some intuitions seem probable, others seem fairly certain, and some seem absolutely certain even before proofs or tests are worked out. Getting an insight or intuitive global solution to a problem is a first step. Then there is the further uphill task of articulating it, arguing it, justifying it through repeated testing. Finally, when it is worked out satisfactorily, one can explain and communicate the solution to others in a downhill movement.[49] But the first global grasp of a correct intuition can sometimes be accompanied by a sense of certainty especially after a person of developed mind has been struggling and long immersed in the relevant material. Once apprehended, intuitive personal convictions about scientific theories can withstand many assaults from conflicting evidence.[50] Scientists can continue working for a long time to prove a theory they intuitively think is correct. It is the same with moral intuitions.

Einstein is reported to have been certain of his general relativity theory even before the results of an eclipse provided empirical evidence that he was correct. When asked what he would have done if the prediction had not been confirmed, he is reported to have said, "Then I would have been sorry for the dear Lord—the theory *is* correct."[51] He later reported that the significance for him of his theory was not in predicting "a few minute observable facts, but rather in the simplicity of its foundation and in its logical consistency."[52] Scientists also talk of beauty as an intuitive criteria for their adherence to one theory over another.[53] Their logical reasoning is complemented by intuitive apprehensions that confer high degrees of certainty.

While scientists may operate at much higher levels of intellectual complexity than most thinkers, the ordinary person also has similar experiences of intuitions. Sometimes, emerging ideas or images are explained by environmental and internal events—images or thoughts of food in the afternoon may remind us that we have forgotten to eat lunch. At other times, we will suddenly be stopped in our tracks by thoughts that we have forgotten something, so we try to remember what it is we're forgetting and find our mislaid keys before we lock ourselves out of the house. At a still-higher level of complexity, ideas can emerge that are similar to the creative solutions of scientists. We wrestle with problems, and in off moments, the solutions arise. Perhaps we suddenly see how the paper we must write should be organized or how to solve long-standing conflicts in projects at work.

We also experience immediate, everyday experiences of nonconscious thinking processes when we begin to talk or to write. We may start out with some general idea of where we are going, but then the correctly chosen words pour out with minimal effort. Later, when we hear a recording of ourselves or read what we have written, we may wonder where all that came from. We didn't know we knew so much or could express our feelings so precisely. Even at its most minimal levels, personal creativity takes us by surprise and seems mysterious. Poets in ancient times described their experience as being inspired by the Muses. These goddesses of creative inspirations were one way to explain the odd experience of receiving unsolicited, spontaneous ideas. Indeed, the voices and inspirations of the gods were sought and were reported as actually heard while awake.[54] In sleep, other messages and portents were thought to come in dreams.

Today, we see these voices, ideas, and messages as coming from the active, nonconscious mind. The mind somehow performs complex tasks of language automatically and works on problems without our notice or awareness. Somehow long-term memory selects and filters information through to consciousness. Intuitions are worth attending to just from an informational point of view, as a clue to what is going on within as we adapt to the ongoing environment. Of course, it must also be remembered that many of the things that pop into our heads seem innocuous, or upon reflection, erroneous, foolish, dangerous, or evil. Ancient ideas of the Muses and the gods were matched by ideas of demons and evil spirits. These were seen as tempting us through the misleading and evil suggestions they intruded into consciousness. In any event, all intuitions or spontaneously emerging ideas do not seem creative, innovative, or correct solutions to problems. Those that arise from environmental signals—the idea of lunch or a nagging reminder—can seem neutral; others can seem random or meaningless.

Mistaken Intuition

Is it perhaps different when an intuition comes with a high degree of subjective certitude or a high confidence level? Unfortunately, we also have subjectively certain hunches, intuitions, flashes of supposed insight, and solutions to problems that turn out to be misguided and mistaken. We do not have to look to the extreme cases of psychotic delusions to find misplaced intuitive certainties. Much evidence from psychological experiments on normal intelligent persons reveals widespread biases in intuitive thinking.[55] People are certain of things that are wrong. There is a tendency to remember our hits and correct guesses, or the evidence that fits our preconceptions, and ignore or forget arrays of disconfirming evidence that rationally should be taken into account. Illusions of control and erroneous estimates of real causes or probabilities are common.[56]

What does not happen is hard to notice, and we tend to ignore missing data or not take into account background or baseline conditions. Worse still, it appears that because our minds are always so active in constructing and ordering reality, we can easily distort our memories without noticing it or meaning to deceive. Even eyewitness accounts are subject to creative reconstructions of the mind.[57] People can be intuitively certain of something in all good faith, yet be quite mistaken in their convictions. Even scientists and experts who are intuitively sure of their convictions sometimes are proved wrong.

Skepticism over the unreliability and limits of the conscious mind are compounded when one is considering the nonconscious mind. Many thinkers dismiss or ignore intuition altogether. We might discount all thinking that does not arise from direct conscious effort and that cannot be rigorously supported by the highest criteria of rational thinking. This drastic strategy, even if possible to carry out, would be a mistake because it would cut off resources of the human mind that have proved their value over and over. Surely there is a way to tap the creativity and richness of intuitive processes and rationally use them.

Here we address the specific question of moral decision making, for moral intuitions are as important in matters of conscience as scientific intuitions are in science. In moral decision making, as in other kinds of thinking, intuition plays a role in initiating problem solving, in pursuing the arguments, and in imparting different degrees of certainty to a solution. Certain innovative moral intuitions, like certain scientific breakthroughs, seem immediately worthy of conviction—even before fully articulated justifications are worked out. These intuitive processes must have taken place often in the history of moral reflection; think of the first person to see that slavery or sexism was immoral, despite the fact that the whole world recognized the practice as inevitable and part of the natural order.

Moral Problem Solving and Intuition

It would appear that the best strategy in moral decision making is to use all the mind's capacities and resources. Once convinced that both directed, rational thinking and intuition are valuable, but not infallible, we can try to devise a means of using both and cross-checking or testing both. To become engaged in rational, directed problem solving, we must first be conscious of a problem. If we are immediately aware of the solutions to moral or ethical questions, then the decision-making process will be brief if not almost automatic. We can instantaneously adjust our thoughts, feelings, and behavior to our internal maps and guides. But if new challenges, internal resistance, or conflicts produce doubt or dilemmas, or even if we simply have leisure for introspection, we may begin the pursuit of the most-adequate solutions for our problems.

A personal moral quest is never static; one feels the internal push to create better and better integrated solutions, just as human reasoning and rationality are often characterized by the seeking of more-complete understandings of truth and reality.[58] But time and energy are limited, and sometimes pragmatic solutions will be the best that can be had. If a less-than-satisfactory solution works now, seems coherent, and can solve the current problem, we will settle for it. If we are very stressed, with many immediate demands made upon us in order to survive, we may use reasoning skills mainly for pragmatic, here-and-now ends. In emergency conditions, we may resort to a form of moral triage. However, given a modicum of leisure and safety, we will be drawn to the search for good solutions.

Once embarked upon an effort to solve a moral problem of conscience, we can employ the general problem-solving steps discussed previously and sanctioned by common sense and the scientific method. As we have seen, the general moves to define, gather information, generate hypotheses, test, and so on, are not simple in actual practice, but are dynamic, subtle, and recursive operations employing many elements. In morality and ethics, the arguments and thinking may include applications of ethical principles, traditional wisdom, and moral arguments. The evidence gathered and used will be more inclusive than that used to solve other problems. But the dynamic reasoning processes are the same. In the back-and-forth, round-and-round steps of problem-solving, spontaneous intuitions may arise automatically and be incorporated into the process.

We can also make conscious efforts to use intuitive resources in moral decision making. Like scientists, we can morally build intuition and induce it with the use of different strategies at different times. We may come up against some impasse and find it difficult to resolve a question. When such a problem has been struggled with for long, frustrating periods, it can be laid aside for a while. We hope that when our attention is in a relaxed state in an unguarded moment, a solution to the problem may emerge. Even if this does not happen, when one returns to the problem, it can often be seen with more clarity.

Other personal moral experiences exemplify spontaneous intuitive movements of ideas into consciousness. In relaxed moments, when we are more or less off duty, hunches, moral intuitions, and innovative ideas about our personal future and future projects can appear from nowhere. These new ideas or flitting images may immediately dissipate and never be heard from again, or they can presage the future. Many moral decisions—such as changes in vocations or careers, marriages, divorces, political and religious conversions—are heralded by early signals that come into the mind as brief, spontaneous images.

In other cases, we may not be conscious of having any moral dilemmas or problems; but because of some intruding intuitions, we may be drawn to rethink moral questions, and thereby initiate some directed problem-solving process. Slightly disturbing but unformed moral ideas or images have been described as stirrings or promptings of conscience. We might, for instance, begin to feel intuitive stirrings that we should take certain moral actions. Or we begin to feel called upon to change our ways. Intuitive promptings may be repeated and can become quite insistent in their entry to awareness. People report that they suddenly found themselves saying something aloud to themselves, heard an inner voice, saw an inner picture of themselves in some new activity, or had a complete certainty that something would come to pass.

Sometimes the intuitive inner sense that something should be avoided or should be pursued is too subtle and inarticulated to even reach the form of an idea or actual feeling. The moral signal is more like a faint odor; we might say, "I sniffed a bad odor about the whole thing." We might refer to the sense of touch—"My skin crawled at the suggestion"—or in a positive vein—"I tingled with the sense that this was what I have been longing for." Rational people seeking to guide themselves morally would want to welcome these subtle signals spontaneously, coming from the self to the self. To know the self, at all levels, has always been judged the better part of wisdom. The faint negative signals may portend things we should confront and examine, but would rather avoid. The positive, innovative thoughts may lead to creative new courses of action.

Persons committed to the moral life do well to encourage sensitive reception of any moral signals from long-term memory or the nonconscious mind. But if there are no signals, can one tap intuition in direct ways? It is interesting that certain techniques for inquiring and listening to one's spontaneous inner stream of consciousness appear over and over in diverse modern psychotherapies.[59] Turning inward to listen also marks traditional Eastern and Western spiritual disciplines. These strategies can be adapted as aids in moral decision making. The first rule always seems to be that quiet time must be set aside for reflection. No one can begin looking inward or listening if caught up in hectic activity or demanding tasks that focus attention away from the self onto external projects.

Traditional Western systems of meditation have often used directed methods to produce imagery in prescribed ways. Eastern techniques have more often emphasized the value of observing whatever spontaneously arises in the mind's operations. Many psychological therapies, building upon the free association techniques of psychoanalysis, have also recommended becoming aware of the spontaneous flow of consciousness and thoughts. Listening to the spontaneous, covert self-talk that flows through the mind is the first step in gaining moral insight and self-control. Much can be learned by just inquiring in general and listening in general to what arises from the inner consciousness. But in moral problem solving, we might ask more of intuition.

When presented with a question or problem, or perhaps when an impasse has been reached, one can articulate the puzzling difficulty and ask for insight. Then one waits and tries to listen for some answer from some source of knowledge that one may possess. Waiting upon one's self can be given a formal shape and procedure. One just sits quietly with unfocused attention and lets whatever comes to mind, come.[60] Whatever emerges into attention and consciousness is accepted and perhaps laid aside—without the immediate deployment of all one's rational critical faculties at once discounting the idea. The permissive acceptance of everything without critique is the essence of all methods, such as brainstorming, which try to tap intuition. Without efforts to be nonjudgmental the active critic or internal censor tends to dismiss any new idea that might emerge. When one welcomes an idea and sets it aside, then one can listen again.

When an intuitive thought emerges that seems to be significant and pertinent, a new thought that gives new insight into one's problem, a sense of intuitive rightness and release is often felt. The intuition's confidence level is high. Something may be felt to shift within as a new perspective on one's problem emerges.[61] At this point, when one feels that new light or awareness has been achieved, then one may return to other more directed ways of thinking to elaborate or criticize. Later, other new ideas may spontaneously emerge from nonconscious processes of thinking or the reordering of knowledge.

Evaluating Intuition

Building intuition like scientists do may have another dimension, which we will explore more fully in future chapters on moral development. Just as scientists struggle and work to intellectually produce a mind ready to produce intuitions, so we can ready ourselves for moral intuitions by preparatory, conscious efforts. Consciously attending to moral questions and moral thinking in pursuit of the good is the way to prepare for worthwhile future intuitions. Before we can be morally creative, we must develop a moral sensibility and the practiced ability to think through moral problems. The nonconscious mind can hardly operate at a level higher than the developed levels of comprehension of the rational, conscious mind.

Receiving intuitions, however, cannot resolve our moral dilemmas automatically. Becoming aware of the spontaneous flow of ideas into consciousness does not settle the question of assessment of ideas. Granted that intuition is a resource, how do we evaluate and select the intuitions, hunches, aspirations, images, and ideas that arise? Here, those committed to the use of reason will once more use the full panoply of reasonable problem-solving techniques and criteria to test and evaluate the quality of the intuitive signals received. When scientists are encouraged to build intuition and guess creatively, they are at the same time taught how to critically doubt, and then rigorously and impartially to test their hunches.[62] The final products and solutions must be able to withstand the scientific community's public scrutiny. One set up one's own ideas and then shoots them down so that errors are weeded out.

I think this process of preparation, incubation, reception, filtering, and critique works in the moral life as well. If we grant that intuitions or spontaneous ideas are metaphorically messages from our nonconscious minds to our conscious selves, we are still not guaranteed of their worth. Since we do not voluntarily choose or deliberately produce them, it is as though they are ideas we have just heard from others— the others being the different parts of ourselves. We can sensibly evaluate the ideas in the way we would evaluate other people's intuitions or spontaneous ideas. The self-self scrutiny here is very much like a self-stranger dialogue. Indeed, many skeptics have thought that those seeking to know the inner self are necessarily confined to using the same strategies used to make inferences about another.[63] While I am more optimistic about ordinary introspection, I think the self-stranger approach can be a good one for judging the value of any intuitions or any dreams that we remember as we wake up. Our minds may have created them, but since the processes of the creation are dim and unknown, we can only assess the message with our conscious awareness.

We can begin our assessment of intuitions with simple questions. Does the intuition, hunch, or dreamed idea accord with reason and common sense? Is it consistent, noncontradictory, in accord with all evidence and reality, and so on? If the hunch or idea seems innovative, we would be more trusting if the stranger thinking it up had a lot of innate brainpower, knew a lot about the matter, had a lot of successful past experience, and had been working very hard to solve the problem or similar problems by traditional rational means. Those persons who had been preparing their minds would be prepared to receive a valuable insight.

When we judge our own spontaneous productions like we would other people's, much depends upon our estimates of ourselves and our known previous efforts in a certain area. Our intuitions that have been most prepared for by previous study and work will obviously have the most weight, since they may more likely be the nonconscious, rational answers to specific rational questions we are ready and capable of answering. Upon testing, these intuitions often turn out to be rationally supported. Intuitive answers to moral dilemmas much wrestled with may have value.

More ad hoc intuitions, as we have seen, will seem less reliable, but are still not to be disregarded. Always our degree of felt certainty has to be matched against everything else we know about ourselves. If we know we are mathematically illiterate, we can dismiss formulas that came into our heads as worthless. And if we are reasonably sane, and undrugged, ideas grossly violating common sense and reason will also be quickly dismissed. From time to time, we may momentarily have the notion that we can really fly, but we do not jump out of windows. Spontaneous intuitions have often been seen as ideas that are closer to wishes and emotions, so some intuitions may clearly be fantasies.[64] Two milliseconds of rational thinking can relegate some hunches to the realm of unreal wish fulfillment or error.

Fantasies of murdering a beloved spouse or holding up a bank are as quickly dismissed as thoughts of flying out a window. Bizarre immoral impulses may be psychological clues to some inner state, but for most people, they are beyond the bounds of possible behavior; only if our thinking or self-control were impaired could such out-of-bounds crimes be committed. Certain essential ethical and common moral principles have the full rational assent of most of us. We would never doubt the core moral obligations that apply to us as we live together in society. But when intuitions, hunches, and aspirations are in the realm of new dilemmas or uniquely private moral choices, the process of appraisal can become subtle and difficult. As we move away from the basics of common morality, the task becomes more difficult.

We have trouble on the boundaries of morality, where different goods may conflict or we have a problem of choosing lesser evils. We have problems most acutely when there is conflict within the society between reasonable persons over the morality of certain actions. Other difficult cases arise from our need to morally direct our own specific lives in a specific time and place. When the general moral rules give no specific guidance about how we are to do good and avoid evil, our consciences must be more creative and innovative. To exercise creativity we must have access to our spontaneous resources, and then rationally test them with more specifically personal criteria.

When we are spontaneously and momentarily morally moved, called, or made uneasy, we should pay attention. Even if we cannot rationally explain, articulate, or substantiate these intuitions, we should note them. If certain spontaneous ideas come up over and over, or begin to increase in frequency, more attention should be paid. Some discrepancy between our nonconscious minds and our conscious awareness is being signaled. Such intuitive signaling deserves the full exploration and rational self-conscious examination of conscience, as well as some effort to induce intuition.

Is there anything we are not noticing, either within or without, upon which the dynamic movements of problem solving should be focused? Here, intuitions might lead us to turn to others for rational counsel; just as we would try to appraise ourselves as if another, so it is effective to have the appraisal of other people. The need for the appraisal of wise counselors is a traditionally recognized truth. The therapist, mentor, spiritual guide, or confessor gives us more-objective rational assessments of our dilemmas. Reasoning together helps us articulate and develop our thinking.

But what if we do not have time to test intuitions, or must act before we are fully convinced and have arrived at some synthesis of reason and intuitions? If we must make moral decisions in split seconds, obviously we rely on intuitive responses because that is all there is time for. These moments of crisis and emergency can be moments of truth, because they reveal what has been produced by all the past decisions that we have made. We can learn much from the revelations afforded by our intuitive moral decisions. When the news is bad, and we are dismayed at our failures, it can be the spur for a new moral quest. If, on the other hand, we responded well or heroically, we may not be considered deserving of much praise, since there was no time to think.

But suppose there is time to think, yet not enough time to reason through to moral convictions completely grounded in both reason and intuitive certainties. In such situations, our present individual moral intuitions may not be in accord with what is commonly accepted or with what seemed reasonable and right in the past. In this case, we have to assess whether we should follow unfounded moral intuitions or follow our more thoroughly grounded past reasons. Much will depend on the content, the circumstances, our assessment of our own capacities, and the degree of our past commitments to, and confidence in, the reasons that now conflict with our new moral intuitions. Also, much will depend upon how strong a degree of certainty, arising from previous mulling and struggle, we accord to the present intuitions. If we follow our more articulated reasons in a conflict, then in the future, we can at least know why we did what we did. If in the future we decide that our intuitions were the beginning of a better moral understanding, we will feel regret and sorrow but not full-blown moral guilt. We can remember the other times when our moral intuitions eventually were judged inadequate, and proved the importance of relying upon our solid foundations of the past.

Over a lifetime, we often experience a change in our rational moral convictions. This seems inevitable, since we live our moral lives in an ongoing flow of time with limited resources; we can never be absolutely certain that at any point our moral decisions of conscience are without error. Perhaps in the future, we will comprehend more of the true and good than we do now—just as we can see from looking back in time that we have changed. Such realizations keep us humble, although they cannot deter those rationally convinced in the present. The more grounded and intuitively certain we are, the more we must stand by our lights. Reason must be served by reasonable persons. But once we know that much of the mind works outside of awareness and can affect it, then it is reasonable to pay attention to intuitions. The best solution to our moral problems will always be a synthesis of dynamic, rational problem solving, informed by intuition, confirmed by intuition, which is, in turn, tested by reason.

Responding to the Challenge

To go back to the original challenge presented at the beginning of this chapter, what do I think of the physician's method of solving her moral problem of conscience by preparing an array of information and then sleeping on it? If I had had my wits about me, what should I have said to her? Now I would tell her that she seemed wise to gather as much information as possible that seemed relevant to the problem. I would add that I hoped she also included as pertinent information the ethical guidelines and applicable decisions and arguments of other moral communities and traditional sources of wisdom. Relevant preparations can be taken by seeking direct counsel with experienced and good persons one knows. I would also commend her decision to allow an interval to pass in order to let intuitive processes develop. Sleeping on it (pondering it, mulling it over, letting ideas marinate in the mind) is an old and good practice, a way of building intuition.

When the physician wakes up and immediately sees her solution, she can be seen as receiving the results of her intuitive processes, which she has prepared and incubated overnight. So far, so good. But I do not think she should stop the process of inquiry at this point, accept her ideas, and consider the problem solved without further ado. Here I would take issue with the claim that she always sees the solution or that she can trust it immediately. Using rational skepticism, one must remember the bias and fallibility of the conscious thinking processes. People forget misses and remember hits, they ignore baseline data, they tend to see what they expect to see, and on and on. All scientific controls and tests are an effort to overcome errors that enter rational thinking unknowingly. Why should the products of the nonconscious thinking mind be any more reliable? All intuitive ideas, like all other ideas, need critical monitoring and testing before acceptance.

I would advise the physician to be more skeptical of her intuitions and proceed to test them. Her solutions that come in dreams or in isolated, private, spontaneous insights should not be considered infallible. I would recommend the full panoply of rational problem-solving strategies described here. Only when my intuitions have been tested and are found in accord with my best thinking can I decide with confidence.[65] My most central convictions are strong blends of reasoning, arguments, evidence, and intuition bound together coherently.

Basically, we become rationally convinced in conscience because of the preponderance of specific and general evidence that is linked with everything else we know and accept from all sources in our life experience. After guessing and testing, building intuition and checking it, all the threads weave together to produce the rope that supports a moral decision.

But the engagement of reason and intuition is not all there is to moral decision making. Emotions and desires affect our conscious directed thinking and our spontaneous intuitions, and we need to know what they are and what roles they play in the moral decision making of conscience.

Chapter 4

Emotions and Moral Decision Making

In my definition of conscience, I stress that wholehearted emotional commitment to the good and right is what distinguishes moral decisions of conscience from other kinds of decisions. I also recognize the importance of the emotions to a sense of self; there is an emotive bedrock of self-consciousness that constitutes the self, the person who makes moral decisions.[1]

The psychological work on emotion is so new that it has not yet been absorbed by many of those developmental and philosophical psychologists who work in another part of the forest, trying to achieve more-integrated models of moral development, moral judgment, and moral education. Nor have philosophers, theologians, or others writing on moral decision making had access to the latest psychological thinking about emotion. The automatic dismissal and neglect of emotion have been prevalent in our Western moral tradition. Certain negative psychological presuppositions and assumptions regularly turn up in both academic and common discourse. When we hear the phrases, "Oh don't be so emotional" or "You're just being emotional," the message is clear: to be emotional makes us inadequate, irrelevant, or wrongheaded in our decisions.

Suspicion of Emotion

The place of emotions—inner feelings or, metaphorically, the heart—in morality has been debated throughout much of Western cultural history. Moralists, from Plato to modern times, often have seen emotions as dangerous or dismissed them as irrelevant and irrational. They authorized reason, or the head as opposed to the heart, as the only reliable guide in life and moral decision making. It is also true, as a feminist critique of philosophy has noted, that they usually characterized reason as male, and

emotions, feelings, sentiments, or passions as arising from our lower animal nature, always stronger in females.[2] The moralists assumed that
women, with their bodily reproductive organs and more sensual natures,
were more biological and less rational. The higher active male power of
reason should master and direct the emotions and body, just as rational
males should govern passive and passionate females.[3]

Passion, emotions, feelings, and desires were judged to be arrayed
adversarially against reason and to rebel against the higher nature of
the soul. While emotions, the body, and the changeable things of earth
will pass away, reason and the soul remain universal and eternal. Anyone who championed the value of emotional feeling as equal to, or
superior to, reason were thought to be endorsing romantic irrationality,
and encouraging anarchy and self-destructive license. Those philosophers or other thinkers who argued that human reason serves the passions whether it knows it or not were seen as denying the dignity of
human nature, as well as disparaging the claims of human reason and
moral freedom. Romantics and the minority of rebels serving the cause
of emotion have been indignantly censured for their views.

Take, for example, a modern reaction to assertions by one of the
great romantic spokesmen for feeling, Dostoevsky. In his 1878 note-
book, he reflects upon a Russian terrorist who balked before an assas-
sination: "What is moral is not completely decided by the simple
concept of consistency with one's conviction, because sometimes it is
more moral not to follow one's convictions . . . one stops short, because
of some feeling, and does not complete the act. One curses oneself and
feels self-contempt, but feeling, that is, conscience, prevents one from
completing the act."[4] Dostoevsky's identification of conscience with feeling is noteworthy, as is his analysis of a divided self in which a powerful
emotion can inhibit an action that reason has sanctioned and directed.

Such romantic Dostoevskian exaltation of feeling is deplored by
Milan Kundera, a modern Czech writer. Fueled perhaps by indignation at Russia's past sins against his native land, he has railed against
Dostoevsky's novelistic universe, "where everything turns into feelings, where feelings are promoted to the rank of value and truth."[5]
Kundera exemplifies the classic rationalist condemnation of the trustworthiness of feelings:

> Man cannot do without feelings, but the moment they are considered
> values in themselves, criteria of truth, justifications for kinds of behav-
> ior, they become frightening. The noblest of national sentiments stand

ready to justify the greatest of horrors, and man, his breast swelling with lyric fervor, commits atrocities in the sacred name of love.[6]

The case against trusting emotions in morality has been made over and over with many variations. When negative feelings are unleashed, they will lead to crimes of passion and group atrocities. But on the other hand, when positive feelings are followed, they too can lead to mistaken sacrifices and misguided altruism. Emotions may inhibit our rational resolutions and convictions as we give in to the tempting desires of the heart. Specific attachments will cloud our commitment to impartial justice and to the universal goals we can reach only through reason and logic.

Not only will emotions attach us to unworthy ends, but more destructively, they will sabotage reason, our only effective means of moral evaluation. Emotions impede moral thinking—"nothing fogs the mind so thoroughly as emotion."[7] Only the detached, calm mind can make rational, trustworthy moral decisions. After all, "arguments are one thing, sentiments another." When sentiment is allowed to reign, we will be led astray by moral decisions marred by the unreliable personal caprice of subjective feelings. For this reason, the primary task of a moral person when making a moral decision should be to suppress emotion in order to be able to follow the light of reason and make more objective, more correct moral decisions. The first goal of a moral decision maker is to achieve a nonemotional state of detachment. Two brief quotations from St. Ignatius and Kant can give the flavor of this tradition as it has dominated great religious and philosophical thinkers.

St. Ignatius, in his advice to those seeking to follow God's will and make a good and correct choice of a way of life, says that the first step is to become completely detached: "I must be indifferent, without any inordinate attachment, so that I am not more inclined or disposed to accept the object in question than to relinquish it, nor to give it up than to accept it. I should be like a balance at equilibrium, without leaning to either side. . . ."[8] Ignatius counseled a long, subtle deliberating process of weighing disadvantages and advantages, but then concludes, "I must come to a decision in the matter under deliberation because of weightier motives presented to my reason, and not because of any sensual inclination."[9] Over the centuries this repudiation of positive feelings became so debased and popularized that persons could be guided by a crude negative moral principle: If you are emotionally drawn to something and want to do it, if it makes you happy, it must be immoral!

Kant was even more stringent in his repudiation of emotions, and to this day his thought affects the philosophical tradition of moral decision making. Kant treats emotions and passions as "probably always an illness of mind because both emotion and passion exclude the sovereignty of reason."[10] Thus one must avoid the toxic illness or intoxicant of passion when making moral decisions. Kant defends the stoic ideal of detachment and apathy: "The principle of apathy, that is, that the prudent man must at no time be in a state of emotion, not even in that of sympathy with the woes of his best friend, is an entirely correct and sublime moral precept of the Stoic school, because emotion makes one more or less blind."[11] Duty done against inclination counts as true morality. The debased popular version of this approach to the moral life is that what's moral makes you miserable, only the painful can be good for you!

The traditional suspicion of the role of emotion in applied moral philosophy persists. Today, opinion seems divided between whether emotions should be totally excised from the moral enterprise as actively dangerous, tolerated as irrelevant, or seen as useful—if rationally tutored, controlled, and kept subordinated in their proper place. Numerous examples of all these shades of negative attitude can be found in those practicing applied ethics.

The totally rationalistic rejection of emotion and feeling is exemplified by the bioethicist H. Tristram Engelhardt, Jr., who can say that affirmations of one's feelings are "irrational, surd;" instead one should seek to become an impartial reasoner "whose only interests are in the consistency and force of rational argument."[12] Only an impartial reasoner can meet other minds and engage in the reasoning process that can come to an agreement on a moral issue. Again the assumption is that emotions are too private, arbitrary, and individualistic to count as evidence or to be helpful in morals.

An example of the just-tolerated but still-suspicious approach is the advice of a moralist who claims begrudgingly that while emotions or gut feelings cannot be avoided, they should be minimized. As James Rachels says, in a discussion of the very emotional topic of euthanasia:

> The idea can not be to avoid reliance on unsupported 'sentiments' (to use Hume's word) altogether . . . that is impossible. The idea is always to be suspicious of them, and to rely on as few as possible, only after examining them critically, and only after pushing the arguments and explanations as far as they will go without them.[13]

In other words, it is a far, far better thing to use only rational analysis and never rely on emotions or intuitions until absolutely forced to do so. Only when the intellectual high-wire act of reason fails should you resort to emotional grounds.

Other warnings against sentimentality and the influence of emotions are more subtle. The president of the American philosophical society, Joel Feinberg, once gave a presidential address devoted to "Sentiment and Sentimentality in Practical Ethics."[14] He expressed appreciation of moral emotions and sees them as essential to our culture, but only if they are always and everywhere evaluated, monitored, and tutored by reason. While moral sentiments or emotions can be the subject of rational argument and used as relevant evidence in an argument, emotions should always be subordinated to reason in *the process* of decision making. Moral emotions can never serve as an ethical criterion; they must always be evaluated solely by rational judgments of the reasonable appropriateness of the feeling to the stimuli and situation.

If rational criteria do not hold sway, then a person making a moral decision of conscience can be the victim of "flawed feelings" such as sentimentality, squeamishness, or romanticism.[15] Wrong actions and, indeed, wrong social policies can be instituted when sentimental attachments are allowed to thwart the actual interests of persons. Inappropriate emotions, even noble emotions, which do not conform to rational considerations of principles, interests, and consequences must not be allowed to direct our applied ethical decisions. For emotions to count in any valid, applied ethical decision, they must be justified on independent grounds. Otherwise, we could never know which emotions are morally reliable. Emotions, even noble sentiments, must be monitored and controlled by a "careful rational superintendency."

Unfortunately, modern moralists' suspicions of emotion are based upon a particular psychological model of human functioning that has not changed much over the past centuries. There is an assumption, first, that reasoning *can* be thoroughly detached from emotion; second, that only detached reasoning will be reliably objective; and third, that emotions will only bias, cloud, and impede moral decision making. Recent psychological approaches to reason, emotion, and their interactions cast doubt on these presuppositions.

Definition and Origins of Emotions

Most of the new work in emotion theory and experimental research has come from experimental psychologists influenced by what has been called the cognitive and consciousness revolution in psychology. As repeatedly noted here, while the founding fathers of psychology were interested in the self and the self-conscious operations of the mind, the subsequent rise and reign of behaviorism declared the mind and consciousness to be a meaningless epiphenomenon. But, once it became clear that human beings are not large white rats, the study of mind and consciousness became dominant again. Along with this movement came the rehabilitation of emotions as well. The thinking, feeling human person, who had been affirmed by philosophy and literature, was rediscovered by scientific psychology.

Once one embarks upon the study of human consciousness, it becomes clear that a large part of what James called the stream of consciousness is "colored" or "charged with" or "heated by" what has traditionally been called emotion or feeling. It is hard to describe or distinguish these feelings using only quantitative measures. There is a qualitative difference between the subjective experience of considering how to rearrange a bookshelf and confronting a lover's betrayal. Recalling one's mother's deathbed is different from remembering the algorithm for solving an equation. Explaining the qualitative difference in consciousness has been the challenge.

Emotions have been called "hot cognitions," because they move us, they press, they motivate.[16] As in the children's game of hot and cool, one gets hotter consciousness the closer one moves to the self. Emotions emerge when we are subjectively and personally concerned and invested in our thoughts and images. This distinctive qualitative difference in consciousness has been attributed to the activation of the limbic system or other brain pathways, or to the arousal of biochemical, muscular, facial, and physiological mechanisms. Emotions seem hotter because they are more arousing, vivid, holistic, and encompassingly, concretely "ours" than other states of consciousness.

In the most dominant psychological theories today, human emotions are seen as the result of a complex, organized emotional or affective system, which is an innately programmed capacity of the human species.[17] The emotional or affective system interacts with other specialized human subsystems geared to perception and thinking, to drives and physiological maintenance, and to motor activity. Emotions, like human rational abilities and the human body, are thought to have been selected through evolution to ensure the survival of individuals and the group.[18] Emotions are seen as the primary motivating system for all activity.[19] Without emotions or affects to amplify physiological drives and infuse cognitive processing with subjective meaning, human beings would not care enough to stay alive, much less mate, nurture offspring, create kinship bonds, or pursue art, politics, science, literature, and moral philosophy. We do things because we emotionally care about them and are personally invested; when we stop being moved, we stop moving.

At one time, all emotions were considered disruptive to the higher mental functions, but it has become clear that only very negative and extremely intense or regressed affective states are disabling: extreme depression, extreme panic, or extreme rage (often due to biochemical and brain disorders) does impair thinking and appropriate action.[20] More generally, emotions are energizing and adaptive, and increase the effectiveness of communication, problem solving, and social bonding. Human beings are far more emotional than other animals, and as the most emotional species, we have outnurtured as well as outwitted the competition. Emotions of love and sympathy make possible the interpersonal bonds and social environments that create, nurture, and socialize new members of the species, thereby ensuring the existence of social groups.

The human emotional system seems to be as universal, and as much a panspecies phenomenon, as human linguistic abilities. Our emotions can be thought of as a protolanguage that we are genetically programmed to learn, encode, and decode from infancy throughout life. Evidence from cross-cultural and infant research points to panhuman constancies in basic emotional responses and expressions.[21] The face and facial configurations of mouth, eyes, brows, and muscles communicate emotion to others, and perhaps through feedback to the brain, partially bring emotions into consciousness.[22] Different emotions can be recognized correctly from characteristic configurations of facial expressions—whether presented to the natives of New Guinea or New York.[23] When movies are made of facial expressions, the initial emotive expression can be seen in a frame analysis, even when there is an immediate attempt to mask the feeling with another facial expression.

Great actors use their faces—and bodily postures and gestures—to make us see a person having emotions. Actors can portray a person having an emotional reaction while simultaneously trying to hide or overcome the feeling. We can read these nonverbal communications because we are innately primed from infancy to send and receive emotional messages; we can comprehend and share the emotional experience of others and be attuned to their emotional states.[24] Our emotional system makes empathy possible, as well as generating all kinds of emotional communication (often below the level of awareness) that affects our behavior and responses to other people and events.[25]

The innate primary emotions appear to be constituted of distinctly patterned responses of the neurochemical, facial, and motor systems

that, when consciously experienced, produce distinct qualitative subjective experiences. Psychologists explore the ways that the subjective
experiences of emotion differ from one another and include built-in
meanings and motivating predispositions: "I am angry and want to
attack"; "I am afraid and want to flee"; "I love and wish to approach."
Sadness differs from joy, which differs from anger, which differs from
shame, and so on.

The limited set of basic emotions that have been described as innately
programmed can, like primary colors, be blended, differentiated, and
elaborated.[26] The primary emotions are often seen as existing upon a continuum of intensity and are usually enumerated as interest-excitement,
enjoyment-joy, surprise-startle, distress-anguish, anger-rage, disgust-
revulsion, contempt-scorn, fear-terror, shame-humiliation, and, for some
theorists, remorse-guilt and affection-love. Researchers in the field argue
over this list, with some holding that startle is not an emotion, but rather
a physiological reaction or reflex, and others seeing love as an early blend
of joy and interest; still others would subsume guilt into shame.

The positive emotions have been grouped together and characterized
as inducing movement toward an object, or motivating continuing contact.[27] The negative emotions induce movement to avoid or overcome obstacles and dangers. Emotions have also been grouped according to
intensity so that highly intense emotions have been seen to have high
arousal in common and perhaps be more subject to excitement transfer or
quick alternation from one to the other. As Freud knew, intense love and
hate are closer to one another, in one sense, than love and indifference.
Of course, in such a new and expanding field, many conflicting theories
and unsolved problems remain. It is difficult to establish the boundaries
and limiting definitions of emotions. How long, for instance, does a true
emotion last? Are emotions brief and acute, as some theorists think, or
do they also come in the form of more diffuse extended experiences which
we label as moods? Must emotions always be conscious?

Since emotions have physiological, behavioral, and informational or
conscious components, and they interact with all the other human functioning systems, it is not always easy to distinguish an emotion from
its associated experiences. The intimate relationships between pain and
suffering, for instance, can produce questions about whether pain
should count as an emotion or be seen as a purely physiological response. At the other extreme, there is the fusion of sexual pleasure and
emotion, which make erotic experience so vivid.

The core of basic emotions seems to be extended by experience so
that a family of emotional phenomena—moods, sentiments, feelings—

appear that reflect complex blends and elaborations occasioned by social learning and intellectual development.[28] Emotions come in various
spectrums, depending upon their purity, intensity, and blends with
other emotions and the other systems of the human organism.[29] Different cultures may elaborate different blends or enact different variations
of the basic emotional themes.[30] The English language is full of emotion
words in which different components are blended. Think of the nu-
ances we distinguish between jealousy and envy, regret and remorse,
homesickness and nostalgia. Basic emotions are blended, elaborated,
and developed so that they operate in complex ways in different individuals and in the particular cultures that shape them.[31] Anthropologists and sociologists in the new field of ethnopsychology are interested
in studying a society's views of emotions, complete with their emotion
rules, conventions, and prescribed patterns for interpreting and managing emotions.[32]

Operations of Emotion

As the individual develops, emotions develop in intimate complex
interaction with all the other innate human capacities. The consciousness of self and personal reality is constituted to a great extent by the
continuity of subjective emotional experience from infancy to old age.
It seems true that "our affective core guarantees our continuity of experience across development in spite of the many ways we change."[33]
Emotions accompany the functioning of the inner subjective self, as
well as offer an important way of communicating with, and responding
to, the world. They provide us with our sense of reality and give vividness to the experience of being alive.[34]

Some theorists of emotion have spoken of an emotional "law of apparent reality," in which "feeling means more than knowing."[35] This
would account for "the powerlessness of verbal reassurance to diminish
phobic anxiety" and the potency of emotional sequences of feeling to
confer reality. On the TV program "Candid Camera," when a person has
been fooled by some elaborate deception, the victim may verbally say that
yes he now comprehends the ruse, but only when the emotional reaction
arrives full force in face, viscera, muscles, and consciousness does the full
understanding of what has happened really hit. In the same way, people
can describe traumas and losses they have undergone, but not feel them
to be real until their emotional reactions become conscious. But while
emotions in their acute stages are intense, they are also thought to contain

within themselves an inhibitory control mechanism, which means that they will wax and then wane naturally. Protective stop rules may normally be built in for each emotional episode.[36]

An asymmetry in emotional experiences has also been noted. The negative emotions are thought to be stronger than the positive emotions. At least, negative emotions and pain seem more attended to. Many have felt that this tendency toward asymmetry has evolved because biological survival is more dependent upon fear, flight, anger, and the communication necessary to flee predators and obtain aid to overcome obstacles. Obviously, part of the power of emotional communication arises from our ability to understand and share emotions. Indeed, emotions are so contagious that we can hardly see another cry without joining in, simply hearing laughter may induce a smile, and anger provokes anger. This contagious aspect may also have induced some of the cultural rules that prescribe the masking and suppression of emotions. But when emotions are absent in a person, there is an eerie feeling that the person is absent. When brain damage or disease causes emotional deficits, persons lose their grasp on reality; they can no longer make vital contact with their own inner experience, and we can no longer make vital contact with them.[37]

Normally, emotions early on in human development become fused, associated with, and interactive with thoughts, images, and ideas in the ongoing stream of consciousness. The subtlety of the quicksilver interplay of thought and emotion is astounding. An instantaneous thought, image, or perception can transform consciousness instantly from one emotion state to another. A thought of a favor done can induce gratitude and joy as quickly as a thought of an injury produces anger; the memory of a transgression can induce shame and guilt; in a moment of calm happiness, a perception of danger can produce fear and distress. Occasionally, the full development of the emotion is postponed during an active emergency so that, while our faces may register the emotional reaction instantly, only after danger has been averted will we experience trembling and waves of conscious fear.

On the other hand, we can begin to feel emotionally reactive before we have a clear perception or explanation of feelings. The most heated debate in emotion research is over how much conscious mental appraisal is necessary to induce an emotion. One influential theorist maintains that the affect system can produce its effects directly, without going through the informational processing system. R. B. Zajonc voiced his ideas in an authoritative article entitled "Feeling and Thinking: Preferences Need No Inferences." He claims that experimental evidence shows that the primary affect system is a "parallel, separate, and partly independent system in the organism," which is engaged in decisions in which the self is implicated.[38] The emotions may provide a separate adaptive way in which human beings decide on actions, attitudes, and reactions, bypassing cognitive appraisal and analysis.

Opponents to the idea of a separated affect system claim that while emotions may help shape and direct attention, there must, at some level, be some rational appraisal made of an event or a situation before the appropriate emotion can be induced and felt.[39] This conflict may be cleared up if it is true, as it now appears to be, that there is a rational nonconscious mind operating below awareness. We may appraise a situation below conscious awareness and then be induced to emotionally react.

The newest work on the mind's nonconscious processing and integrating of information (taken up in the previous chapter on intuition) can help explain why emotions, like thoughts or images, seem to pop into our consciousness without conscious effort or deliberation. We do not have conscious access to much of our mind's processing and filtering of information. Our long-term memory may determine what will get through to our limited resources of conscious attention. In a way, what spontaneously emerges into consciousness, whether emotion, intuition, or image, is a message that one part of my system sends, or allows to get through, to my present awareness. This is one reason why emotions, like intuitions, are worth attending to; they are, in a sense, "vital signs" or signals from myself to myself.[40]

The newest research on memory shows that emotions, in their turn, can apparently shape thinking and information processing. Our long-term memories may consist of networks in which emotions and information are stored together or in associative units.[41] Things, and our feelings about them, may be stored together; narratives and scenes may be stored as units along with their associated emotions. Thus, when either a feeling or an idea is activated, so are the associated networks. Thinking about death may activate sad feelings, but feeling sad may also activate thoughts of death. When we are happy, we remember happy things and make optimistic predictions about the future and other persons. Our present emotions and thoughts will go into our memories to shape future responses and our streams of consciousness.

Some of the most exciting research in the relationship between emotions and thought has shown how emotional states affect memory and other thinking processes.[42] Emotions have been seen to affect selective content of memory, efficiency of memory, social evaluations of persons, learning ability, and even perception of physical stimuli in the environment.[43] But these interactions of thought and emotion may not be operating in conscious awareness, and there seems to be no clear one-way direction of cause and effect.

Perhaps the best image of this dynamic interaction of thought and feeling in the stream of consciousness is that developed by Michael Lewis and Linda Michalson, two astute students of infants. Finding linear models of one-way directional causation inadequate, they developed a more two-way interactive model in the image of a musical fugue. As they express it: "We have developed a third model based on the metaphor of a musical fugue . . . in this model, the cognitive-emotional relationship is depicted as a complex interplay of processes, similar to the themes of a fugue, which are often lost and reappear."[44]

Other investigators have found that this interweaving of thought and feeling, along with fusions of thought and feelings, continues throughout life.[45] Emotions induce thoughts, which induce emotion, which may induce other thoughts or emotions, and so on. (Automatic physiological reactions, along with voluntary behavior, also become a part of the interplay and stream of responses.) The complexity of an individual's past experience creates a person who thinks and emotionally responds in characteristic ways. Our emotional reactions, as much as our thoughts, express who we are.

Long before experimental psychologists or psychoanalysts began their investigations, the stream of consciousness was open to human introspection and was the focus of poetic expression. Art and religion testify to the interplay of the inner fugue of thoughts and feelings. The psalms are great subjective expressions of thought and feeling, equalled by later works such as Augustine's confessions, in which a voice moves from facts remembered to feelings invoked, and then back again to ideas. Poetry, epics, Greek drama, myths, and later literature such as novels and autobiographies, along with opera, also interweave a narrative and the feelings the narrative invokes. Film is another potent medium for conveying the emotive stream of consciousness with all its subtleties, combining visual imagery, music, and the human voice. Part of the power of narratives lies in their ability to compel attention as the story invokes suspense and emotional response.

Problems in Emotional Functioning

In an individual's emotional functioning, many distortions are possible—excesses and deficits, along with regressions to immature, infantile states, all of which warp the inner signals and social interactions. Since thought and feeling are so interwoven, most emotional distortions and regressions are also marked by distorted, irrational thinking patterns. One often-overlooked problem area is the lack of sufficient emotional responses. Without love or empathy, without guilt or shame, persons become morally impaired. In such cases, persons may have high IQs and be able to verbally articulate moral rules, but they cannot really feel the moral imperative or oughtness of the rules as part of their own reactions. They do not feel the emotional "mustness" or demand of conscience, nor do they feel anxiety or fear over possible transgressions. Finally, they feel no guilt or shame when they intellectually know that they have transgressed. Their verbal cognitive symbolic reasoning may be functioning, but it has become separated from their personal affective system, which is either stunted or not functioning. Persons who are deficient in love, sympathy, moral anxiety, guilt, and shame have been labeled psychopaths and seen to be suffering from a severe mental disorder.[46] For whatever reason, they are numbed or tone-deaf to moral feelings.[47]

Another more-frequent problem with emotional responses is not a deficit problem but the appearance of infantile emotions and thought patterns that arise when persons regress under stress. Freud called the primitive thinking and feeling untouched by maturing influences of reality the id. Today, instead of speaking about the id as though it were a thing or a miniperson inside of person, theorists speak of a way of acting that is childish in feeling and thought. As Roy Schafer, one of the major theorists reinterpreting psychoanalytic language, puts it, the regressed way of acting known as the id

> "is a way of acting erotically or aggressively that is more or less infantile in its being irrational, unmodulated, unrestrained, heedless of consequences and contradiction, thoroughly egocentric, and more than likely associated with those vivid and diffuse physiological processes that fall under the common heading of excitement or arousal.[48]

The emotions and thinking displayed are those of a child, whether the person is a bright young physician under stress, an old person facing death, an adolescent newly facing life, or even a middle-aged philosopher in a second adolescence.

Unfortunately, at any time in the life cycle, irrational emotions can fuse with irrational thinking, so that "reasoning with a person suffering from mania, is like reasoning with a five year old."[49] Severely depressed persons are equally resistant to rational influence and the counsels of reality. When the disorder becomes extreme, a diagnostic label is attached and psychotherapy and/or drug treatment prescribed. There are many degrees of disturbance, ranging from normal ups and downs to neurosis, to psychosis where contact with ordinary reality is lost completely. The most unsettling thing about severe disturbances is that people may not be aware that they are disturbed.

It is more often the case, however, that when certain distorted emotional states appear in our own stream of consciousness, we can tell that qualitatively something is amiss. When we are under stress, our conditions of disordered emotion and thinking result in a sense of addictive, obsessive excess; our feelings and thoughts seem out of control.[50] The stream of consciousness can be repeatedly flooded with intrusive recycling of "primitive" thoughts and feelings. Such experiences of high emotional intensity are recognized, but the irrational thought patterns that accompany them draw less attention. Thus emotions have been blamed as the sole cause of such deterioration and so have been held as morally suspect. Rational moralists have identified all emotional influences with these regressed infantile patterns of behaving.

It has gone unnoticed that the moral conflict supposedly between head and heart, or mind and emotion, is usually between one immature-thinking, emotive scenario in conflict with another more-mature moral scenario involving more-positive emotions and more-rational thoughts. Conflicts can occur when we wish to overcome some emotions, while seeking and welcoming other emotions as more acceptable to our self-image.

The desire not to feel certain personally threatening emotions leads to another complication in assessing emotions. Can there be pseudo-emotions that are not what they seem? In psychoanalytic theory, it is claimed that an emotion can be defended against not only by suppression and denial, but also by transformation, or consciously feeling another less threatening emotion.[51] Better to feel anger than shame or guilt. This defensive transformation of emotions implies a subconscious or preconscious filtering and a lightning ability of the self to transform one feeling into another. There are probably some limits to, and some laws governing, these self-protective manipulations of feeling, at least in nonimpaired adults.

Every day we see people deny that they feel emotions when everyone around them can observe that they are feeling angry or sad. But do the people themselves know their emotional state at some preconscious level? If so, the effort to repress or hide from experience should exact a price in energy. To deny emotions or keep them acceptably transformed must tax the inner personal system. Most theorists would hold that in order to defend against an emotion, the person must first know at some level of processing what is to be defended against. Thus energy to keep from knowing or to transform knowledge would have to be expended. Different parts of the brain may even have to be kept in conflict and not allowed to operate in the usual integrated way. Integrity and nondefensive functioning may be more efficient for a person than the costly strategy of self-deception.

Covert self-deception seems different, however, from the conscious decision to select one aspect of an emotion in an ambivalent situation and thereby edit or shape an emotional reaction. With children, this editing process has been observed and called "social referencing."[52] A baby may be attracted by a toy and also be afraid of a visual cliff. The infant looks to the mother, and if she is unafraid and smiling, the infant resolves the ambivalence in favor of pleasurable attraction and a feeling of joy. High-arousal experiences can be on the edge of fear or joyful excitement, with one of the components finally becoming dominant—the roller-coaster ride is a thrilling pleasure rather than a terrifying ordeal.

The interesting point is whether we as adults can consciously shape our emotions without self-deception. Can we emotionally tutor ourselves in adulthood as was done for us in the past? Can we, within the constraints of the innate human program, voluntarily control, select, edit, and engender emotional consciousness, shaping our present and future and perhaps even redoing emotional reactions to events in our past? I think we can.

Voluntary Control of Emotion

One of the reasons emotions have been considered so suspect in the moral life is that they have been seen as involuntary, passive, and beyond personal control. If emotions are states of consciousness that simply happen to us, or are suffered passively like eye blinks or heartbeats, then how can we be responsible for them? The best that can be expected is to avoid and suppress emotions and occasions of emotion, and seek to follow reason alone. But once emotions and the emotional system are seen as partially under control and responsive to the agency of the self, the picture changes.[53] Emotions become more important and central to personal motivation, inextricably interwoven with self-consciousness and moral thinking.

The involuntary emergence of many of our felt emotions is not the whole story of our emotional system. Yes, we need biologically programmed lightning, responses such as signals of fear, in order to escape danger and survive; the involuntary characteristics of many emotions cued by environmental stimuli can serve adaptive purposes. Also, spontaneous emotions can reveal things about our inner selves that we need to know. Emotions spontaneously enter consciousness as signals, just as perceptions, thoughts, and intuitions emerge from preconscious processing as information that seems to come effortlessly to our conscious attention. But despite their apparent reality and vividness, emotions can be disregarded and, once judged to be irrelevant, allowed to naturally wane. Just as we see some intuitions as wrongheaded, we can see that some emotional feelings are wronghearted or inappropriate. On the other hand, other emotions can be personally appropriated, developed, selectively encouraged, directed, and shaped.

I also claim, more controversially, that emotions, especially positive love, can be initiated and engendered at will from a state of rest or ground zero. I am not as sure about voluntarily engendering negative emotions. Can we will to be afraid, to be angry, to hate, or to feel contempt or disgust when we start out feeling neutral and safe? Perhaps we need an Iago, a Hitler, or a demagogue acting from the outside to work up negative emotions. But positive emotions of goodwill and love can be engendered, just as a person can decide to speak certain words or initiate a rational process of creative imagination or problem solving. Often we hear persons testify how they tried and managed to love someone they once hated or finally became able to confront a person they once feared.

In other acts of emotional control, we speak of not wallowing in self-pity or not letting anger get hold of us. It is significant that we regularly blame our friends and family for their emotional reactions.[54] We judge that they should have controlled or suppressed some emotion, or have grown beyond feeling certain childish or negative emotions. We even go further and demand that friends, family, and ourselves become more adept and practiced at other mature or positive feelings.

When we talk of someone's good character or virtue, we imply that they have shaped and directed their natural involuntary temperament and emotions in certain positive ways. We recognize that certain emotional tasks are much more difficult for some people than others, because of the raw material with which they started: "It's been hard for Joe to learn to be calm" or "Jane has had a hard time getting up the courage to be assertive." But we still hold them to it, and I think rightly so. Emotions are not outside the realm of moral responsibility.

Since emotions emerge from different causes, they can be controlled in many different ways. Emotions can be suppressed, shaped, controlled, directed, and engendered by all the other functioning sub-systems available to the self as self-conscious agent. The great advantage of being a complicated multisystem organism is that one system can correct, check, supplement, and compensate for another. The innate, preprogrammed primary emotional reactions that arise from the biological organism may be suppressed or engendered by physiological means. Yoga practitioners and other native peoples with access to traditional ascetic practices had perfected physiological training and control of bodily reactions long before modern means of behavioral conditioning were developed. Before there were modern pain clinics or biofeedback methods of self-control, Native Americans were trained to courageously sing their death songs while being tortured.

Today, behavioral medicine is interested in the interconnections between emotion and the underlying physiological mechanisms of the body. Emotion is explored in its interactions with the immune system and the progress of disease and pain. All sorts of new interventions are investigated, as the proliferation of support groups, phobia clinics, and stress-reduction programs attest. Persons learn to control emotions through relaxation, breathing routines, exercise, biofeedback, and other reactive and proactive strategies.[55] People are taught to run in order to control depression and get the brain to release the chemicals for a runner's high. They learn to breath, pant, relax, and employ therapeutic touch to control the fear of childbirth or other panic states. These intentional physiological coping strategies are often employed along with medicine's traditional use of drugs to dampen or engender emotional states.

Other equally traditional but newly rediscovered strategies for voluntary emotional control employ rational and verbal coping strategies. From the Stoics to the latest cognitive therapy or rational emotive techniques, the control strategy focuses upon using thought or inner speech to induce different emotional reactions.[56] Since in the natural spontaneous stream of consciousness thoughts and perceptions induce emotions, a rational strategy can change emotions by producing thoughts and images at will. One can give self-directed commands, such as "stop," or repeat counterassertions to the stream of covert inner dialogue that is producing the undesirable irrational emotions: "No, I am not a worthless failure"; "No, everything does not have to be perfect for me at all times"; "No, I do not have to do what mother says if I don't agree."

Cognitive therapies stress learning and rehearsing rational inner speech and thoughts as replacements for irrational, self-defeating, and emotionally debilitating thoughts: "Yes, I can do it, or give it a good try" (remember the little engine that could!); "Yes, I am worthwhile and do not need to be unhappy to be good." In much of cognitive therapy, the ancient Stoic philosophers are revered and directly quoted for their prowess in teaching self-control and the way to happiness. Marcus Aurelius declared that "happiness is an inward power of the soul," and cognitive therapy would agree that the rational thinker can shape emotional reactions. Freud also aimed to have the ego or rational self-direction replace the irrational id. The rise of rational therapies has aimed for the same goal of reality acceptance, using more direct, overt methods of conscious confrontation and self-direction.

In rational therapies and in much self-help writing, the strategies of self-control that appear resemble traditional moral and religious treatises on self-control. The key means of control is the human ability to freely deploy attention. William James considered this ability to direct attention the critical means by which what we call the "will" can function. Once attention is focused on an object and held steady, then emotions and action can follow. Self-control and willpower turn on the human ability to direct attention and focus consciousness. Of course, the more stress being endured, and the more vulnerable or unformed the personality, the more difficult it is to hold attention steady.

Human powers of attention and will are tested in ordinary living when illness and losses are present. We also have the dramatic testimony of many who have endured extraordinary circumstances of torture, interrogations, deprivations, and imprisonment. The mental resistance of some modern prisoners—in concentration camps, communist prisons, fascist prisons, hostage situations, and other situations of extreme physical and psychological pressure—provides evidence of the ways thought and focused attention can control emotional reactions of fear and depression, and the urge to surrender to the forces of oppression.

Directed thought has been used to outwit the enemy's intimidation, to adapt to pain, to distract from present misery, to fight boredom, to review sustaining beliefs and ideologies, to remember the past to strengthen identity, and to imagine and plan a better future. The ability to direct attention backward and forward in time, to disengage from one object of attention and move to another, gives human beings immense potential resources of self-direction and control. (Of course, humans also have the ability to suffer anxiety and morally fail as no other animal can.) The mental strategies used in extreme situations are the same strategies often taught or induced in psychotherapy and moral instruction. These methods of self-management are also often discovered by normal children as they develop coping strategies and learn to delay gratification and control themselves.[57]

But as we have seen, emotions also influence thinking. The emphasis has always been upon how negative and infantile emotions distort thinking, but this is only half the story. Prisoners and persons undergoing extreme stress report the power love and joy have to shape and energize thoughts and overcome stress and the power of negative emotions. Attention is directed to what one loves, even more than to what one fears. When prisoners were tempted to despair and give up, they were reenergized by recalling and reexperiencing love of spouses and family, and the mutual support of friends.[58] Reliving past happiness, taking joy in kindnesses, small pleasures, and events in nature all reinvigorated hope, belief, and the continued employment of rational strategies to survive.

It has long been recognized in religion and psychotherapy, as well as moral education, that positive emotions can overcome negative emotions. The desired goal or ideal has been to become the kind of person able to feel certain emotions, such as love and joy, which can overcome emotions such as fear and anxiety. Progress toward that goal has been seen as a large part of the moral life. It has also been universally recognized that achieving moral self-transformation of emotions is not easy.

Emotions, reason, and intuition should be fully integrated and engaged to produce a complex approach to moral decision making. We need to make decisions in a holistic way that does justice to all our moral resources.

Chapter 5

Making Moral Decisions

I think we best make decisions of conscience through an integrated, recursive process in which we direct and focus attention back and forth, within and without, activating, mutually testing, and monitoring all our human capacities of thinking, feeling, and self-consciousness. We can consciously use our reason to test our reasons, emotions, and intuitions, and use emotions and induced intuitions to monitor our reasoning and other emotions. We can simultaneously pursue overt, rational problem-solving strategies, while activating and paying attention to our inner, psychological subjective processes of intuition and feeling, which may be no less important. In a decision of conscience, I seek a holistic fusion and unified resolution of the different levels and different capacities of my self-consciousness and moral agency.

Different Kinds of Decisions of Conscience

I have defined conscience as the making of moral decisions in which we self-consciously commit ourselves by integrating emotional self-investment with our reasoning on behalf of the good and the right. These decisions are different from other personal decisions because we ask ourselves what we, or others, ought to do, and give ourselves over to answers made in the light of what we hold to be good and true. Deciding what is the morally right thing to do is different from deciding what is the most efficient thing to do, the most enjoyable or preferable thing to do, or the most elegantly beautiful thing to do.

Moreover, deciding moral questions that demand a personal response as to what is the right and good thing to do is not the same as producing an abstract analysis of the ethical issues present in a dilemma. As noted earlier, a professional ethicist, be it a philosopher or theologian, can set out all the issues, describe the pros and cons and the underlying considerations and methods of moral decision making, but never move to a self-commitment or to a personal decision as to what ought to be done. As Edmond Cahn, a philosopher of the law, once remarked (referring to talmudic scholars), there is a difference between an "answer" and a "decision."[1] An answer can be more purely intellectual and abstract, but a decision is "a disposition of some specific human predicament to which the attitudes and evaluations developed in the answer might become applicable in one way or another."[2] When individuals decide specific moral questions, they commit themselves to those acts that ought to be applied; they thereby act in conscience.

Philosophers from Aristotle on have noted that the act of moral judgment is difficult to understand. As Charles Larmore, a modern philosopher, expresses it, "The nature of moral judgment is a peculiarly difficult phenomenon to describe, partly because the tradition of moral philosophy, by so often neglecting the importance of judgment, has handed down to us so few attempts to make sense of it."[3] I think the actual process of judgment has been difficult to understand because morally deciding is a holistic act of subjective personal consciousness. Deciding is a free, personal act of human consciousness, which, being self-reflexive, cannot be programmed in the same way as a formulaic deductive answer.[4] Morally deciding is always more than a logical or rational operation; it is also an intuitive, emotional self-commitment to standards of worth. When a rationalistic approach to morality attempts to excise active personal subjectivity (intuition and emotion) from the moral life, then there is no way to understand moral judgment and a decision of the self on behalf of the good.

The self's decision about what "ought" to be done means that a particular, specific, subjective self is making an active commitment to what is affirmed as good or the best choice in the circumstances. We infuse a rational analysis with a personal emotional commitment to bring to pass "what ought to be" if it is in our power to do so. Our inner sense of self both chooses and is compelled by the felt moral demand; we are most inwardly active and yet, at the same time, most responsive or responsible to a perceived reality beyond ourselves.

I also include in my definition of human action the capacity to think, feel, and imagine at will, as well as move about physically. We can decide what we ought to do, think, or feel. Thus, active moral decisions of conscience can be very different, depending upon the circumstances and what is required. Should we join a protest march against nuclear weapons and break the law of trespass? Ought we to give money to an alcoholic brother when he hasn't paid old debts and we know he will use the money for drink? We may also have to decide our moral positions and our votes on abortion, what our roles in a union's strike will be, or what our country, church, or company should decide on some public issue. There are innumerable potential moral decisions that can be the focus of what we and others ought to do. Decisions become more complicated as the number and complexity of variables that must be taken into account increase.

But direct decisions about what is to be done are often less complex than the inwardly self-directed decisions regarding our personal moral processing of decisions. How adequate or honest were we in making specific moral decisions? We can examine and morally judge the quality and effectiveness of our own moral self-governance. These inwardly focused decisions, with the self and its functioning as object, are seen as subtle challenges of conscience, since it is so difficult to know one's self completely.[5] These more self-focused, specific decisions devoted to our psychological processes and motivation might address questions such as "When I decided not to disobey the law and not to join the protest march, was I doing what I thought was right, or did I decide to refuse because I was afraid of being arrested?" "When I did march and break the law, was I doing what I thought I ought to, or was I trying to gain glory and prove my moral superiority?" If our motives were mixed, how mixed were they, and do our mixed motives make moral difference in the long run?

When we focus upon ourselves and our moral functioning, we are making a complex, inward-directed decision of conscience. Of course, we are also judging the content of our actions to some degree: the moral process is almost always a correlated, blended, double-pronged, interactive exercise of personal consciousness. Our thinking, its content, and our motivations will be entwined in myriad and subtle ways. Moral decisions are always personal to some degree, for even our moral decisions directed to what ought to be done or thought by others in the world are still self-consciously directed acts of our personal attention. Who we are and how we subjectively proceed to decide can never be excised from the decision-making process, or totally isolated from objective content and facts. The dream of pure reason may have aspired to objective, impersonal, impartial moral decision making by some ideal observer or archangel, but we actually make judgments by employing our embodied, emotional, contextual human consciousness and capacities.

A human being can also engage in a kind of metamoral decision in which a person decides the long-term direction of his or her future.

When we are sane and not in an ecstatic trance or a drugged state, we know that we operate in an ongoing, future-directed arrow of time. The present is informed by memory of our past and anticipation of our future. As temporal beings, we can look back on past decisions as well as anticipate the general direction of the future. At particular moments in time, we can make negative moral evaluations of our pasts, decide to change, and begin to pursue different courses for the future. Or alternatively, we can decide to continue in the same overall courses, with or without modifications.

In other words, we can morally reflect and make large decisions about our life stories as narratives in progress.[6] We can change the plots and rewrite the scripts. Reflecting upon our stories is a constant human cultural motif and a form of moral learning and dialogue. In Western culture, the tale of the self's moral journey is an inescapable theme. Our forebears read and meditated upon epic Greek journeys, Biblical pilgrimages of faith, and *Pilgrim's Progress.* Today, we encounter the moral narratives of people's lives everywhere—on TV talk shows, at AA meetings, in autobiographies and self-help books.

Developmental psychology has been stimulated to articulate the "life-span approach" to persons, complete with talk of life scripts, stages, passages and crises—but these ideas are as old as traditional literature. We progress through time and are in the midst of creating our stories; we give moral accounts to ourselves and to others. We revise, appraise, and morally reflect on our progress, and are capable of large decisions of conscience. Our personal stories are partly about what happens to us beyond our control, but they become moral narratives when we make crucial personal decisions that determine the general direction of the plots. We may start out the recipients of environmental influence, but end up the owners and creators, or the destroyers, of our lives. A character in William Faulkner's novel *The Town* is described by his neighbor who says: "Things, circumstances and conditions didn't happen to people like Mr. de Spain; people like him happened to circumstances and conditions." But Mr. de Spain, to a lesser or greater degree is Everyone; character, not anatomy, is destiny.

The self as heroic journeyer will meet many chance events—good fortune and disasters—but how the self aspires and copes with circumstance constitutes the moral substance of the tale. As the self-interpreting animal, we can each ask ourselves, Who do I want to become? What are my moral aspirations? Our largest decisions of conscience are proactive and future oriented. As the psychologist Gordon Allport once remarked, people are living their lives into the future while psychologists are busily explaining their pasts.[7] We experience ourselves as free moral agents, desiring, aspiring, and exercising free will, despite the fact that many psychologists, constricted by scientific ideologies of material determinism, deny that humans possess the freedom to make moral decisions about their future lives.

Recognizing the Need for Moral Decisions

Human beings experience themselves striving to achieve personally important life goals, or what Allport called propriate or self-invested goals. In moral striving, these goals and decisions concern questions such as How shall I live—how good shall I be? What is my life's story all about? Are my moral desires and standards of worth, worthwhile? Some of us may seek to avoid these questions as too puzzling or demanding, and perhaps some of us do manage to immerse ourselves in daily routine and follow custom and convention while drifting through our lives; perhaps a few even avoid the proverbial mid-life crisis or near-death self-confrontations of integrity. One thinks here of the sad protagonist in an autobiographical novel of a butler, who at the end of his life of total service and trust in his employer, Lord Darlington, a Nazi sympathizer, allows himself this reflection:

> Lord Darlington wasn't a bad man. He wasn't a bad man at all. And at least he had the privilege of being able to say at the end of his life that he made his own mistakes. . . . As for myself, I can't even claim that . . . I can't even say I made my own mistakes.[8]

But as readers of the novel can see, the butler has made his own mistakes. Repeatedly he avoided human contact, drew back, and refused to become emotionally involved with others. His mistakes were refusals to take action and, like all acts of omission, were less noticeable than others. His life story was morally decided in repeated moments when he refused to either go forward and act or take the time to reflect with honest feeling about the microdecisions that were cutting him off from love.

Moral decisions demand emotional energy and time; they take self-consciousness and unflinching attention and reflection upon our experiences. Our larger life decisions (avoided, inarticulated, or not) inform and shape the small daily decisions, while at the same time, countless small decisions shape the larger story. Who we think we are and who or what we aspire to be will influence our moral actions in the world; our moral self-judgment of these acts, and their effects, will in turn influence who we want to be. The continuing round of interactions will either move us toward our larger moral goals or not. Circularity is unavoidable. Just as rational thinking and problem solving always circle back and forth from implicit, personal knowledge to the pursuit of facts and arguments, so a person's moral life is both global and specific, external and inward in focused activity.

Personal acts of attention, as we have seen in previous chapters, are the key components of decision and moral self-direction. Making a decision is basically an act of fixing personal attention on a goal in time, with the purpose to produce the act of thinking, feeling, or behaving. Psychologists, following William James, have understood how the focusing of attention shapes a person's current stream of consciousness.[9] James, as we have said, equated freedom of the will with the human ability to freely direct the focus of attention and hold it steady. Thus, one can shape and will an act or attitude in the present.

As Viktor Frankl, a modern proponent of humanity's psychological freedom, puts it, the one freedom that can never be taken away is the freedom to take up an attitude toward what is happening to us.[10] The claim for moral freedom asserts that, short of psychotic breakdown, toxic poisoning, or brain injury, a human being can direct attention and so decide or will acts in the present. The depth of processing in a decision, the perseverance in the struggle, and the "strength of will" displayed in adhering to the resulting conclusions are directly caused by the individual's deployment of attention despite distraction or inner conflict.

Present decisions create our present consciousness, but also create the future self. What we steadily attend to in the present will be encoded in long-term memory. As Kenneth Pope and Jerome Singer, two preeminent modern psychological researchers on consciousness, put it, "attention exerts a dual control: not only over what is appearing in consciousness at present but also over what consequently passes into short and longterm memory (against which future incoming stimuli will be matched."[11] Our long-term memory appears to be the part of the mind that selects and filters what reaches conscious awareness.

What's disturbing is how much we can be limited by our past decisions and past environmental contingencies, encoded in long-term memory. The good news is that as we freely deploy attention in the present, we can not only shape our present, but lay down new long-term memories that will shape our future consciousness. Through freely focused acts of personal attention, we can learn, grow, and develop over time. Within certain limits, the constraints of the past can be transformed.

The philosopher Iris Murdoch perceptively describes the way a person morally creates a self by ongoing acts of attention. Writing long before new psychological theories were formulated, she said:

> If we consider what the work of attention is like, how continuously it goes on, and how imperceptibly it builds up structures of value round about us, we shall not be surprised that at crucial moments of choice most of the business of choosing is already over. This does not imply that we are not free, certainly not. But it implies that the exercise of our freedom is a small piecemeal business which goes on all the time and not a grandiose leaping about unimpeded at important moments. The moral life in this view is something that goes on continually.[12]

We now realize that thinking and feeling are so continuous that they go on without being noticed in myriad nonconscious processes. Emotions, intuitions, and thoughts that spontaneously come into consciousness are partly the products of past emotions, thinking, and decisions. Instant emotional feelings of acceptance or rejection appear in consciousness, and intuitive responses and appraisals appear that seem to predate any informational and intellectual deliberative process.[13] Inevitably, one begins many processes of moral decision making with given predispositions and frameworks built up from the past.[14]

The fact that a quandary or the need for a decision reaches consciousness reflects the fact that the perceived situation is somehow challenging enough to attract our attention and effort. Discontinuity or dissonance, uncertainty or ambivalence—something must produce the sense that a real moral question exists and demands some attention. Few normally socialized adults, for instance, would even consider whether or not they should torture innocent children or whether they ought to knock down old ladies in the street. Such questions would simply never come up.

Of course, for anthropologists or critics of a society, the omissions in a given system are as revealing as what is evident. In morality, what does not even arise in a culture as a question shows the basic assumptions and moral consensus of the group. So too for individuals; much is revealed about people's moral characters by what does or doesn't appear as a moral question. What we can perceive or recognize as a moral question or dilemma displays a level of accrued moral awareness that is the precursor to decision making. Some persons never become engaged in moral decision making because they seem morally tone-deaf; a certain awareness and perception of a challenging moral problem must occur before anything else can happen.

On the other hand, instant altruism and heroic deeds also reflect past habits and patterns of behavior. Researchers on altruism have claimed that there is an instinctive response to help in emergencies, and heroes often report that they just rushed into an emergency rescue attempt without a thought. These heroes are often hesitant to take credit for what they did so unreflectively. But other individuals, faced with similar crises, instantly repress or defer any altruistic impulses; they may have built up habits of avoiding altruistic risks. Thus, heroes can be seen to deserve praise for having become the kind of persons who automatically act to help others.

The time available for deciding does make a difference in the kind of decisions we make—a millisecond, an hour, a week, or a forty-day retreat provide different operating frameworks. We have different time frames in which decisions can be made and then applied. It may be that we must act and decide instantaneously in morally challenging situations. In these cases, as with acts of altruism, spontaneous decisions are mostly the result of our past development of feelings, thoughts, aspirations, and habits of action. On the other hand, as great tragic drama convincingly portrays, sudden moral lapses, betrayals, and flawed decisions are never as sudden as they seem. Sudden stress uncovers hidden moral weaknesses—or strengths.

Moral decisions can also be differentiated by how difficult they are to make. Usually this consciousness of difficulty will be a result of the uncertainties or the complexity of factors involved, as well as the degree of inner conflict they may arouse. At one extreme, some moral decisions are easy, emerging in a fairly effortless way. Long-debated decisions can be resolved so incrementally that in their end stages, it is as if fruit is just dropping from a tree that has been watered, pruned, and fertilized over a season. The inner psychological efforts to decide finally seem to reach equilibrium—or to use some new computer talk for achieving an outcome, the aggregated system relaxes.[15] Certain emergent or bottom-up decisions do seem made up of many small incremental decisions that gradually weight the larger networks toward a particular outcome. The actual moment of decision may be almost impossible to denote; it is more as if the tide is coming in, or going out, an inch at a time in a continuous direction.

But if a person begins to think in a direction different from the prevailing process—starts going against the tide—there will be a disturbance, a conflict, and a conscious sense of effort will ensue. Discontinuity and reversals of directions produce strain and call more attention to the process. Ignatius Loyola analyzed the difference in psychological characteristics between a smoothly continuous decision-making process and the strife encountered by reversing the moral direction of thinking. He described the continuing movement toward a goal, either good or bad in nature, as like a drop of water quietly and smoothly being absorbed in a sponge. But a change in direction produces a noisy disturbing splash, like water hitting a resistant stone.[16] Attention is aroused, and more conscious effort will be required in the decision process.

Indeed, many moral decisions of conscience will require a fair degree of personal work.[17] These decisions will be more like top-down executive programs initiated and directed by the self as conscious agent and problem solver. As we have previously discussed, these executive decisions are not as simple as following decision trees and executing steps one, two, and three of the program. Instead, they are constituted of back-and-forth strategies, with alternative shifts of attention from one method of thinking to another. Intuition may play an unsung role in the process and in the final evaluations of solutions. But if all goes well, a general sense of orderly progress to a solution or goal can be had without a great deal of conflict.

Other decisions of conscience are not so orderly. Some decisions give testimony to the root meaning of the word *decision*—a "cutting off" of a process. There is no step-by-step progress, for deciding is more like giving a rending lurch or grinding into high gear. We may oscillate in the throes of competing reasoning and emotional pulls. We are torn because we see the cost of committing ourselves in particular decisions—but we must decide. William James speaks of this kind of effortful decision as consisting of "a slow dead heave of the will," in which one must choose as "a desolate and acrid sort of act . . . full of inward effort."[18]

The commitment involved may change a person's life forever, for the choosing of one alternative means giving up the other with all its attractions and opportunities. James says one must almost murder the potential self, who can no longer exist after the fateful decision. Such climactic decisions of conscience are the stuff of novels and drama. I would interpret the difficulty of these decisions as arising from inner conflict within the multidimensioned self. The core avowed self, encompassing most of a person's most cherished values and goals, may be challenged by other valued dimensions of the self that rebelliously contest integration into the whole. We are not in full control of ourselves; our moral agency and integration are weakened. The struggle to direct the whole person and organism toward our most avowed goals provides the inner conflict with what has long been recognized as a part of us in rebellion. As one familiar metaphor has it, "The spirit is willing but the flesh is weak."

What James calls the slow dead heave of the will is the final struggle of the core self—with one's most appropriated, deepest desires and moral purposes—to act, to fix attention and cut off the less-valued part-selves or alternative desires.[19] After a variety of experiences in our moral lives, we learn about the full range of moral decision making.

Strategies for Integrated Moral Decision Making

A decision-making process is initiated because in the course of a flow of events we become conscious that we face moral questions of what we ought to do. The questions, problems, or decisions may have slowly emerged over time, or been precipitated by events at work or at home. Perhaps we have been criticized or attacked as immoral for something we are doing. Perhaps we have been urged by other people to make moral decisions. Perhaps we must decide ethical quandaries that arise in our professional roles. Our consciences are engaged when we consciously recognize that, yes, there is a moral problem to solve; yes, a decision or judgment should be made about what ought to be done.

At this point, our first decisive moral act will be to continue attending to the moral dilemma. We might turn away from the decision process by using a panoply of evasive maneuvers. But if we choose to go forward and stay with our dilemma, we begin an active moral quest. As moral agents seeking to make moral decisions, we can direct our consciousness and observe our spontaneous consciousness in a complex, dynamic process of problem solving.

The dramatic metaphor of moral thinking provided by the moral philosopher R. M. Hare is instructive and true to what actually takes place. He depicts and defends a person's ability to integrate intuitive and principled thinking much as a general on a battlefield can do many things at once:

> To say that it is impossible to keep intuitive and critical thinking going in the same thought process is like saying that in a battle a commander cannot at the same time be thinking of the details of tactics, the overall aim of victory, and the principles (economy of force, concentration of force, offensive action, etc.) which he has learnt when learning his trade. Good generals do it.[20]

Indeed, most successful rational problem solvers will be able to engage in oscillating rational strategies.

The self as moral decision maker can be seen as a general able to direct and engage in many different acts of consciousness that are needed, but I would expand the picture to include the ability to process subjective emotions concerning the decision, as well as intuitions and critical thought. Unimpaired, sane adults can direct the flow of oscillating, dynamic movements of consciousness, which can include spontaneous and directed acts of emotional feeling, as well as thinking and acting. We can direct our consciousness—circling and doubling back, going within and turning back outward, seeking and assessing information and reasoning—while integrating emotions, images, intuitions, and arguments into our moral decision making. Just as we can observe and direct our thoughts, so we can also observe and direct our emotions within the fluctuating stream of consciousness.

Within the rich, complex processes of thinking and feeling—complete with both spontaneous and directed play of attention—in moral decision making, reason judges and tests what reason marshalls into operation, as well as judging the spontaneous intuitions and emotions that appear. We test and discard, test and retain; we can also try to induce creative intuitions and call up appropriate emotions. We projectively move back and forth from different inner perspectives and test different bases of knowledge. The rational processes of moral problem solving can in turn be monitored, judged, and even tutored by emotions and intuition. I claim that the best, most fully human and enriched way to make a moral decision is to enter into a full personal engagement, using all one's inner resources of consciousness. While much happens with the speed of light in the self's inner life, or is alternatively slow and incremental, it is helpful to analyze the different strategies that can enter into the process.

Reason Judges Reasoning and Intuitions

I vigorously defend the traditional Western claims of the value of reason and rationality, and want to repeat once more how important it is in moral decision making. I assume that moral problemsolving is a form of problemsolving and so the rational strategies that work in other problems should be used by those facing a moral dilemma. This entails engaging in a dynamic but ordered process of problem definition, information gathering, assessment, analysis into parts, partial subroutines, reflexive returns to larger frames and networks of general

knowledge and problem redefinitions.[21] While there are serious philosophical problems about what constitutes rationality, and what is the
reality to which rationality conforms, we also possess great consensus
within our common Western cultural tradition about rationality. Even a
philosopher like Alasdair MacIntyre, who emphasizes the difference in
different traditions of rationality, concedes that all the different rational
traditions have logic in common.[22] Thomas Kuhn, in his study of changing scientific paradigms and the conflicts surrounding scientific revolutions, also maintains that all paradigms use rational methods in their
reasoning.[23] There is a common core of logical thinking and agreement
that persists in operation, even though thinkers and scientists argue
over which theories best fit and most accurately interpret the evidence.

Rational criteria of good thinking traditionally have been consistency, logic, rules of evidence, appropriateness, coherence, clarity, completeness, and congruence with received reality and meaning. These
are the criteria we should use to judge our own rational productions.
In assessing human thinking, many observers can agree. It is usually
apparent when deficits, erroneous arguments, or distorted assessments
of reality arise in the thought disturbances we then characterize as logical fallacies, demagoguery, manic-depressive thinking, mental retardation, psychosis, brain disease, and dementia.

An assessment of a reasoning process and its outcome is made by
seeing how the specific arguments and evidence presented cohere with
everything else that the problem solver knows. The larger paradigms,
frameworks, traditions, or maps that we use influence the weightings,
evaluations, and interpretations of specifics. Common sense follows the
same kinds of assessments as scientific or directed rational reasoning;
the difference may be in the explicitness, detailed care, orderliness, and
completeness of scientific methodologies and tests.

In our moral decision making and judgments, we should struggle
to the best of our intellectual abilities to think as well and as rationally
as we can. We should be good generals, deploying all our forces and
different kinds of thinking abilities. We will seek and assess facts, and
test arguments of our own and arguments of others by rational criteria.
We will also seek to know what other informed, intellectually disciplined persons have to say pertaining to a particular moral problem. If
it is a professional dilemma, public question, or familial question, we
can research the current thinking on the subject by looking at the moral
reflections of philosophers, theologians, psychologists, or other experts. What moral principles have been articulated by moralists and
ethicists in and out of our moral or religious communities? We will also

seek counsel from those friends and colleagues whose judgment we respect.

During the process, we will seek to build intuition as we seek to think through the question and arrive at a decision. Then our intuitive appraisals and hypotheses will be tested, just as we would test other tentative conclusions. We will look at different perspectives, try out different solutions, compare arguments, and so use the full panoply of the tools for rational thinking. Reasoning is active, and reflectively assesses its own productions and operations in recursive strategies of skeptical double-checking.

Reason Judges and Tutors Emotions

As we think in a directed way, emotions will be part of the dynamic process in consciousness. We can be conscious of the rise and fall of feelings in the effort to arrive at a moral decision. We can also rationally judge, assess, and shape these emotions while being affected by them during the moral decision-making process. Since interest is accounted an emotion, and desire for the truth and caring about the good are emotional, the search for moral solutions is fueled and energized by emotions felt or induced. We keep pursuing problems because we want to know the truth and want good to prevail. If we think the pursuit is morally important, we will induce interest, care, and the desire for truth if they should flag.

Negative emotions may also come into play during the process and be suppressed or shaped accordingly. Perhaps we become afraid when we see trouble ahead if we keep going with a line of argument. We can judge these feelings and recognize when we become tired and distracted and are tempted to stop caring about getting to the truth, to stop making the required effort. Rationally dedicated to the truth, or not fooling ourselves, we can also see when we may want to believe something so much that we will search only for confirming evidence or ignore contrary findings. We have to suppress the emotional impulse to settle for what we want to be the case.

In moral decision making, as in other uses of the intellect, it is important for the self to assess and develop the proper desires, emotions, and actions. Our reason assesses, judges, and shapes the requisite emotional motivations and methods of problem solving. Michael Stocker, a philosopher writing of intellectual desire, emotion, and action, says:

We must, for example, learn intellectual discipline, we must master and develop those forces and tendencies connected with directing the mind as opposed to letting it wander; we must learn to recognize and keep to the point; not to stop thinking when the problem is too easy or too difficult; not to be satisfied with just any answer, but to press on for a correct or important answer; not to be too concerned with detail and the expense of the general nor the general at the expense of detail. And so on and so on.[24]

As reasonable moral agents, we rationally judge and control the emotional and rational processes involved in the moral decision-making process. As we go through our subroutines of inquiry and reasoning, we may have inappropriate emotional reactions to facts, conclusions, or implications of an argument that must be disciplined or mastered. Does disgust, joy, or another emotional reaction to proposed solutions to our moral dilemmas seem rationally founded? We will assess our emotions by such rational criteria as whether they are based upon correct or sufficient evidence, or whether they seem in proportion to the precipitating stimuli.

As rational moral agents, we will also assess whether our emotional reactions to a proposed course of action are inconsistent with our larger moral purposes, or integrated with our other personal moral goals and emotional commitments. We may judge certain emotional reactions, such as envy, contempt, or cowardice, to be intrinsically reprehensible, and some emotions, such as goodwill, to be intrinsically helpful. Other emotions would be judged by their moral appropriateness to the events or situations that invoke them. An inappropriate lacunae or emotional void of indifferent apathy in the self can also be appraised. We might worry a great deal if we, or others, remain numb, especially if we have no emotive reactions at all when confronted with reprehensible acts. Indeed, those who even can consider cheating without anticipatory shame or propose stealing or bearing false witness without a tremor of anxious guilt should be troubled. Those who actually do so without moral emotions are in a worse state.

It is far easier to shape, sublimate, and control emotions than it is to induce them in burned-out or numbed persons whose imagination and empathy have either failed to develop or ceased to operate. In my opinion, the fact that our national leaders can talk of the nuclear destruction of cities, or countenance the exporting of killing and torture techniques to allies, without visible emotive reaction casts an oddly psychopathic tone to the policy deliberations of our society. Apathy and the lack of moral emotions is one way the world can end in ice and fire at the same time.

More happily, inducing, enacting, educating, and controlling emotions are possible through rational tutoring. Stoic philosophers, religious mystics, modern psychotherapists emphasizing cognitive therapy, and ordinary persons who reach maturity testify to the fact that their emotions can be induced and tutored by personal strategies. In fact, emotional self-control is so pervasive that some critics have claimed that there is too much emotional control required in much of American professional life. According to some, in the interests of successful business practices, we have been asked to produce "the managed heart" too often.[25] Whether this is true or not, the complaint of too much emotional self-management is testimony to the fact that we can learn to control our feelings, without becoming method actors or Zen masters.

We can tutor our emotions by thinking of certain images and beliefs, or calling up certain remembered states of feeling. These controls can sometimes break down when and if some event surprises us, concerns us deeply, or arises when other stress is present. Trauma, shock, and the suddenness of an event can make it harder to exert our normal controls over emotions—but not impossible. As stated earlier, the emotional system motivates and produces apparent reality and vividness, but emotions may also have built-in limits to their effects upon us.

All in all, I believe the normal adult human being to be adept at using the rational, thinking informational system to test, judge, tutor, and control the emotional or affect system when there is enough time to engage in a moral decision-making procedure. When we are not neurotic, psychotic, drugged, retarded, or under some extreme stress that induces regression to a childlike state, we can self-consciously and rationally assess the emotions involved. We can tutor the emotions arising in the process as well as the emotional reactions to the content of moral thinking. This ability to engage in reflective rational testing and judging of our reasoning, intuitions, and emotions is what we mean by saying that someone is adult, mature, or stable. When the rational tutoring and control of emotions serves the good, we say a person is of good moral character.

Our culture has traditionally valued the role of reasoned self-direction of emotions—as it should. We have been less sure of whether emotions and intuitions can contribute to conscience and moral decision making.

Emotion Tests and Tutors Reason

Emotions can tutor and monitor reasoning in both negative and positive ways. As we have seen, emotions emerge into a person's stream of consciousness in different ways. Some emotions may be strongly programmed biologically and innately linked to certain environmental cues—fear of sudden loud noises, attraction to the human face, or empathy for the pain of others. Through empathy, emotions are contagious to a certain extent—your crying induces tears in me, and so on. Other emotions emerge from the constant preconscious filtering of inner and external information that seems to be governed by long-term memory. In some cases, the original emotion may be threatening, so in a self-defensive move, the emotion allowed through to consciousness may be instantly transformed into an acceptable substitute. We can quickly turn sadness into anger, or vice versa.

Still other emotions may be obvious conscious responses to environmental challenges. We have feelings that are stimulated by, and fused with, a multitude of built-up ideas, concepts, images, narratives, and personal readings of the social environment. These feelings and emotions, signaling various subjective states, wax and wane, and come in different blends and degrees of clarity and strength, but like intuitions, they are reflexive, personal signals or "vital signs" of our inner processing of the present and the past. These signals, often blending with our spontaneous intuitions, can be morally helpful and even tutorial in both positive and negative ways.

Emotion may negatively inhibit or warn us as we think through moral arguments (or more accurately, mull things over), trying to arrive at a decision. As we think, we may be signaled in consciousness by feelings of negative emotional responses, which may range from mild aversion to intense repugnance. A rational argument without any apparent logical flaws may be proposed, such as for the use of torture, the harvesting of organs from living bodies, the refusal to treat AIDS patients, or the severing of some relationship with a troublesome family member.

We can feel that the arguments, solutions, or line of reasoning is wrong, wrong, wrong—even disgusting or contemptible—although we cannot rationally articulate any reasons why we feel as we do. Our discomfort or emotional aversion induces us to withhold consent and continue looking beyond the proposed arguments, to keep on searching, scanning, and broadening the quest for an acceptable solution. Later, we may be able to understand the reasons why we should not have assented, and feel profoundly grateful we were protected and not carried away by the abstract argumentation. Obviously, there are times when pure logic can run amok. While in certain situations, we can say that two minutes of thought would have saved the day, but two minutes is a long time, so at other times, we can say that two minutes of proper human feeling could have saved us from an ethical or moral disaster.

Philosophers since Aristotle have recognized that a good and wise person, properly brought up, has emotions and intuitive reactions that can be morally trusted. According to new psychological approaches to the mind, these appropriate emotions emerge because the good person's past deployments of attention and previous moral decisions ensure a good preconscious self-filtering system in the present. The person of good character has built up values in long-term memory and so possesses a pattern of preconscious processing of information that will produce the proper emotions. The nonconscious functionings of the mind, which we do not have access to, could constitute what has been called "the heart's reasons which reason cannot know." Humanity has always been mystified by the way emotional and intuitive moral guidance often comes without conscious effort. Perhaps this is why the voice of conscience has been seen as the voice of God or as emanating from guardian angels or good spirits.

The negative, censoring voice of emotions and intuitions has often been given more weight than the positive. One remembers that Socrates is reported to have had a voice that told him what not to do, but not what to do. Perhaps as the eighteenth-century Bishop Butler has told us, this is generally true because in actuality we can do more harm to others than good.[26] We cannot make others happy, virtuous, or successful, but we can harm others. Modern theorists of emotions also claim that there is an asymmetry in emotional life, but aver that this is because in evolution, stronger negative emotions and warning signals are needed to ensure survival and avoid danger.[27] Fear, disgust, guilt, and shame are fairly potent in their aversive effects on consciousness and attention.

I would speculate that the negative emotions and censoring intuitions have been accorded more status by all cultures because they better conserve the group's approved moral standards. Moral innovation is more problematic. When conscience induces rebellion against the status quo, there are more social repercussions. But it is important to grant that emotions and intuitions play a large part in moral innovation. Emotions can tutor and monitor reasoning processes in a positive way.

Much of our creativity in moral thinking emerges as ideas and emotions are activated in memory and induce new intellectual reverberations, images, or narratives. As stated previously, feelings and emotions can activate memory networks and call up scenarios and ideas that have been stored with or near the emotions. These thoughts then enter the ongoing stream of consciousness and have further effects. Anger, for instance, at mistreatment of self or loved ones has provoked moral awakenings and revisions of moral ideas. Anger blended with a desire for fairness and an idea of equality becomes moral indignation and sparks resistance to oppression. Righteous anger motivates efforts to restore or change oppressive conditions. From the days of the Hebrew prophets to the latest civil rights activists or revolutionary freedom fighters, anger and moral indignation have sparked new moral visions of liberation.

The emotions of empathy and sympathy are also built into human nature, and these spontaneous feelings can fuel efforts to think new thoughts.[28] Many moral revolutions have been initiated by empathy felt for previously excluded or disregarded groups: slaves, women, workers, abused children, the handicapped, experimental subjects, patients in institutions. Experience and familiarity with others produce liking and affection.[29] As we emotionally respond positively to another person or group, we may be forced to confront a conflicting negative concept or received moral idea concerning the group. Novel emotional responses of sympathy and identification clash with previously accepted moral principles or habitual thoughts. An inner inconsistency and unsettling discrepancy can prompt a creative moral readjustment.

The emotion of love is the great moral educator because it makes us pay attention to and value what we love. Love can be defined minimally as joyful interest with a predisposition to attend, approach, unite with, and care about the love object.[30] While infatuation and intense desire wish the love object to fulfill selfish needs, love engenders attention, care, and concern for the other. As art critic Kenneth Clark has noted, in a comment as apt for morality as for art, "Most errors of judgment arise from an absence of love, a lack of fine perception and inability to withstand the pressure and prejudices of the time."[31] Love motivates fine and careful perception, which works against stereotypes, automatic dismissals, or habitual arguments made from inertia or carelessness.

Love makes us think by expanding our focus, perspectives, and commitments. When we love and admire a person, we want to be like them, and so we try to think as they think, feel as they feel. When Augustine said one should love God and do what you will, he understood that love can transform the moral life of the lover. The great power of parents to morally educate their children arises through the child's love and desire to identify with the beloved parent. But moral influence through love, attachment, and increased attentiveness to those who morally inspire us continues throughout life. Our emotions continually interact with our moral decision making.

Emotion Tutors Emotion

In a more subtle process, even more difficult to elucidate or articulate, one emotion can monitor or tutor another emotion. Love and sympathy neutralize many negative emotions, as when in the treatment of the diseased or handicapped, sympathy wells up spontaneously and overcomes disgust. It has been taught that "love casts out fear" and, in modern therapeutic practice, that a relaxed, secure state is incompatible with anxiety. Behaviorist therapists induce relaxation and positive imagery and feelings to overcome fears. Love can also quell anger or mitigate the contempt felt for a person's moral lapse or betrayal. On the other hand, anger can transform sadness, depression, and apathetic hopelessness into active assertiveness or aspiration. Much of both psychotherapy and moral socialization can be seen not only as teaching rational control but also as trying to replace or transform one emotion by inducing or enacting another emotion. As Iris Murdoch has expressed it:

> It is also a psychological fact, and one of importance in moral philosophy, that we can all receive moral help by focusing our attention upon things which are valuable: virtuous people, great art, perhaps the idea of goodness itself. Human beings are naturally "attached" and when an attachment seems painful or bad it is most readily displaced by another attachment . . .[32]

An attachment, or emotion, can be experienced as painful or bad, both by its intrinsic experience of awfulness, as in envy, cowardice or, guilty shame, and/or because our reason has judged it to be wronghearted in this situation or destructive in its social consequences.

One can envision moral progress in moral decision making, the achievement of virtue, or personal moral transformation as becoming a person who feels more intrinsically good emotions, such as nurturing love, and fewer despicable or inappropriate emotions that lead to destructive consequences for self and others. When emotions have been self-tutored by love and attentive attachment to the good, a person is less subject to deformations of moral decision making. Moral failures arise when regressed, infantile, or selfishly willful persons undergo stress or encounter conflict. The wise and good care about others and care about moral goodness and truth. They are better prepared through their good hearts to be able to attend carefully, see clearly, be unbiased, and stand by their moral commitments.

The Art of Integrating and Balancing
Reasoning and Emotion

In order to achieve integration, we must recognize what the philosopher Mary Midgley has called "the unity of the moral enterprise."[33] In her view, solving moral problems involves "three inseparable aspects—(1) a changing view of 'the fact,' (2) a change of feeling, and (3) a change in action, arising out of a changing sense of what action can decently be contemplated and what cannot." She thinks it has been a "real misfortune: that many philosophers have tended to concentrate entirely on separating these factors and putting them in competition as if they were alternatives, rather than on investigating the highly complex relation between them and pointing out where it goes wrong."[34]

The most adequate moral decision making of conscience must achieve congruence or a fusion of thinking, feeling, and willing into a unified whole. As we engage in moral quests, we begin the inner moves and recursive operations toward decision and resolution. All of the back-and-forth self-conscious mutual testing and monitoring described previously should be induced and pursued. We can build intuition, pursue arguments, pay attention to and assess our emotions, enact other emotions, and flexibly change rational strategies in the process. This inner engagement and dialogue proceeding toward a moral decision of conscience has been described as "consulting conscience," "pondering it in my heart," "wrestling with my problem," or "mulling it over in my mind."

These phrases describe the interaction of the numerous recursive inner operations and testings of reason, intuition, and emotion going on as the self as moral agent "attempts to get it all together." We can define and redefine our problems; note our instant intuitions, hypotheses, positive or negative emotional reactions; begin to seek out facts and the applicable moral principles and arguments and critically assess them. As we think critically, we can also consult our emotional and intuitive responses to arguments, and note where we are drawn on, and where and how we shrink from proceeding. Why here, why there, why now? Our personal assessments and interventions to ensure the integrity of our individual searches will be both reasoned and emotive. Reactions to our own emotional reactions can be sought, other emotions enacted, and a numbed, shallow, or qualitatively fevered emotional response be felt as suspect. We may recognize infatuation or ambition as distorting our thinking or our other emotional responses.

Again, we can judge and test ourselves the way we do others from whom we seek counsel: Are we, or they, biased, blinded, careless, or maturely formed in personality? As we consult with others, we judge their moral and ethical knowledge, their competence in rational argument, and our emotional response to them. Our holistic response to them includes an affective intuitive assessment of the integrity and quality of their inner moral processing. Do they seem wise and good, and at the same time to desire to be better and seek more wisdom? Are we moved by them as people whose grasp of morality and personal integrity we can trust? When heart speaks to heart, one is intuitively responding to another person as a whole person. While a diseased physician can cure a sick patient, it is unlikely that an amoral or evil person could make consistently wise and good ethical judgments and give good moral counsel.

In the midst of many other strategies, we may also project ourselves forward into the different moral narratives that our decision might create. We can imagine different outcomes and the effects upon others of our actions. The emotions that we and others would feel are a great part of these projections (certainly as much as rational calculations of other consequences), and we can emotionally anticipate how we would feel in the future if we do this or that. We can also imagine how those we love and admire would emotionally respond in various projected scenarios. Thus, our present emotions may be modified, overridden, or trumped by our imagined enactments of future emotions.

As we deploy our attention, we will be most emotionally drawn to the past, present, and future emotions that we appropriate as most completely ours. We can enact those emotions that express the whole "me," the fruit of our own life stories, with our own aspirations and identifications with admired and loved mentors. The weighted influence of past and future emotions may either validate a present emotion we experience in our moral decision making, or reduce the force and power of the present feeling. The apparent reality of this emotional moment of consciousness can be modulated by larger desires and deeper feelings.

Mutually monitoring all the movements of consciousness for the sake of an integrated moral synthesis means being both respectful and skeptical of all our capacities and reactions. During the processes of decision, there should repeatedly be what has been called "the important pause," when cross-checking can go on.[35] The philosopher Jonathan Bennett discusses the interaction of affect and reason in a famous article devoted to the moral crisis of conscience experienced by Huckleberry Finn.[36] In one of the most famous passages in American literature, Mark Twain shows Huck in an intense inner struggle over whether he should turn in Jim, the runaway slave who is his friend. Huck's emotions, imagination, and reasoning circle back and forth as he anguishes over what he should do.

He has been taught that following his conscience means he should uphold the moral principle of slavery and give Jim up. But after much tortuous oscillating between different courses of action, he chooses to follow his emotion of love for Jim and saves him from the slave catchers. Huck interprets his decision as shucking off the moral burden of conscience as too onerous for a human to bear. He does not conclude that the reasoning of his conscience was too rigid, static, and narrow. Huck cannot see, and I doubt Twain did either, that what is happening in such situations is that emotional experience is tutoring conscience to moral action that supersedes the conventional morality one has been taught.

Bennett uses Twain's comic masterpiece of moral irony to argue for the value of what I call the art of mutual monitoring. Bennett recommends "checking of one's principles in the light of one's sympathies. . . . It can happen that a certain moral principle becomes untenable—meaning one cannot hold it any longer—because it conflicts intolerably with the pity or revulsion or whatever that one feels when one sees what the principle leads to."[37] Even more provocatively, Bennett sees principles themselves

> as embodiments of one's best feelings, one's broadest and keenest sympathies. On that view principles can help one across intervals when one's feelings are at less than their best, that is through periods of misanthropy or meanness or self-centeredness or depression or anger.[38]

In a view that our principles are partially our crystallized, most self-owned and avowedly worthy emotions, there is a built-in fusion of the rational and emotive in moral thinking that frequently occurs. At a very fundamental level, reason and emotion can become fused in the basic concepts or tools of moral thinking. The best, most appropriate moral emotions we can have and aspire to are incorporated into the moral rule, which in its turn tutors and controls the less worthy, less personally appropriated emotional reactions we may have.[39] I think we can call to mind moral principles such as beneficence, respect for autonomy, and justice, and proceed to analyze the worthy, best-felt emotions they crystallize. In a sense, an emphasis upon the emotions we feel in order to be motivated to act on principle is another mediating link between the rational, principled approach to morality and ethics and an approach that emphasizes personal virtue and character.

Our discordant emotions, like our intuitions, can signal to our selves that a proposed act or solution can no longer be wholehearted or congruent with everything else we know and feel. This discordance will, in turn, be judged and tested by reason and emotions. We will continue to probe emotional reactions, seek information and arguments, reasonably assess our processes, listen to hunches, test them, take counsel with others, and be guided negatively and positively by our feelings and thoughts. This process of coming to inner integration and decision can, as discussed earlier, be either orderly or filled with various struggles and difficulties.

We must continue the inner dialogue until we can bring our different inner voices into some unity. We must weave the many threads of thought and feeling into coherent personal designs. The most satisfying moral decisions of conscience will be designs in which all the multi-colored threads are carefully worked and tightly interwoven into a whole; ideally, even the underside of the cloth is beautifully finished and worthy of display. Or, to use high-tech language, when all systems test positively, when all systems are go, then we launch our ships into space—we morally decide. We commit ourselves in wholehearted decisions of conscience when we achieve a fully congruent, reflective equilibrium of reason, intuition, and emotion.[40] The picture finally comes into focus. After a fully personal engagement, there is nothing held back, suppressed, or untested in the struggle. We act at full capacity, as morally competent as we can be.

When we make such wholehearted, reasoned moral decisions, they will not easily be overturned. We will remain steadfast in conscience, as the saying goes. Here we stand, because we can do no other and be whole persons true to ourselves and the goods that we serve. If we are dedicated to truth, we cannot retract or bear false witness to our own moral decisions, unless otherwise convinced. If we yield or dissemble out of fear or expediency, we know that we are lying and betraying our integrity. When we have tested, been skeptical, and self-consciously included our own moral self-probings in the process, we can fear self-deception or our unknown faults and limitations, but we will have done all we can do to guard against error and serve the truth and the good.

Of course, we must always be willing to admit that as fallible human beings, we may be wrong. Unfortunately, we know we have been mistaken in the past, and we have seen other people and institutions be wrong, so we know we could be mistaken now. What do we do when conflict arises? If we are morally convinced and opposition comes from outside, that is one challenge. But what if the conflict is within, and despite all our efforts, we cannot come to an inner congruence or equilibrium?

Conflict, Character, and Community

If despite prolonged effort we cannot reach inner accord or integration of mind and heart, we cannot decide wholeheartedly. The unconvinced conscience, or an undecided and morally ambivalent state of mind, can be torturous. Some persons may seek to be rid of the anxiety that moral indecision produces and simply quit the field in flight and avoidance. Others may jump one way or another in order to end the ordeal. I do not think either flight or ungrounded leaps into decision are morally justified. If a matter is morally serious enough to struggle over, it is too serious to avoid, or to decide as one might decide some indifferent matter. Our moral freedom should not be squandered by arbitrary endorsements in order to relieve the anxious burden of indecision.

Occasionally in emergencies, we must make moral decisions, no matter how unsettled or incomplete the inner process. When absolutely forced, what should we do with our inner lack of reasoned wholeheartedness? If no known evil action is involved, we might decide upon the grounds of our most prevailing or most strongly grounded inner tendencies, even if we are not completely convinced. Looking at the inner preponderance of thought and feeling, we can see the balance weighted in one direction, so we choose what appears to be the most probably correct decision. As with other intuitive choices that later appear incorrect, we may feel great regret over such decisions, but it is regret rather than guilt. We can consider the mistake in personal judgment in the same sorrowful way we do those past emergencies in which we were forced to act without reflection and failed to choose correctly.

In true forced-choice quandaries, when there is outright conflict that produces oscillations between strong emotional feelings and strong reason, should we choose the emotional, intuitive pull, or the reasoned course? The answer is not a foregone conclusion, as the rationalist tradition's estimation of reasoning would aver. As in the question of judging intuitions, a reading of the person having the intuition is involved before making a decision. Whose intuition or emotional pull is this, and in which context and content—even if the person one is judging is oneself? Perhaps we wholeheartedly know ourselves to be poor thinkers, ill educated, or with painful past experiences of having been easily swayed by what we can now deem were fallacious moral arguments. Still, we have time and again found that our emotional responses were morally superior to our arguments.

We sense that our habits of the heart, nurtured perhaps by good family and good traditional community, have been proved more morally trustworthy over time than our naivete in intellectual argumentation. In such conflicted emergencies, when there is no obvious moral wrong involved, we could risk choosing what we are emotionally drawn to as a probably more correct course than our present reasoning. Huck Finn is not the only character in the world who chose correctly following his heart! If, on the other hand, we know ourselves to be more intelligent than good-hearted, we might trust our reasoning as more probably correct. In such serious inner conflicts, when forced to premature decisions, our own moral judgments or conscientious assessments of our general character becomes a factor in the specific decision. How much, and in what ways, do we trust and distrust ourselves? And the next question may well be, are there no others to whom we can look for help, whose moral guidance or communal moral tradition we could trust?

If we are unconvinced, we might also decide by following those persons admired as wise and good—if as far as we can see, their convictions are not morally wrong and they are strongly convinced. If most of the wise and good moral mentors we admire belong to a traditional community, and/or we hold a moral allegiance to an ideological group, we may in conscience listen and follow the community's guidance—if in a particular instance it does not seem morally wrong to us. Indeed, if there is a long-standing moral consensus within our community, this would provide some moral surety and guidance for personal conscience. Moral consensus operates much as consensus arising from repeated experiments, and argumentation in scientific and intellectual questions builds up grounds for intellectual assent.[41]

To freely choose to follow the guidance of a moral tradition on specific decisions is not morally irresponsible or an escape from freedom. We can responsibly and autonomously give our informed consent to a moral decision made by our community, when we do not actively dissent and have no better alternative moral solution.[42] We are not turning over our whole past and future conscience to another, as in totalitarian states or cults. The Nazi's oath, with its motto of "My honor is my loyalty to the fuhrer," was unlimited and uncritical. One pledged to do whatever the leader ordered for whatever reason. There is a world of difference between absconding from all personal moral responsibility, and voluntarily seeking moral guidance and taking direction from a moral community or tradition. After all, we choose or maintain membership in a community because we agree with the tradition's wisdom and moral guidance; thus we naturally seek help and guidance from our fellow members as a resource for our own moral deliberations.

In moral crises, moral conflicts, and personal dilemmas, the question of how we have chosen our communities and built our characters becomes crucial. How much do we love, admire, and rationally respect and trust the moral competence of the communities and traditions that have shaped our characters? Filial piety has always been seen as important in communities because each individual person cannot possibly have the capacity, energy, or time to adequately decide every moral question starting from scratch. Yet the community must continue to function and morally educate new generations. No parents or group can raise children in a value-free, open morality without having made value decisions. Certain stories, narratives, values, and virtues will have to be passed on as part of the tradition. A socialized person, who is not a psychopath, will arrive at adulthood with some inculcated moral system in place.

The question then becomes one of the degree to which the individual person recognizes, appreciates, and decides to appropriate what he or she has been given in the way of moral guidance and vision of the good life. All moral communities have those who dissent, those who are deficient, those who embody the norm, and those who challenge the sufficiency of the norm in the service of some higher moral ideal they wish the community to follow. There is a tension between a group's need to be open to reform and improvement of their moral vision and the need to conserve and pass on their traditional morality. As one astute observer of the moral education of virtues has put it:

> Communities that seek simply to remain "open" and that do not inculcate virtuous habits of behavior will utterly fail at the task of moral education. Communities that do not permit the virtues they inculcate to be transcended by the good will ultimately cut themselves off from the very source that inspired their efforts to shape character.[43]

From the individual's subjective point of view as a self-conscious moral decision maker of conscience, one of the larger metamoral decisions involved in deciding what kind of person to become, what kind of life to live, is about the kind of community and moral tradition one will appropriate or repudiate. A pluralistic, individualistic society like the United States presents the moral challenge of choosing communities most forcefully. An array of competing moral visions and communities are constantly presenting their claims. Will we stay within the family or communal traditions that shaped us, or try to transcend our traditions by giving our allegiance to other moral communities?

Conversions to new moral visions happen in our society and are acceptable as expressions of our need to create our character and appropriate the values by which our lives will be guided. But such transfers of moral allegiance are rarely the result of purely analytic or rationalistic reasoning processes. The movement from one vision of the good to another is like a specific moral decision, infused with personal emotion and moral intuitions as well as reasons. If we change our group, it is usually because we are changing our views of our selves, or aspiring to different, more emotionally compelling moral ideals.

In moral conversions or moral recommitments to our filial groups, we choose communities in which we feel we can morally flourish. Our feelings of love and admiration, and our desire to emulate the life we see being lived by others, lead us to move toward new groups, or consciously reaffirm loyalty to our own. We may oscillate and struggle through many of the same testing processes that go into all decisions of conscience. A myriad of personal interactions during our lives have been encoded in our memories, and these implicit and explicit impressions influence our choice of a moral ideal community. The self or proprium that is ours and self-appropriated is a dynamic, ongoing creation of our attention and consciousness, which in turn are shaped by our emotions, reason, and willed decisions.

However, becoming more and more self-created, self-controlling, and self-directed is not always the same thing as progressing toward the morally good. Just as we are not determined by our initial family conditioning, so we are not inevitably programmed to keep progressing toward the good. We may increase in intelligence, strength of will, and competence without increasing in virtue. Moral freedom means that moral regressions, free choices of evil over good, and stagnation are always possible; moral decline and fall is an optional plot in our life stories. The cooling and curtailment of moral aspirations can also propel us to choose different communities. We can move from one social group to another to find less-morally demanding standards of action. The rake's progress or the addict's habits lead to the choice of new companions, and newfound affinities that help deaden conscience.

No matter how well we understand the strategies of moral decision making, we may not always use them to effect. Sometimes, we will refuse to make any moral decision; sometimes, we will make the wrong moral decision. In coming to grips with the action of conscience, we must face the nearly intractable problem of moral failure and evil.

Chapter 6

Moral Failure and Self-Deception

How and why does the personal moral decision making of conscience fail? If we understand how things go wrong, perhaps we can help ourselves and other persons in their moral development and moral functioning.

I define moral failure as failure in moral decision making and contend that there can be many different kinds of failure. A failure in the inadequate or erroneous outcome or content of a decision is different from a failure in the deciding process or the moral effort made by an individual. There is a difference between *what* is decided and *why and how* it is decided. Assessing moral failure in the content of an outcome is a negative evaluation of the quality or adequacy of the moral decision made. The assessment of content is a judgment using philosophical, ethical, or theological criteria, and it is usually a judgment made within a community exercising the moral standards of a moral tradition. But since individuals and communities live in time, they can change in their understanding of the requirements of an adequate morality.

No matter how conscientious the process, human error can occur because we are limited, fallible, and bound by the social conditions or potential intellectual knowledge of our historical time and period. In the cultural evolution of ideas, there are precursors, developments, and local periods of regression in group life that affect what a single individual could ordinarily know. The sociology of knowledge, or an analysis of what ideas can be accessible to whom, is a factor in determining the possible moral functioning of an ordinary human being.[1] There are always exceptional persons who exhibit moral genius or moral prophecy in their countercultural insights, but they are rare.

Another inevitable source of moral failure through ignorance is the individual's developmental history. Moral development is a process that takes place over the life course, from infancy to old age. Looking back on our individual pasts, we can see that each of us made inadequate moral decisions and moral mistakes, despite our trying as hard as we could at particular times. Knowing what we *now* know, the moral decisions would be different.

We can look back upon an earlier stage of moral development and see that all the components of good moral decision making were in an immature state of development. Despite all-out efforts, our reasoning abilities, emotional sensitivities, caring, and commitment were still childish and primitive. The self as moral agent may have also been weakly integrated, unpracticed in self-direction, self-evaluation, and self-knowledge. An immature moral agent employing inadequate moral understandings produces moral failure. We can now see that personal decisions about what ought to be done in the world, and about what ought to be done in our own lives, were objectively wrong. Yet since the prior decisions were made in honest ignorance, we cannot feel deep guilt, but rather regret and sorrow.[2]

Regret rather than condemnation can also accompany evaluations of past moral failures of various communities in history. We can't blame them now for not knowing then what it would have been impossible for them to realize at the time. Of course, there are limits to what can be claimed as justifiable ignorance. Some persons and communities claim retrospective innocence of things that they could, and should, have known.

Reflections upon moral failure and the limitations of humankind can induce humility. When making moral decisions, the wisest persons will never claim absolute certainty or moral infallibility. It is far better to be modest and claim only that one is deciding on the better course or the best decisions that I or we collectively can achieve with our present moral understanding. Many moral problems are multidimensional and complex. Even if the moral decision-making process has been sincere, informed, searching, nuanced, and done by emotionally mature, highly rational persons with the highest motivation and ideals, persons can, in retrospect, be objectively judged to have failed in the content or outcome of their decisions. Ethics and morality is not an exact science—and for that matter, even exact science often fails in its progress toward a fuller understanding of the physical universe.

Since we live in time and limited space, all possible future truths and events can not be known in the present. We are always working with incomplete information—about the world, about other human beings, and about ourselves. Human beings and the human brain are such complex organisms that even our own self-consciousness is not always accurately reading our own situation, or our own motives and desires. Moreover, uncertainty about the future also means that we cannot predict with certainty the consequences of moral decisions. Dealing with uncertainty and assessing risks make it even more difficult to decide what ought to be done. Then too, the good, or the relationship of various goods and duties, can rarely be so thoroughly understood by any one individual or community at one moment of historical time that infallible moral decisions can be guaranteed.

But given the human condition, ignorance and error are not the only forms of moral failure. At the other end of the spectrum, it appears that persons with full knowledge and consent can freely choose to do what they know to be morally wrong. These choices are made in many different ways, with different degrees of personal dedication to wrongdoing.

Freely Choosing Evil

If persons are free moral agents, then they can morally fail through free and deliberate acts. Perhaps the worst cases arise when strong personalities, despite all their capacities and talents, repudiate morality at a fundamental level and commit themselves to evil. In literature, we have Milton's Lucifer, who, in his pride, envy, and rebellion against God, declares, "Evil, be thou my good." In real life, we have demonic serial killers and sadists who defiantly go to prison or death extolling their evil deeds. They, like Hitler, openly despise conscience and traditional morality.

Choosing evil as a good still includes an element of choosing a good, but in this fundamental choice, whatever the good recognize as evil will be substituted for traditional goods. Evil must, in reality, always be parasitic on good through some perversion or failure. This dependence arises because good is based upon the reality of our positive human capacities and nature; evil can only be negative in denying, distorting, or perverting what in other circumstances enables good acts.[3] Thus the more intelligence and freedom, the more potential for moral failure.

In the truly wicked, there is an avowal of immorality for its own sake, as a form of rebellion and revenge against moral standards and civilization. In an inverted moral system, cruelty, slaughter, rape, torture, and degradation of others in the service of personal goals, or even personal whims, can be embraced without hesitation. All traditional moral taboos may be broken; the only requirement is that there be no weak-willed turning back or acceptance of moral judgment by self or others. The most admired values are strength of will and accruing the power that enables one to overturn all opposition and outwit and overcome all moral restraints. A conscious commitment is made to harden the heart and abandon moral standards.

It takes very strong, driving persons to deliberately fashion themselves into monsters of evil. Such people can draw others to them by their perverse charisma. Those who are attracted to an evil leader are promised many spoils in addition to liberation from traditional morality. However, at the same time that they are allowed to renounce the constraints of conscience, they must blindly submit to the will of the powerful leader. The motto of the Nazi SS was "My honor is loyalty"; their operative morality was ensured by their oath of obedience to the will of Hitler. In the Haitian dictatorship of Papa Doc, the same cult of the leader's will as law reigned, producing atrocities and terror. In Hitler's case, he alone assumed moral command in the name of the mystic Germanic race or volk.[4] Other demonic leaders such as Stalin, or on a lesser scale Charles Manson and Jim Jones of Jonestown, also demanded absolute obedience, complete with atrocities assigned as loyalty tests, or "blood cement," through which previous moral standards, values, and loyalties could be repudiated. The followers, in the long run, usually meet their own betrayal and destruction, since in systems in which there are no restraining moral standards, a leader or one's fellow rebels recognize no obligation to fair treatment.

Moral lawlessness weakens the operations of a completely dedicated evil person or evil cultlike group. The thousand-year immortal Reich lasted hardly more than a decade. Even if external forces are not provoked into counterattack and rebellion, inner moral disintegration and corruption take their toll. The strong personalities who can commit themselves to wickedness find that it is hard to keep responses compartmentalized. The existence of interpersonal dimensions of the self means that there is a predisposition toward consistency between self-self interactions and self-other relationships. A person constructs a concept of the the self using his or her own person as evidence; then the concept becomes a template, or filter, to interpret other persons in the environment. Lying, deceiving, abusing, and manipulating others breed the conviction that others too must be liars and in their turn out to manipulate, secretly betray, and attack. Paranoiac thinking comes from projecting onto others one's own aggressive characteristics.

Overthrowing rational morality's thrust and demand for consistency leads to inconsistency and irrational mental operations. If severe contradictions of logic are permitted within a self's own conscious operations, and no objective standards are recognized as obligatory, then rational thinking processes begin to erode. The pleasure principle and magical thinking overcome the reality principle. Megalomania affects rational problem-solving skills. Autistic moral standards and personal selfishness trap the self in one obstinate point of view; as one becomes more cut off from others and general standards, there is an increase in mental claustrophobia and isolation from the facts.

While many individuals may fawn upon a powerful evil person, few real friends remain who can provide the corrective interplay of intimate truth telling. Only free, equal, and secure friends and colleagues will tell a person the unpleasant news necessary to make successful strategic moves. With tyrants, reality recedes behind the lies of fear. So many evil monsters descend into a type of paranoia and madness that observers are tempted to say that they must have been insane to begin with. This may not be so; persons can freely choose to pursue and repeat evil acts that at some point take on a destructive dynamism of their own. As in some physical addictions, somewhere along the way the ability to control self-destruction can be lost.

But persons so completely dedicated to evil as their good may be rare. Those who take defiant pleasure in the evil they do and seek its triumph stand out as exceptions. Most wicked people are not true believers; they are not committed to evil as a crusade against good. More evil is done by shrewd, amoral pragmatists who may make conscious and free decisions to repudiate morality, but act amorally only when it serves their purposes. They choose evil by default, because they abandon all commitment to moral values. The self's will is autistically enthroned, and moral indifference serves as a protection from outside interference or restraint. Traditional moral standards or a commitment to transcendent goods would entail accepting moral obligations; morality requires self-evaluation beyond self-interest.[5] In order to avoid moral duties or demands, the amoral evil person ruthlessly suppresses all tendencies toward moral reasoning, moral emotions, and moral actions.

But in this freely chosen cultivation of moral apathy, there is no fanatic zeal—that too might require effort and lead to danger. If other nonmoral values such as beauty, sentiment, or efficiency are appealing and conveniently self-enhancing, then they can be espoused. To avoid trouble, amoral persons will shrewdly obey moral conventions and even engage in moral talk. The most selfish and indulgent life-styles can usually be obtained by a certain amount of external conformity and moderation. No excessive acts of cruelty or needless violent trampling of others will take place; amoral pragmatists will only employ whatever amoral behavior it takes to get what they want when they want it. By a tempered, shrewd, amoral approach, a person can more easily avoid external disasters and internal mental deterioration.

Consciously, one may have decided that all questions of moral obligation or signals from moral feelings will be repudiated; but this private and total abandonment of the moral enterprise is neither advertised nor revealed to others. This careful, contained kind of amoral person rarely disintegrates into a mental shambles, or even provokes opposition or prosecution. Such individuals can even succeed and progress up a career ladder in many enterprises. If their abandonment of morality shows outwardly, it is only in the fact that they seem strangely compartmentalized, somewhat deadened in tone, and narrowly one-dimensional in motivation.

Only moral conflict with another person, or some inadvertent public lapse, reveals the moral barrenness within. Their intimates and family members inevitably find out more about the antisocial consequences of amorality—much to their sorrow. But it is hard to prove an absence of conscience, and given good manners, outsiders and casual acquaintances may find it hard to believe the moral indictment of intimates and family members.[6] But even these chilling instances of completely amoral pragmatism are rare types of moral failure. Much more typical are the everyday moral failures of basically good people who are weak.

Moral Failures from Weakness

I think most moral failure does not arise from the completely conscious choices of amoralists. Most ordinary, normal people have made a fundamental choice to be moral and to be good, or at least morally good enough to be acceptable as a passing member of their human community. Yet despite their general commitment and desire to be good, they do wrong. Individuals can freely, while in full consciousness and full capacity, carry out an act they know to be morally wrong.[7] Persons differ in how often they morally fail or how serious the matters are in which they fail. The good person fails less often in less serious matters, but the old saying may be true that even the just man falls seven times a day. Even when persons do nothing that they judge is morally wrong, it is still improbable that they do everything that they think they ought to do. They fail by omission, if not by commission.

It seems easier to fail by not acting, by refraining from doing something. A morally wrong outcome can be effected by freely choosing not to act when we know that we could and should. But these immoral decisions not to act are different from overtly initiating wrongdoing. For one thing, it is easier to avoid punitive external consequences for something we refrain from doing. Inaction is less noticeable and legally harder to prove. It also takes less initiative to refrain from acts in the ongoing flow of complex social interactions and behavior. To delay an action may mean that events and the opportunity pass, and one has effectively chosen inaction. Much grievous injury in the world arises from omission and the avoidance of moral action by good people. Inertia is morally insidious. Using purposeful passivity to gain aggressive ends is also quite common.

But on a deeper level, what is happening when we describe moral failure from weakness? This is not a case of ignorance, or not being able to decide what ought to be done in a complex moral dilemma. We know already, but still fail. What seems to happen is that one part of the person or self rebels against the central core self's commitment to the good embodied in the morally recognized duty. I, who am my most deeply avowed, most completely appropriated self, am committed to the good, but another part of me impedes the act, or does something else that I know is wrong.

There are many inner dimensions of self that are usually integrated as a whole, but we, as agents, must supply the energy or psychic glue to act as a whole using our capacities appropriately. The self's multiple dimensions, modes, functions, subsystems, or parts can come into conflict with the executive agent or with each other. The result is inner conflict and incoherence if parts break away, break down, or fail to follow the order given. Self-consciousness also varies dynamically along a continuum as one lives from moment to moment, so in a particular situation, different dimensions within can be more salient, stronger, or weakened. We, as self-directing subjects, are subject to bodily fatigue, hunger, pain, and illness.

Stressful social interactions and emotions such as anxiety, anger, or desire may exert pulls toward an action we judge to be wrong. Some stressor from without, combined with some inner conflicting desire or some part-function, can interfere with the moral self-direction we aspire to enact. Moral agency weakens if there are strongly conflicting emotions or opposing rational considerations working against our commitment to the good moral action. This inner conflict and opposing pull are experienced in their duration as temptation. The whole self-identity we most value, the self most consistent with what we have learned in the past and aspire to be in the future, demands moral acts that will be the best in the long run. But in the short run, during a momentary "weakness of will" arising from some counterattraction, some part-self or subsystem rebels and takes control.[8]

Moral failure does not mean that we repudiate or abandon the good forever—it is just that at particular moments, we do not submit to the moral obligations that we recognize. Part of us refuses to obey or serve the inner moral commands we give ourselves. In the inner division, we watch ourselves do what we know and feel is morally wrong, even as we do it. Such counterconscience acts, be they thoughts, feelings, words, or deeds, may be done in a host of different circumstances. There are different degrees of rebellion against our own moral standards, concerning different matters and producing different subsequent aftereffects.

If someone is defiantly initiating, embracing, and rejoicing in an intention to hurt or destroy another, then we rightly speak of an evil and wicked deed. We humans, knowing the good and desiring to be good, can still freely will to do evil to others and to ourselves. This contradictory quandary of human moral existence has produced efforts at explanation in many cultures. Different myths personify a devil, demons, or fallen angels who employ supernatural forces to engineer the fall of humankind and then tempt us into evil acts. Secular theories that repudiate the supernatural try to explain the evil that persons do by positing unconscious forces in humans that rise up and take over conscious, rational control. The unconscious—in an innate death instinct, an aggressive instinct, the collective Shadow, or the eruption of conflicted and repressed desires— produces the evil behavior we repudiate. But these theories are hard-pressed to satisfactorily explain the fact that we can know we are rebelling and choosing the wrong we do—as we do it. We can hardly excuse ourselves by blaming unconscious, biologically determined forces, as if we were suffering psychotic episodes or epileptic seizures.[9]

It seems unlikely that the excessive sadism, evil, and gratuitous cruelty found in the world could be due to biologically programmed, unconscious mechanisms. Animals, who are morally unconscious and instinctually programmed, never commit destructive acts equal to the excesses of human beings. Human selves, who can know the good and be conscious of their own freedom, can use their knowledge and imagination to fuel evil, cruel, and gratuitously excessive acts impossible for other species. Once knowing the good and one's freedom to destroy and self-destruct, a self can rebel with elaborated, destructive acts, which then escalate in number and degree.

The human tendency to escalation and excess in immoral acts may arise, ironically, from the human development of conscience. In most

normal persons, the choosing of known, recognized wrongdoing usually requires rebelling against and overcoming the core self's own moral
standards. Therefore, the immoral act is often done with a frenzied,
excessive quality because the violence and frenzy are needed to drown
out the inner self's reproving voice. So-called crimes of passion may not
be so much energized by the passion as by the energy it takes to act
against our moral self-knowledge. Atrocities breed more atrocities because the betrayal of our own moral self must also be avenged. Once
the line is crossed, the moral standard overthrown, a person goes further and further in order to stave off feelings of guilt, shame, remorse,
and anxiety. Fear of the self's disintegration is countered by more hasty
action. Once the deed is done, it can only be justified by further deeds.

This same dynamic of excess and escalation can characterize other
less-serious rebellions against conscience, which are done with less-
malicious intent. If we are regretfully letting desire, fear, or external interests overwhelm the demands of conscience, there ensues a certain "Oh,
to hell with it, let's get this over with quickly" quality to the moral surrender. Shame and despair can produce enough self-loathing so that what
starts as a minor lapse becomes a general rout and debacle. We cannot
care enough about our avowed, long-term self-goals to resist the pressures
of the present. Psychologists working to help people control their addictive and binging behaviors understand the inner dynamics of relapses.[10]

Another very different kind of emotional strategy can be used when
persons knowingly act against their own moral standards. Instead of
using violent impulsiveness to drown out inner incoherence, persons
try to silence the moral imperative through withdrawal of attention and
feeling. If we do not notice or allow our emotions to react then this
immoral act is not real. These inner psychological distancing and with-
drawing actions have been seen as combinations of psychic numbing,
derealization, and disavowal.[11] The self is divided so that while we can
see that part of the self is doing the immoral action, we are acting as if
it is not really happening.[12] We are awake, conscious, and freely con-
senting to our own immoral behavior, but we are trying our best to
dissociate the real self from the immoral acts that part of us is performing. We are numb and function like machines, or as if we were actors
in a play or people in a dream.

In the most extreme withdrawals and splitting off of part of us, we
can achieve what some psychiatrists have termed "doubling."[13] We remain ourselves, and our disavowed doubles are doing the unacceptable
acts. Others would explain this splitting of the conscious self as letting
the social self or the role-playing self become dissociated from the core

subjective agent self. The psychic glue of the self as an "I" who acts as a whole loses its hold on the parts. One is not yet totally disassociated from one's self-identity, as in multiple personality, amnesiac, or other mentally ill states, but inner coherence is breaking down.

A free personal act of rejection of what we, upon reflection, avow to be the good and true course for us is an experience of inner self-contradiction. Some unauthorized part of us, some subsystem, has gained control in some division created by an obsession, or in an oscillating flux between contesting selves and identities. Words and deeds are at odds, contradictory emotions war, or part-selves are in conflict. Such confusions produce anxiety and can induce new moral decisions to resolve the pain and chaos. Sometimes there can be an inner confrontation, and the self as moral agent reasserts moral responsibility. Sometimes there are further moves to avoid the shame and guilt of self-judgment, and a morally debilitating dynamic can occur. Moral sensibility and moral reasoning become sources of pain and anxiety, therefore they are avoided. Just as with the muscles of the body, the unused capacities of conscience can begin to deteriorate and become blunted. An arm put in a cast withers away, and the moral sense may also atrophy.

Free choices to do what we avow to be wrong, when not repudiated and accompanied by efforts to reform, increase the probabilities of more such choices of increasing moral seriousness. Habituation helps the slide down the slippery slope, for inertia and repetition are powerful forces. Many life stories repeat the narrative of the rake's progress or the prodigal son—modern versions can be heard at AA meetings or read about in autobiographies. Each wrong step and free choice to act against conscience work to lessen moral sensitivity while increasing susceptibility for the next surrender. The behavioral law of repetition is fairly inexorable—what is done tends to be repeated.[14] With the atrophy of central moral controls, a person begins to become less and less alert to moral signals. Individuals can morally decline—slowly, perhaps plateauing at some point, or continuing on to collapse. Metaphorically, these moral self-betrayals have been described as "dimming the inner light," or "hardening the heart."

Moral hardening occurs when any emerging moral concern is dismissed from the person's stream of consciousness. The individual on an immoral trajectory will find it easier and easier to dismiss moral questions as irrelevant. "Ought I to do this?" or "What is the good and right thing to do?" become meaningless questions. Moral demands or claims of goodness or truth beyond the person's own immediate interests and plans are dismissed as more and more illusory or irrelevant. Eventually, some persons may reach the amoralists' final abandonment of the moral quest, described earlier. They no longer choose to be good; they are morally indifferent and apathetic. If they go the next step and become converted to evil as the inversion of morality, then they can not only dismiss moral concerns, but be ashamed of their previous feelings of guilt and remorse. They can see conscience as but a remnant of a slave morality that the weak espouse because of their resentment of the strong and free.

But for most ordinary persons who do not abandon the fundamental desire to be good, the effort to avoid guilt and shame through various strategies becomes increasingly distressing. Pressure builds up either to face reality and reform one's life or to find some other solution to the perpetual inner conflict. A normally socialized, moral person is threatened and demoralized by the consciousness that one is constantly violating one's own moral standards. The desire to be good and acceptable in our own eyes is strong; the need to be integrated and consistent also seems built into our rational nature.[15] Self-contradiction, inner conflict, and ambivalence are torturous. The perception that one seems to be disintegrating adds fear and anxiety to the pain of shame and guilt. A person can feel caught in a bind—one refuses to abandon morality and yet is threatened and distressed by consciousness of moral failure. Flight is a common form of escape. A person can flee psychological distress by psychological manipulations of reality; a person is drawn toward self-deception.

Self-Deception and Moral Failure

There are different kinds of self-deception, and in all likelihood, some self-deception permeates all forms of moral failure. Those of us who are neither saints nor morally indifferent find that our most frequent experiences of moral failure involve self-deception or bad faith, in varying manner and degree. But what is self-deception? Self-deception, in its broadest sense, has been defined as refusing self-acknowledgment through motivated evasive strategies of different kinds—and then trying to evade the knowledge that one has done so.[16] The cover-up of a cover-up can use the evasive techniques we learn to employ in deceiving others.[17]

But there is a problem in using one particular interpersonal model, or self-other relationship, as a model for self-self deception. Can the outright, calculating, conscious lie be used on one's self? Those who have denied the existence of self-deception have claimed that since the deceiver and deceived are one and the same person, a sane, rational person will find it impossible to know and not know at the same time. If we think of self-deception as defined only by actively accepting two contradictory beliefs at the same moment in time, then it must indeed be rare, if not impossible, for anyone who follows Western logic and its definition of rationality. But there are many other ways we can evade acknowledging things that do not involve accepting outright lies and overt logical contradictions.[18]

Humans learn to deceptively manipulate others through use of words, use of silence, persuasive rationalization, emotional manipulations and behavioral strategies of distraction, substitution, delays of timing in giving information, and so on. All these strategies can be used in motivated evasions of reality by the self to the self. A description of all the infinite permutations of such strategies would take a whole book, but some brief sketch of self-deception is necessary to understand the pervasiveness of moral failure in basically good people.

Self-Deceptive Strategies

Self-deceptive strategies can range from the passive to the more active. We can avoid finding out things, or systematically ignore what we can't help knowing. More actively, we can selectively bias our thoughts and feelings or hastily rationalize them. Finally, we can create false accounts and try to pretend stories are true by selectively forgetting inconvenient facts. Some persons who fall deeply into inveterate self-deceptive habits manage to convince themselves of outright lies that they first told in an effort to protect or aggrandize themselves in some way. (The ironic question then arises whether a person who performs a spectacular feat of self-deception has achieved the status of the authentically ignorant who morally fails because they do not know any better!)

At least we would recognize as culpable ignorance or pseudoinnocence those cases involving incomplete self-deception. Just as we blame persons for excessive carelessness, negligence, and avoidance of their duties, so we can see that persons could have, indeed should have, made efforts to find out what they ought to have known. As the Nazi Albert Speer said about the death camps, "I didn't inquire because I didn't want to know."[19] Such self-deceptive ignorance is blameworthy because it is the result of motivated active avoidance. Knowing enough to know that one doesn't want to inquire is symptomatic of motivated, culpable ignorance.

A premonition or enough general intuitive knowledge tempts a person not to pursue further. This is not a new human failing, for it was noted by Joseph Butler in his acute eighteenth-century treatise on self-deception. He describes a situation in which men find that their own lives and behavior are unsatisfactory, but "their general knowledge, that matters were not well with them, prevented their looking into particulars . . . they turn away, will not go over particulars, or look deeper lest they should find more amiss."[20]

There is operating here a self-deception motivated by the desire not to face morally demanding truths that are suspected or already halfway known. In our complex mental functioning, which includes a preconscious filtering system, there seem to be hazy states that exist as forms of intuitive knowing, falling somewhere between explicit knowledge and true ignorance. These in-between conditions have been called "middle knowledge."[21] The claim is made that culpable ignorance is middle knowledge, and that it blends into more active forms of self-deception and bad faith.

More active forms of avoidance are necessary when painful reality becomes clearer, and closer to home. Evidence begins to present more of a demand upon attention. Systematic ignoring or developing selective blind spots may occur.[22] Persons may begin to use avoidance strategies employing overlooking, forgetting, and systematic biasing of thoughts or feeling. They can even use partial truths to quickly rationalize or veil the unpleasant perception, or as discussed earlier, emotionally withdraw or even transform one emotion into another more-acceptable one. There can be delays, distractions, blurring vagueness, and use of slogans to avoid paying closer attention. By twisting and turning, using words and feelings as excuses and dodges, the self can manipulate the stream of consciousness and the focus of attention.

All sorts of evasive maneuvers can be used to keep from full moral self-acknowledgment—at the beginning of a morally unacceptable act, in the middle of it, or after it is over. Memories can be selectively edited to aid in self-deception. One can avoid seeking the company and counsel of others who might be helpful, since they might expose self-deceptive maneuvers and distortions. In the struggle for moral self-esteem, it is tempting to bias and transform reality. Occasionally, those seeking neurotic abasement will also use self-deception to bias evidence against one's achievements, but this may be more rare.[23]

Self-deceptive mental operations are possible because of the complexity of self-consciousness and thought. There are so many complex interstices in informational processing that can be exploited for self-deceptive purposes.[24] A magician can trick us because she or he understands the ins and outs of the perceptual operations of the mind and eye. These same complexities can allow us to become master magicians in the cause of avoiding moral confrontation and self-acknowledgment.

Our wide-awake, attentive, focused consciousness is only one of our personal modes of operation. Our inner stream of consciousness flows through time with many different thoughts, images, and emotions, and many different states and stages of arousal, alertness, and focus. Undergirding the conscious flow are many nonconscious and preconscious informational processes filtering and selecting what will emerge into perceived consciousness. A person's stream of consciousness is the product of much preconscious selection from the overwhelming amount of stimuli that bombards the conscious mind from within and without. Long-term memory may guide the filtering process.[25] But memory itself is organized in complex ways, and the structures and content of knowledge seems to be separated into different categories or filing systems, as it were.

Everyone has experienced the problem of trying to remember things, and gradually warming to the task or getting cognitively tuned as one penetrates the store of what one knows about, say Roman history, or whatever the topic at hand. A person who is sincerely *trying* to function at full power has trouble maintaining focus, recalling, remembering, overcoming the vagaries of the wandering mind's creative reconstructions. New investigations of eyewitness memories and cognitive biases in thinking reveal how much active construal of reality we engage in when we think.[26] Every mental construction and reconstruction is subject to bias and error in the best of cases because it takes place in time and requires different forms of encoding and processing. Fooling ourselves is possible because we obviously do not have instantaneous, clear access to all that we know or can remember at any one moment in time.

Moreover, these many levels of the cognitive preconscious and cognitive unconscious are also linked to the emotional system. Perception is affected by emotions, particularly anxiety, fear, and desire. In such complex inner processes, there is room enough and time enough for strategic interruptions, distortions, selective perceptions, selective amnesias, and failed connections. Self-deceptive strategies of avoidance or bias are easily effected given the problems of paying full attention and pursuing a focused train of thought that may be emotionally threatening. Threats to our safety, security and self-esteem create fear and stress, which produce predictable distortions in consciousness.[27]

Painful knowledge or the unpleasant connotations or implications of certain acknowledgments about one's self and reality can induce what have been called psychological defenses. While some posttraumatic amnesias exist, other distortions of reality are the result of instantaneous microdecisions made with awareness. As threatening information begins to come into consciousness, there is enough knowledge to make the choice that we must take some evasive measure and then try to forget that we did so. At the top of the filtering system, on the edge of complete clarity of consciousness, we can begin to shape or censor the bad news we cannot bear to attend to. The self can distort, deny, or suppress what is painful; when the self's security operations are severely threatened, it is possible to distract, displace, or bias incoming information and feelings.

Psychoanalysis has produced a vast clinical literature devoted to the defensive self-protective tricks of consciousness management. Psychoanalytic theorists, following the work of Anna Freud, analyze these defensive processes used by the self.[28] They are often called ego defenses and recognized by the way threatening information and feelings can be transformed in various operations. If the threat cannot be forgotten, denied, or compartmentalized, then what is inside can be projected outside as the characteristic of another, not me. Other reversals, switches, transformations, and distortions can be made to avoid painful realities.

Since all these inner defensive processes must be inside a person, can they manifest themselves to an observer? Like all forms of inner moral failure (or for that matter, all activities of a good conscience), they are hard to assess accurately, since no one can have all the relevant facts affecting another's self-consciousness and flow of inner experience. Metaphorically, this has been expressed as the inability of any human being to infallibly read the human heart. However, long before psychologists began their experimental studies of self-deceit, people were observed by dramatists, poets, novelists, philosophers, religious masters, and clinicians. As long as morality has been considered, so has the problem of self-deception; the question is whether one can, or can not, "know thyself" or "to thyself be true."

Acute observers discern signs of defensive strategies to avoid self-threatening information in cognitive, affective, and bodily clues. The study of lying and deception offers insights into self-deception.[29] In self-deceptive, evasive dialogue, patterns emerge of quick switches of topics, rapid slides into contradictory reasoning, or sudden forgettings—as well as selective distortions of the content of information.[30] There can be bodily changes, facial signals, odd actions, or slips of the

tongue. Blatant self-contradictions and logical inconsistencies are overlooked, discrepancies between thoughts and feelings or words and behavior remain unnoticed. Odd changes in emotions, substitutions, or
moves from intense to bland to blank can also give a clue to the way
painful reality is being dimmed, distorted, or suppressed by a person.
Once the deception has been effected, the person can further save face
by forgetting the distortions that have been made.[31]

While therapists or counselors listen for defensive strategies with
the third ear, ordinary persons in social interactions also get messages
revealing self-deception. But in trying to get along, or to be charitable,
persons smooth interpersonal interactions; they usually disregard in-
congruities and continue to play their roles to keep the social drama
going.[32] Watching the TV show "Candid Camera" reveals how far people will go to maintain normality and try to keep the protective rules
of the game in play. We all "save face" for one another, and protect a
person who has made a social gaffe or seems self-deluded. We will
pretend it didn't happen, or quickly pass things off with humor or
some distracting maneuver aimed at keeping conflict or social disrup-
tion from occurring. The show must go on, so we are trained to overlook, not notice, and practice a form of socially approved blindness. We
learn various subtle silencing strategies that operate to keep dangerous
information at bay. Only an untutored child blurts out that the emperor
is without any new clothes and is parading around naked.

In a much more dangerous way, we save face for ourselves in the
moral domain. It has been noted by some psychoanalytic thinkers that
a severe early socialization full of punishment for the slightest moral
infraction may be more likely to produce liars, antisocial persons, and
self-deceptive strategies.[33] The child internalizes expectations and experiences with an intractable parent who can only be placated by lies,
deceptive strategies, and disparate manipulative efforts. The hopelessness of the external situation produces an inner moral struggle that also
favors self-deception, moral rebellion, and perhaps a gradual suppression of the whole anxiety-producing moral enterprise.

But the moral self-deceptive abilities of average people raised with
good enough parenting also develop apace. Persons become adept at
ways of coping with moral lapses or moral challenges by internal personal shifts of attention, thoughts, and feelings. The distorted version
of reality is quickly taken up and integrated into other firmly erected
defensive bastions, and then is increasingly difficult to budge or
change. Psychotherapists, for instance, can spend many hours slowly
and gently getting persons to confront what their self-imposed blinders

hide from themselves. When one's self-esteem or safety is threatened, self-deceptive oversight and denial can be extraordinary.

In isolation defenses, different knowledge can be kept separated and isolated from other contradictory information. If one never compares the inconsistent views, one is not disturbed by dissonance or logical contradictions. This kind of self-deception can be achieved by the minimal inattentiveness needed to keep from seeing the whole picture at once. We play many roles as we progress through the drama of our lives. Some theorists have claimed that we all actually have multiple selves, but even those who reject the strongest version of this claim admit that we play many different roles in our social existence. Some lack of integration of multiple roles and other self-identities may be inevitable in complex modern lives and institutions.[34]

Some persons are less given to introspective efforts toward consistency and can more easily use compartmentalization to avoid unpleasant truths. In less-severe instances of the "doubling" processes of evil persons (described earlier), good family men can go to work in a police state's bureaucracy and cooperate with its institutionalized oppression of others deemed outside their own group. Their consciences are circumscribed to operate only within their own private circles; public political enemies are alien, morally excluded, beyond the pale. Often the excluded groups, such as Jews, Communists, blacks, natives, or whomever, are not accorded full human status.

Internal inconsistencies are defended against in several ways. If the police interrogator is accused of being a complete amoral monster, but knows he is a loving family man and patriotic to boot, he can use his partial innocence to dismiss and defend against the charge. As Bishop Butler so shrewdly remarked in his classic treatise on self-deceit, "such general and undistinguishing censure of their whole character" confirms self-deceit in many, because "they know that the whole censure is not true; and so take for granted that no part of it is."[35]

Humans are clever at using partial truths and subtle but slipshod reasoning to project and avoid moral responsibility. The major move in most self-deception is to keep attention focused outward, away from one's own inner suspicions. The closer one's self-focused attention comes to dangerous moral self-confrontation, or clearly inescapable knowledge, the more frantic the defensive activity becomes. Again, as Bishop Butler said long ago, the partiality to ourselves results in the most flagrant flaws being overlooked within, while the same faults are vigorously criticized in others. He did not talk, as the Freudians do, of defensive projection and displacement or scapegoating, but he understood the psychological mechanisms involved. As the gospel query put it even earlier, "Why do you see the speck in the eye of another and ignore the beam in your own eye?"

In the effort to avoid self-knowledge, all sorts of outward-oriented behavioral distractions can be used, such as coping with self-generated emergencies, throwing oneself into demanding work, or joining crusades and/or witch-hunts against the moral faults of others.[36] Drugs, food, and sexual addictions can also serve to blunt perception and distract attention.

Paradoxically, a few persons can even avoid real moral self-confrontation by continually examining and obsessively worrying over their moral status. Excessive moral rumination, or a bad case of scruples, arises from the need to avoid guilt and blame. Other proud persons become obsessed with achieving moral perfection. Their self-deception operates in their substitution of continual moral analysis for the more-pressing demands for personal action and emotional commitment. The endless moral talk becomes another smoke screen to hide behind, one more subtle, self-deceptive ploy to avoid acknowledging the whole self's moral responsibility.

Some people embrace a similar strategy of avoidance through other partial operations. They begin to take their moral feelings and emotions as substitutes for moral action, and cultivate moral fantasies that never intersect with either rational thinking or behavior. Such sentimentality or reliance on moral feelings has been considered morally culpable self-deception if a person basks in good intentions and warm feelings but does not try to think through what acts are morally required, much less follow through. Tyrants like Idi Amin and Henry VIII seemed to be masters of self-deceptive sentimentality. The separation of any subsystem or part-self from the integrated whole person is morally dangerous.

Evaluating Self-Deception

Is not some self-deception inevitable and necessary in human life? If self-deception is built into our nature, isn't there an adaptive purpose served by illusions? Many observers have defended the necessity of so-called "vital lies," or those life fictions that make human life possible amidst harsh reality.[37] Self-protective denials of stress and refusals to face unpleasant truths are necessary, it is claimed, for hope, love, and psychological survival. Those theorists who argue in this vein do not seem to notice that their underlying assumption is that reality must be harsh, negative, and unbearable.

I do not grant that any reality is ever so harsh and bereft of meaning that it must be distorted for psychological survival, or for altruism and love to exist. I hold with those who discount the need for vital lies and believe that truth can only liberate, and enlarge consciousness. Even with misfortune, evil, and suffering, there can be more positive value found in facing reality than in lying to oneself. It is better to face suffering and death—it clarifies the mind wonderfully.[38] Innovative psychological experiments find that thinking of one's death intensifies personal moral values.[39] Worse still, according to shrewd analysts, humanity's denial of death and other human limitations lead to moral danger.[40] Not accepting reality leads to defensive moves of narcissistic aggrandizement at the expense of others. Accepting oneself, accepting the reality of suffering, evil, and limitation, is the beginning of wisdom and virtue. Good people can better hope, believe, and morally aspire toward ideals when they acknowledge themselves to themselves and give up illusions about others.

Moreover, permissiveness toward self-deception is morally debilitating. Given the human predisposition for avoiding unpleasant truths, it is doubtful that a person can keep habits of self-deception isolated in harmless nonmoral domains. How can a person decide beforehand which self-deception is going to be a beneficial "vital lie" and which will be morally deforming and destructive to self and others? The recommendation that self-deception can be a temporary coping mechanism is equally flawed. How can one know when to begin the deception and when to quit distorting reality? If it goes on too long, can it be easily given up, and will it not do harm in the meantime? Since one's self-self inner transactions become patterns for interpersonal transactions, self-deception soon leads to deceiving others, and one has the problem of restoring real trust. Those who champion self-deception as a necessary coping skill underestimate the psychological and moral price to be paid.

Another interesting question is whether self-deception depletes valuable psychological energy needed to shape attention, perception, feelings, and behavior. If the self-deception process has not been completely successful in suppression, then avoiding what we half-know will require effort.[41] Our complex minds may still remember at some level when we are self-deceiving ourselves. Although our conscious, alert self may be able to avoid confronting the truth head-on it seems to take a mental and an emotional toll to engage in the informational processes necessary to avoid knowing.

Self-deceivers must make constant, careful efforts never to bear down on the thin ice; it proves exhausting to maneuver around obstacles while pretending they do not exist. One must distort some-thing, then be sure to deny one is distorting it, and then try to forget the whole operation.[42] The short-term advantages of avoiding pain and self-criticism blunt, fog over, and in the long run atrophy a person's mental antennae and acuteness. Habits of avoidance and the cultivation of self-deception produce a constricted personality that cannot sponta-neously risk being too curious or going too broadly or deeply into per-sonal inquiries. Perhaps the worst moral effect of self-deception is that the better it works, the more complacent one becomes. No one can grow or morally develop if every call to change or stirring of self-doubt is quieted, blunted, or enfeebled by inner strategies of avoidance.

Obviously, the pain of self-criticism becomes more pronounced as there is more to criticize. As in all deception, more and more evasive lies are needed to cover up the lies already told. In lies to oneself, more and more dangerous topics must be avoided. Attention narrows; scan-ning and exploration of moral ideals and moral thinking must be con-strained to fit the constructed version of acceptable illusion. Only the self-deceptive use of approved language and terminology can be used in thinking to oneself. More and more miscalculations are made. Moral deterioration and personality deformation interact and influence each other when reality is avoided. One popular psychiatrist, M. Scott Peck, accurately describes the need for a dedication to truth and reality:

> The more clearly we see the reality of the world, the better equipped we are to deal with the world. The less clearly we see the reality of the world—the more our minds are befuddled by falsehood, misper-ceptions and illusions—the less able we will be to determine correct courses of action and make wise decisions.[43]

If our map of the world and our inner reality is distorted, we cannot get from place to place effectively. The worst thing imaginable is to have our consciousness corrupted.[44] If we are caught on a darkening plain, how can we begin to see more clearly? Are there some strategies for avoiding self-deception and other forms of moral failure?

Strategies to Avoid Moral Failure

Since an active, effective conscience consists of the whole person's ability as an agent to integrate and commit one's emotive, intuitive, ra-tional, and behavioral capacities in the service of moral standards of worth, all these diverse personal capacities must be developed and strength-ened in an effort to avoid moral failure. The best strategy is, as always, preventive, and in this case, this means the moral development of conscientious persons from childhood (discussed in the next chapters). Maturity and moral knowledge guard against failures from ignorance. But strategies are needed to avoid moral failure after one is an adult, with weaknesses and tendencies to self-deception already in place.

These remedial strategies overlap many of the techniques of psychotherapy, which also address the problems of lack of personal integration and defensive self-deception. Moral psychology can benefit from the accrued knowledge of psychological operations. Indeed, great moral counselors of the past, often in religious traditions, have used many of the same techniques as modern therapists and self-help movements. But those dedicated to the development of personal conscience must necessarily eschew the psychological techniques used in brainwashing and indoctrination. Brainwashing may induce behavioral conformity and a minimal moral socialization out of fear of punishment. But coercion cannot produce free inner acts of conscious moral commitment. In the end, individual adults freely choose whether they will or won't try to avoid moral weakness and self-deception. It is by definition a voluntary enterprise.

Those who freely and defiantly embrace wrongdoing, or those who have abandoned morality, will not care about being morally better persons. Amoralists will dismiss the whole moral enterprise as illusory, and expend their energy on obtaining safety, power, self-expression, pleasure, and other nonmoral goods. Unfortunately, those who are inveterate self-deceivers will also be too defensive and morally threatened to give attention or energy to moral self-transformations. Those who feel a need to dispel their ignorance and be better will make an effort, along with those who recognize that they must change and amend their morally unsatisfactory lives. The already-good and those in pain will be most ready to seek to overcome moral failure and self-deception.

A person must be aware of ignorance and failure to begin to overcome it. Only those who desire the good and can still feel morally ignorant, ashamed, guilty, uneasy, or generally dissatisfied are open to change. In response to a moral conflict or a moral lapse, a person open to change will accept the painful emotions of guilt, shame, or inadequacy. These emotions serve as signals to a morally socialized person that a personal standard of worth has been violated. Shame and guilt, which appear to be innately programmed emotions, have been extensively analyzed in literature and psychological work.

Guilt and shame are marks that a self-conscious self is present and operating as a moral evaluator. In some classical analyses, shame and guilt are considered to be different emotions.[45] Shame is supposedly more oriented to outward social failure. Shame is induced by being exposed and found wanting, usually in the eyes of observers. Shame is displayed in a desire to hide, to sink into the ground or be covered over, so one covers one's face or hangs one's head. Shame is thought to be very close to embarrassment and can have a nonmoral cause, as when one commits a social blunder or fails some test of achievement. One can be ashamed of things that one did not do, could not help, nor had any control over—such as class status or physical appearance. But one can also be ashamed of one's moral ignorance, moral failure, and self-deception, when and if they are exposed and recognized.

Guilt, by contrast, is described as a feeling of individual, personal responsibility in which one's moral responsibility for wrongdoing is salient. We know we should have, and could have, acted differently, but chose not to. The emotion is experienced as self-directed, accompanied by a desire for confession, reparation, and atonement. Guilt is always thought to be morally relevant, and more highly developed in cultures that stress self-consciousness, free will, and individual moral responsibility. Shame is thought to be more amoral and associated with cultures in which collective self-consciousness and social membership or ascribed status are more important than individual responsibility.

But the classic analyses seem misguided, since the self always possesses a social dimension, is always mentally intertwined with others, as well as inevitably engaged in taking various roles within a community. The social dimension of the self and the fact that an infant's self is largely developed through engaging in interpersonal relationships indicate that social shame will be important in the moral life.[46] In our internalized memory, we can carry our inner, unseen audience of beloved and admired moral tutors and exemplars, whom we do not wish to disappoint or morally betray, by betraying the standards of worth they have imparted to us. Even if we have no community of mentors and witnesses in our heads, we can be ashamed of ourselves when we do wrong. Shame can be fused with guilt, because the individual's guilty action must be judged a moral failure before the self's own inner court. We are guilty when we indict ourselves by our own standards, and in the self-reflective judgment, we can hardly avoid being ashamed.

Inappropriate feelings of guilt and shame can be held over from childhood that do not accord with present realities or with a person's present mature standards of moral judgment. If these are entrenched, they can often induce emotional reactions that are considered by the mature self to be irrational and unwarranted. But since the whole core self as moral agent does not endorse this part reaction, these guilts or shames are not considered truly moral activities of conscience but simply old conditioned reflexes to be outgrown or overcome by concerted effort. These disconnected irrational pangs of feeling, irrational fears, or forebodings can sometimes hinder mature conscience by providing a confusing distraction or a ready excuse to discount all moral emotions or thoughts as infantile. To make moral progress as an adult, one can never outgrow reacting to moral failure with "good guilt" and "good shame," that is, feelings that are reality oriented and not excessive.

A peculiar psychological paradox is characteristic of successful efforts to avoid moral failure. Movements like AA or religiously inspired efforts toward self-reformation and self-control require as a first step the admission of failure and giving up control. After personal failure and helplessness are acknowledged, a person makes an affirmative act to give over personal control to a beneficent, higher power. Psychological strategies of pain control and addiction control have recommended similar techniques, calling them employment of the law of least effort.[47] The idea is that in seeking self-control over some flawed behavior or pain, it is counterproductive to fight fiercely and thereby focus all one's attention and will upon the struggle with pain or desire. The increased effort and tension produce increased focus of attention upon the undesired phenomenon, giving it more reality and force in the field of consciousness.

What we attend to seems real while we attend to it; attention invests its object with subjective reality. There is also a tendency toward psychological reactance—or reasserting a freedom that is threatened.[48] Thus the more one fights to exert control, the more reactive counterforce is generated. A person becomes burned out, overwhelmed, and exhausted by the inner struggle. Letting go, giving up, and turning attention to positive alternative thoughts and activity release the energy being spent in the debilitating inner struggle. Ceasing to focus on control detaches and frees the mental consciousness from the dominance of the unwelcome obsession.

Strategies to avoid moral failure make use of these same dynamics. Moral failures, other than clearly avowed amorality, often arise from a lack of personal integration; parts of the person are isolated or rebelling against core identities, long-term values, and moral self-directives. If divided controls and inner conflict constitute the problem, the best cure can hardly be to increase inner divisiveness and conflict by setting up one more obsessive effort to beat a part-self into submission. As the inner division and struggle increase, integrated, wholehearted moral decisions and concerted, consistent actions become ever-more difficult. Attention is narrowed and locked into dominance struggles, more often lost than won. If a person becomes fiercely fixated on achieving perfect self-control, failure is foreordained—followed by depression, self-reproach, and anger, often projected onto the failings of others.

Moral exemplars who overcome moral failure take another course. They begin by affirming failure and powerlessness over sin, suffering, illusion, neurosis, alcoholism, compulsions, or whatever. The surrender of all efforts at self-deception is accompanied not by despair but by an act dependent on trust in some larger flow of reality as a source of help beyond the self. This expanded awareness brings calm, peace, personal integration, and most paradoxically, a new self-control over avoiding habitual failures as one works at reflection and change.

To maintain the new awareness, a person must be willing to continually search and examine the conscience and correct the inevitable failings—slowly, calmly, patiently, one at a time, one day at a time. The self-examination and effort required for maintaining a sense of powerlessness and trust is not like the older fight for control, which was like an angry, obsessive, violent attack and search by a prosecuting attorney. Gentle self-reminding to pay attention is more like maternal nurturing, or being softly licked into shape. These self-self interactions are more like the counsel of a good friend or wise mentor. The inner moral dialogue can give direction gently, peacefully, and with full awareness and self-acceptance of appropriate guilt or shame; frantic defensive and reactive rebellions are unnecessary.

The Buddhists speak of achieving mindfulness, which appears to be a gentle recalling of what is important, a patient recalibration when one is off course. Other spiritual traditions speak of recollection and directing attention to the good. These gentle forms of self-conscious, clear-eyed acceptance of moral weakness seem the most effective way for persons to overcome moral failures—without lies. As in pain control or prepared childbirth, a person does not anxiously fight against the oncoming waves, but accepts reality, focuses attention, and floats free. Just enough attention and effort is expended to keep attention focused; there is no anxious panic, no test of wills that results so often in being upended by a more powerful force and nearly drowning. Easy does it; the strategy is one of moment-by-moment, day-by-day perseverance.

Why do these paradoxical strategies of giving up self-control work? Is it the trust and sense of beneficence in reality that banishes primeval anxieties, restores hope, builds self-confidence, and so makes effort more effective? Fear and anxiety over one's powerlessness and helplessness seem defused by actively embracing their inevitability, and transforming lack of control into dependent trust. Perhaps reducing conscious controls and struggle allows long-suppressed, positive, preconscious tendencies to operate more autonomously and more efficiently? Another explanation of the paradox may be that admission of failure and limits relieves the need for self-deception and cover-ups and furthers the energy available for moral agency. The cessation of inner war gives new power to the core self who morally decides.

Social relations will also be affected, for a new unity and openness within the self engenders more-integrated, open dealings with others. When we have nothing to hide or defend, we are less socially constrained and elusive; others, in their turn, can be freer to respond honestly. Nothing may be as helpful in overcoming self-deception as opening up the self to dialogue and the scrutiny and corrective responses of trusted others. The therapeutic movement toward what has been called "the transparent self" is built upon the theory that openness, honesty, or transparency to everything within the self is necessarily connected with openness to others without.[49] As we open ourselves to others, we get support and social confirmation. Inner freedom gives flexibility, encourages risk taking, and garners instructive feedback about reality. Some or all of these processes (along with unknown others) may be operating to produce the moral conversions and moral transformations we witness when persons change their lives for the better.

There are intrinsic rewards for moral improvement that appear to escalate liberating processes, operating much as do the opposite dynamics of the slippery slope and moral deterioration. Once experiencing a positive difference, a person can understand the testimony of others that nothing is as important as the effort to mind the self. Self-consciousness is the key to moral self-direction. And given the power of defensive maneuvers and external distractions, persons have to set aside time, make the effort, to engage in moral self-reflection. Traditional recommendations to examine one's conscience daily, or set aside time for meditation and reflection were psychologically wise. Longer periods of reflection can also be necessary at crisis points in a life.

To question one's actions and motives is difficult enough when particular acts are involved. It is more arduous and takes more sustained thought to examine one's whole life course and direction. While it is important to reflect upon one's immediate desires, feelings, and motivations, it is more crucial to reflect on what desires one desires to have in the long run. One's "second order desires" and self-goals will set a life's direction.[50] Living an examined life and making efforts to avoid self-deception must go on continually.

The human capacity for using imagery and projective imagination can be used in moral reflection and self-guidance.[51] Some tried-and-true methods recommend observing ourselves as we would another, or to put ourselves in another's place. The imaginary reversals of view-points induce empathy and different, wider perspectives. The vicarious subjectivity helps us grasp the traditional moral principles of equality of moral worth, and justice. The effort can be made to use imagination and feeling to avoid any selfish biases or partiality of vision.

So too in moral dilemmas, we can try to imagine a good man or woman in the same situation in which we find ourselves, and imagine what they would do.[52] Does this tell us something helpful? Or we can try to imagine ourselves into the future, perhaps at the end of life looking back on this moment.[53] What would we then wish we had done in this situation? Other imaginative strategies instruct us to act out scenarios, playing all the roles, in order to think about consequences and other potential side effects of different moral decisions.

When we observe our own thoughts, feelings, and actions as we would someone else's, we can spot the same subtle cues and clues that point to avoidance of painful truths and realities. All the ways by which we know when others are deceiving themselves can be used to monitor our own consciousness and behavior. We can be alert for discrepancies, inconsistencies, switches, forgettings, unusual reactions, and biases that serve our need for self-justification. Some people have learned that when they get highly indignant or upset over some other person's fault or shortcoming, they should be suspicious. Is this intense critical reaction because we too have this moral failing and can only avoid painful self-confrontation by flailing at the evil when it appears in another? Or are we distracting our attention from our own shortcoming by being particularly sensitive to a particular problem in another person?

When the temperature of moral indignation heats up, is it because objectively something is a more-serious moral problem, or because this moral failing is closer to home? One must test the idea, just as one might in another's case. It might happen that we have struggled and overcome some tendency and that is why we are so attuned to the failing in others. Self-help movements like Alcoholics Anonymous operate on the principle that someone who has experienced all the self-deceptive ploys available can most truly penetrate another's excuses and defensive denials. At any rate, conscious attention is drawn to more personally meaningful events. We know that lovers see traces of the beloved everywhere, the innocent see no evil, and wrongdoers see their own faults in others. Wise persons learn to go in and out, back and forth, relating their own subjective reactions to their reactions to others.

But if overcoming self-deception is so arduous and moral failure through ignorance is inevitable, how can we avoid despair. It seems so difficult to tell good guilt from neurotic guilt, or achieve assurance when we reach an inner truth. Can we ever be sure that we have gotten to the bottom of some strategic effort to avoid what we should be confronting. The good person or person with a "delicate conscience" is always alert to the fact that she or he may be failing, and be unaware of it. Deliver me from my secret sins, or the benighted state of self-deception. It does seem that one can never be infallible or absolutely certain in the effort to avoid self-deception; but it also seems possible to affirm that one can get better at moral self-discernment.

Many observers affirm that certain experiential signs indicate when one reaches the bedrock of a personal truth. When one penetrates beyond a self-deceptive strategy and admits something heretofore denied, one can feel a sense of release of energy and a sense of insight. Whatever wiles of rationalization or denial that it took to keep this bit of self-knowledge inoperative are now removed. Some counselors have spoken of the holistic felt sense of a shift within, a wholehearted "aha experience" of yes, this is really true—a sense that the scales fall from our eyes.

Long before psychotherapy, preconscious theories of information processing, and ego defense theory, Joseph Butler articulated this experience:

> Truth, and real good sense, and thorough integrity, carry along with
> them a peculiar consciousness of their own genuineness: there is a
> feeling belonging to them, which does not accompany their counter-
> feits, error, folly, half-honesty, partial and slight regards to virtue and
> right . . .[54]

We know that it is as easy to close the eyes of the mind as to close the eyes of the body. But keeping them closed or at least squint-eyed requires an uneasy effort. When we open our eyes and search for the truth within, we can encounter an inner sense of self-confirmation. The "real good sense" and thoroughness of our intuitive, moral integrity can then be tested over time and by other confirming patterns of evidence. Opening ourselves to truth and reality means a freer access to self-observation of behavior, thoughts, feelings, and the observation of others. But the sense of having done the best we can do in our examination of conscience does give a certain peace, authenticity, or wholeness. I think we recognize this wholeness and lack of self-deception in other morally developed persons, and we recognize it in ourselves. In the end, we must stand on our own moral integrity, for we have nothing else of comparable value upon which to stake our lives.

The ultimate strategy for avoiding moral failure is to be true to what we already know and understand. Each person is called to act in accord with his or her conscience. Each positive moral action, each step taken in accordance with conscience, will affect the next steps. We grow in virtue and moral strength through the self-initiated practice and exercise of following through on reflective moral decisions. With the smallest step, we move our position in the world, and a different orientation produces a new perspective. The smallest act can have large consequences. Moral perseverance produces hope and empowers the moral actor. When we act in conscience, we know ourselves as persons who make moral decisions. Moral confidence and competence grow little by little.

Spiritual masters, along with moral mentors, self-help programs, behaviorists, and other therapists, have always been enthusiastic over the step-by-step, active way to self-transformation. This has sometimes been known as the little way—one day at a time, or for the more dedicated or desperate, one moment at a time. The present moment is the best candidate for the transforming moment, for it alone is actually present to us to do something about. To pick up a pin, to refrain from one scornful word, to initiate one small moral act of integrity strengthens moral purpose. In a moral dilemma, the extra effort to find out new relevant facts or information that may lead to the best solution is an exercise of intellectual integrity. One micromove is never a small thing in moral decision making because inertia is potent and delay and procrastination abort action. As all evil seducers, brainwashers, and salespeople know, the smallest hook landed in the quarry can herald eventual victory—for either good or evil.

A new thought, a new feeling, a new moral action can be the first step in self-transformation and moral change for the better. A good conscience is like a stream of water flowing from the innermost heart of a person. Self-consciousness changes constantly. Moral optimists have affirmed that seeking the true and the good is liberating. The effort to become wise and good, truthful and wholehearted is a never-ending process, but the first phases and choices of moral development begin early in life.

Chapter 7

Moral Development: The Birth and Growth of Conscience

Moral development enables a person to make moral decisions. The more advanced one's moral development, the better chance there is for good moral decision making. By understanding this development process, we can better understand ourselves and others, and may be able to help engender moral competence.

The amount of theoretical and research material on moral development and moral education is overwhelming. I will extract the essentials from different approaches in order to forge integrated answers to central questions.

What Is Moral Development and How Can It Be Assessed?

Moral development is a term used to describe existing patterns and predispositions for a kind of self-conscious activity; but moral development can also refer to the past history of these active processes in an individual case. Is moral development, then, the same as conscience development? Yes, in the sense that moral development describes the potential or readiness for engaging in active moral decision making of conscience. I have defined and discussed conscience as self-conscious, integrated, and committed decision making on behalf of moral standards of worth; thus conscience development and moral development can be seen as roughly referring to the same reality.

A person with a highly developed conscience has certain characteristics. The more morally developed self is a self more and more consciously integrated, more and more capable of free self-direction, and more and more committed to the good and the right in personal acts. A morally developed person of good conscience can readily and easily activate and integrate her or his reasoning, intuition, imagination, and emotions, in order to effect good and right outcomes.

Over time, a developing self becomes more and more differentiated and more highly competent in many diverse capacities. The component functionings of self—such as reasoning, empathetic feeling, and creative imagining—increase, yet at the same time the self as moral agent becomes more and more capable of freely, and at will, exercising central hierarchical controls. We, at the center, can mobilize our part functions to produce complex but coherent moral decisions. The more highly developed a self, the more the self can become an autonomous, free agent oriented to the good.

What counts in moral development is how adequately our differentiated complexity of mind and heart can be holistically marshaled. We will deliberate, test, and retest in order to actively commit ourselves to the goods we value. When there is a high level of moral development, the self has many circuits and capacities to call upon, and the self as agent is equal to the task of integration. The highly developed moral agent is dedicated in wholehearted commitment to standards of worth beyond the self. Caring and emotional dedication to the good and the right increase. Thus, the compelling, overriding quality of moral obligation in a good conscience is attended to with a ready responsiveness.

In the desire to become morally better and continually grow, the person of good conscience is ready to evaluate and reevaluate his or her past and present moral functioning. Inevitably, the ongoing inner self-dialogue open to being tutored and tested will turn to trusted others. If we are serious about the moral quest, we will seek counsel and seriously attend to traditional sources of wisdom in the community. A person of highly developed conscience constantly seeks to be open to moral self-transformations, to be ready to respond to some moral truth and good not yet perceived.

In this dynamic view of moral development and growth of conscience, the process is as much one of constant personal conversion as it is a gaining of new information, moral knowledge, or moral reasoning skills. In developing a personal self who can make good moral decisions, everything counts. All dimensions of the self have to be changed in what is really a process of critical consciousness raising. The process of moral development is not like going through a course teaching statistics or electrical engineering. It is more like engaging in some lifelong, value-oriented educational psychotherapy, or like being in the novitiate of a religious order. Learning a set of moral rules, principles, or even sophisticated philosophical reasoning skills can only be a part of the process.

As we have seen over and over in the previous discussions of moral decision making and its failures, the subjective processing of thinking and motivation is all-important. A single act or external outcome can be a misleading clue to the whole inner process. Any single human act observed only from the outside may be the result of chance or some simple primitive reaction—such as a conditioned reflex, or in the case of spoken words, an uncomprehended formula from rote memory. As philosophers of social science explain personal acts, "We cannot explain an action till we know what action it is. We cannot know this unless we know how the agent views it. . . ."[1]

A child parroting words could respond to a moral challenge in the same way as a Zen master who has achieved the "gift to be simple." Only after a long struggle of self-discipline and philosophical meditation do some persons reach a "second naivete," in which they master a return to childlike simplicity of expression—which can be misunderstood. In the comic movie *Being There*, Peter Sellers played a retarded, misfit gardener whose simpleminded, literal answers appeared to be the morally profound gems of a wise guru—for a time.

Inner mental, moral, and personality processes are notoriously hard to assess without interacting with an individual for an extended period. And even then, it is hard. Unlike physical development and physiological functioning, which can be measured concretely, even recorded on film or with other probing diagnostic methods, moral development is invisible. A characteristic moral operation of self-consciousness can be manifested only in actions that must be interpreted. Admittedly, brain scans and new methods of producing computer images that map the operation of the brain can show activity in the appropriate brain areas (the frontal lobes?) to certify an alert, self-conscious, thinking, operating state. Films of the face and measurements of eye movements and micromuscular activation may reveal emotional configurations that may also be manifested in measures of physiological and biochemical responses. Behavior, including verbal behavior, also can be observed and recorded. But the inner stream of self-reflective consciousness and self-commitment of an agent's moral decision making and conscience is hidden.

Moreover, the concept of development, by itself, presents perplexing difficulties for assessment. Is development continuous and gradual, or does it progress unevenly by jumps in qualitative reorganizations of the mind? Or, as more likely, by both patterns of growth? Are there invariant stages of progress? The claim is made that we cannot understand "higher" moral reasoning unless we have moved in sequence through various preparatory stages. But then, are the developed capacities to be judged by the highest level of potential ever achieved, by what a person can do, or by what a person most often does?[2] Another provocative measure of moral development is by the lowest level of functioning a person may occasionally sink to. Perhaps we should measure by some average or range measure between highest and lowest benchmarks. The difficulty is deciding which displays of activity, in which environments and with whom, should count as evidence.

Assessing moral development shares in the general difficulties of all psychological efforts to assess human beings. There are long-standing scientific and intellectual debates over whether, or how, an observer can assess higher functions of persons, such as intelligence, personality, or mental health. The complexity, freedom, and flexibility of the self-reflecting human organism living in time, but with memories of the past and goals for the future, make any assessments of human consciousness fraught with problems. Human beings can deceive, lie, fail to cooperate through hostility, fear, or disinterest, or on the other hand, overcompensate to meet social demands when observed.

Assessment Tools and Methods

All sorts of assessment tools and methods have been used to try to get an accurate picture of a human person; they all have both advantages and disadvantages. Psychological testing has faced tremendous theoretical and pragmatic obstacles, as seen, for instance, in the current arguments over the validity of intelligence tests. Psychiatric diagnoses of mental dysfunction have been equally disputed. In the end, perhaps the structured clinical interview by a knowledgeable, well-functioning, unbiased, wise, and good expert (!) can be as successful as any other time-limited method of personal assessment.

Unfortunately, in moral development research, serious difficulties with disputed theories and research methodologies abound. Here, too, structured interviews, sometimes combined with lab and field observations of actual behavior, have been used. Asking people to make moral judgments, using questionnaires and interviews, and putting persons in controlled situations and observing the outcomes have all been employed in attempts to assess moral functioning. Often the basic problem, from the perspective of a holistic approach to moral development, is the narrowness of most theoretical definitions of morality that are employed as a guide to research.

Some researchers have stressed primarily the achievement of moral reasoning and moral judgments to the exclusion of developed emotional responses.[3] More behavioristically inclined investigators slight moral reasoning and focus upon behaviors, such as cheating, resistance to temptation, delay of gratification, altruism, and disobedience to rules.[4] Other researchers, in either interviews or laboratory or field studies, look for evidence of caring, emotional empathy, or interpersonal sensitivity to context.[5] Psychoanalytic researchers approach morality confined within the Freudian or neo-Freudian system of superego, ego, id conflicts, and defense mechanisms.[6] Those who see socialization and large cultural forces as the most important determinants of moral behavior look for cross-cultural differences in child rearing and different social constructions of moral rules.[7]

Obviously, despite the theoretical and empirical research and assessment difficulties of behavioral scientists, people in ordinary daily life continue to make interpersonal assessments and predictions about the moral development of other persons. However it is done, everyone has to make moral assessments simply to survive and function in a community. In countless situations, we must judge persons either as morally developed and reliable or as inadequate for any serious undertaking, or even to be avoided as dangerous. It may be that we use many of our intuitive, nonverbal skills and the interpersonal communication capacities of our social selves in this task. These social skills in person perception, however hard to consciously or verbally articulate, do filter and process interpersonal signals that help us in our intuitive readings of persons.

However, I maintain that in judging personality and moral character, we are quite sure that we are judging *something* that, although invisible to the human eye, exists. Some theorists have claimed that a consistent personality hardly exists, much less a distinctive moral character reflecting levels of moral development; for them, human behavior is really determined by the past history of conditioning and the different environmental variables operating in different socially scripted situations.[8] A particular environment, situation, or setting cues the different rules proscribed for different social roles, roles in scripts that we have previously learned from social conditioning. The individual is always predominantly shaped by the demands of the situation rather than by some consistency of traits, or inner self-regulation and character.

These theorists have lately been challenged by evidence of personality consistency over time and over varying situations.[9] Internal individual differences are accorded new weight in determining social outcomes. The social environment is a powerful influence on human beings, but the human individual also controls or shapes her or his own environment. At the very least, the individual can selectively attend to, or interpret, the environment. Thus in a return to "folk psychology" and common sense, the consensus grows that the individual's consistent configuration of patterned actions and reactions exists within persons. Given enough time, our assessments of persons and their moral character are shaped by who they are and the desires and beliefs that affect what they do.

Our judgments may be qualitative, holistic assessments, much like the assessments of experts judging musicians or seeding tennis players. It is not every note or every shot that counts, but the repeated performances produced over time add up to a whole that is greater than the sum of its parts. In tennis or music, a fairly close agreement among experts can be reached as to who is playing at what qualitative level of performance. Given enough time to observe, attentive fans can also tell when people are making progress and when they are falling off and declining. So too moral assessment becomes fairly reliable. Certainly at the extreme ends of the continuum, after death closes a life performance, it is fairly easy; we do not have much trouble ranking a Hitler or a Gandhi in their degree of moral development. In the middle range in the midst of an ongoing personal story, assessment is more difficult.

People who know better do stupid things, take "moral holidays," and experience regressions and lapses in the adequacy of their moral decision making. As discussed in the chapter on moral failure, it is difficult to know exactly what is happening, or why. Does a lapse from a generally high level of personal and moral functioning reveal hidden structural weaknesses of underlying immaturity or a basic lack of consolidated development? Does a lapse signal only the temporary interference of extreme stress or other factors that create temporary forms of self-deception? Or is such a failure a freely chosen act of wrongdoing counter to conscience, done in weakness or defiance?

Since the human self is free to choose over time and in changing circumstances, life stories or moral careers roll on. There will be unpredictable moral failures. More happily, there are also positive moral surprises. Criminals repent and reform their lives. Seemingly mediocre moral conformists grow into moral giants. War, concentration camps, civil-rights struggles, and revolutions provide some of the unusual stimuli for the most surprising moral changes. But most mysterious are the appearances "out of the blue" of moral monsters, or conversely of the Mozarts and

and Einsteins of moral development. One is forced to confront the nature of human nature: With the raw material available, is the effort to morally educate conscience in everyone, everywhere, worth the trouble?

Does Moral Development Arise from a Universal Human Nature?

Is the development of conscience a universal phenomenon, following certain common patterns? Pragmatically, the effort to further moral education for all is supported by the belief that there are universal, deep structures undergirding human moral development. If there is an innate human nature that gives rise to common social realities, then there is more hope for rational convergence and moral consensus about attempts to develop moral competence. A struggle to hammer out concrete agreements about moral education will not seem doomed to failure if we are convinced that we have common moral equipment. When there is despair over the possibility of achieving moral and rational consensus, the temptation is to retreat to familial or sectarian enclaves. At best, one can only draw up the protective walls and cultivate one's moral garden with one's own kind.

The news is good for those who assert an innately programmed, species-specific universal human nature predisposed to moral competence—as well as to certain moral failings. There is evidence that persons and self-consciousness exist in all cultures, that innate human intelligence and reasoning powers exist everywhere, and that innate emotional programs are everywhere the same.[10] These aspects of human nature predispose the human being to moral decision making always and everywhere. As new infant studies reveal, by the age of two, children in every culture are beginning to evaluate behavior according to standards of achievement and moral goodness. A noted child psychologist, Jerome Kagan, has stated: "Humans are driven to invent moral criteria, as newly hatched turtles move toward water and moths toward light."[11]

Evidence from many sources reveals that questions of conscience appear in all places and times that have been recorded; an inner sense of right and wrong comes with the birth of the self and self-consciousness. And the social experience of humans, the most social of all animals, leads to further common experiences. These experiences arise from innate species-specific human emotions and reasoning powers. We have discussed the cross-cultural importance of emotions and seen how all the emotions are involved in conscience—love, guilt, shame, anger, contempt, and so on.[12] Here again, Kagan's testimony is powerful. In his acclaimed book on the nature of the child, he goes so far as to defend the idea of a universal morality built upon universal human experiences of emotions.

Kagan states his refutation of cross-cultural moral relativism in strong words:

> I believe, however, that, beneath the extraordinary variety in surface behavior and consciously articulated ideals, there is a set of emotional states that form the bases for a limited number of universal moral categories that transcend time and locality.[13]

In other words, the preprogrammed human organism will achieve certain outcomes in different social environments. If, as the saying goes, you cut off someone's nose, that person's child will still be born with a nose. Some constancies of conscience and moral development may be inevitable in every culture.

Certain moral-development researchers have come to the same conclusion. Today in cross-cultural work in moral development, much moral consensus does appear. One of the foremost cognitivist, developmentalist researchers, James Rest, concludes, "We find the similarities between cultures much more striking than the differences between them."[14] Such similarities occur, he claims, because despite different surface characteristics, "there are certain basic conceptions and categories in the social world that are common throughout various cultures." The fundamental conceptions that structure human understanding of the social world are

> awareness of individual differences in social power and capacity; awareness that each self has an internal consciousness, along with his/her own point of view, desires, interests; awareness of human relationships of affection, loyalty, mutual caring; awareness of group expectations and norms, social roles, customs and laws.[15]

Researchers find similarities in developmental stages of moral reasoning in all the cultures they study, from the United States to Taiwan to Tibet.[16] It seems reasonable to suppose that rational, emotionally bonding individuals could construct similar moral responses adaptive for the common human organism and common human condition. Everywhere there is a similarly structured physical world of space, volume, weight, density, time, and cause and effect, and a similarly structured psychosocial interpersonal world in which persons must function if they are going to survive and flourish. Certain basic moral understandings should be similar in all long-term surviving human groups. Since certain modern Western cultural ideas are also spreading with the spread of modern industrialization and communication media, it is even less surprising that there are constancies in moral development.

There are further encouragements to accepting panhuman characteristics arising from new studies of mind and intelligence. A strong case can be made that the human species comes with a brain preprogrammed to be an abstract-thinking, rule-following organism. Deep structures of rational functioning programmed in the brain may account for the spectacular feats of learning seen in infants everywhere. The readiness to learn the rules of language is matched by the readiness to master social rules and a moral rule system. Implicit language learning through immersion in a community may perhaps serve as the best analogy for moral learning. Infants respond to the rhythms of human language from birth and can tell when there are discrepancies between the words spoken and the lips they are watching. Complex language rules are learned inductively through immersion in the interactions within a family. Similar processes probably produce a child's early sense of rules and standards through which guilt and shame can be felt.

The general theoretical acceptance of common models of mind and innate intelligence by cognitive psychologists supports the idea of a panhuman rational human nature. Howard Gardner, a noted chronicler of the new growth of cognitive science, speaks of "the universal mind."[17] Gardner thinks there are different innate modes of innate intelligence, or "frames of mind," which appear in all cultures. The existence of these intelligences is supported by evidence from brain science, empirical findings of core operations, developmental histories, similar end performances, and evolutionary plausibility.[18]

The multiple intelligences that appear constantly and crossculturally in his model are linguistic, musical, logical-mathematical, spatial, bodily-kinesthetic, and the personal intelligences. The last two of his modes of universally appearing intelligence are an intrapersonal sense of self, or "access to one's own feeling life,"[19] which is necessarily related to an interpersonal intelligence, and the "ability to notice and make distinctions among other individuals, in particular among their moods, temperaments, motivations and intentions."[20]

These personal intelligences, developed together, appear everywhere and always, and some persons in every culture develop an extraordinary ability to socially interact and guide others, and become apt in reading and managing the inner life of the self. Gardner does not indicate that these forms of personal intelligences are relevant to morality. (In fact, Gardner has no listing for "morality" in his index.) But in their descriptions, the personal intelligences sound like prerequisite components for moral development. As we have seen previously, similar universal characteristics make their appearance in the psychology of the self. These personal intelligences, when conjoined with linguistic and logical intelligence, would provide the necessary universal capacities for moral decision making.

It would appear that in order to synthesize and apply such intelligences, or care enough to do so, persons would have to possess not only a developed sense of self, but also a developed sense of self-agency operating with highly developed emotional commitments to moral ideals and standards. Having the complexes of crucial intelligences function together coherently is important. To achieve such integration there must be an agent director of the personal stream of consciousness, free to engage in committing the whole self in moral decision making. While Gardner ignores the concept of the self as free, self-directing agent, an important achievement of his work is his magisterial mustering of the evidence to support cross-cultural constancies in human nature.

It is interesting to consider Gardner's ideas as an example of how the evolutionary thinking that started with Darwin is developing theories of a brain selected for self-consciousness and rational thinking. One theory is that if the universe runs by mathematical laws, then through the eons of development, the human species will have had mathematical ability imprinted upon the human brain with advantageous results in selection and survival. If human survival is served by intelligent self-consciousness, then self-conscious rationality will be selected for, and appear in, all members of the human species.

Others, who are biologically oriented, like the sociobiologists, have also insisted upon species-specific behavior, but usually discounted rationality in favor of nonconsciously genetically programmed behaviors aimed at successful mating and reproduction.[21] In their views of universal human nature, dominance, aggression, competition, and indeed bonding and altruism are built-in methods to get more of the organism's genes selected for the next generation. If what we now call morality constantly appears, it is not because of the mind's free exercise of intelligence and commitment to values, but because certain behaviors serve evolutionary, selective processes. Bonding behavior is not chosen because it is good, but because it is adaptive for survival and consequently becomes built in through the genes.

In the sociobiological perspective, there are positive species characteristics predisposing to "moral behavior." An innate altruism exists that propels individuals to protect and give their lives for their offspring and the group—and thereby get their own and their relatives' genes into the next generation. Parental altruism is also a case of innately programmed behavior that has direct selective value. Humans share with their fellow primates high investments of maternal and parental nurturing and care for offspring. In humans, with their large-brained abilities to be aware of kinship ties, affective bonding with one's family and group produces an investment that sets the stage for the development of cooperative norms and moral rules.

The universal negative predispositions that come with species membership and create universal social challenges include dominance struggles, aggression, competition for resources, and a tendency toward self-deception.[22] The claim that human self-deception has selective advantages may be moot, but is explained on the grounds that if human beings, otherwise socially pressured to cooperate, can deceive themselves about the selfish acts they are actually performing, they can then, with more energy and conviction, garner more resources and gain a reproductive advantage for offspring. Overall, sociobiology emphasizes the recognition of humans as a common species with universal species-specific characteristics, but denigrates the idea of self-conscious rational agency or allegiance to moral standards. The unconscious drives of the "selfish genes" are really the most important underlying realities.

Psychoanalytic thinkers, in all their different existing variations from orthodox to revisionary self theorists, have also posited universal mechanisms of human development that arise out of the matrix of the inherited unconscious and preconscious affective transactions necessary between infants and caretakers. Here too, common universal patterns are claimed predisposing to both positive and selfish behaviors—from universal, unconscious life and death instincts to the conflicts between sex, aggression, and a superego. Humanity is species programmed through the inherited operations of the instincts, the reproductive matrix, and the operations of the dynamic conflicts of the unconscious and conscious ego.

Indeed, Jungians and others, in a field of psychology that is labeled "transpersonal psychology," go further and actually claim the existence of a collective unconscious. All individual humans are deeply interconnected through their common participation in the collective unconscious. The collective unconscious is manifested in dynamic, unconscious "archetypes," which undergird the universal patterns of human individual development, complete with positive growth tendencies to good developments and corresponding tendencies to evil or the shadow of each individual. In its most developed forms, transpersonal psychology has affirmed much of the worldview and perspectives on the self found in Buddhism and other eastern religions.[23] But here too, in the emphasis upon deep unconscious forces and contrast schemas alternating in transfers of energies, the individual's self-conscious rational moral agency has been given less of a role. In systems in which the play of unconscious dynamic energies, or the play of genetic selective forces, are emphasized, individual moral self-direction and moral agency are seen more as surface phenomena.

Western developmental psychologists are more ready to countenance the development of human intelligence and self-directing agency, but they have also been interested in exploring species-specific patterns and common stages of physical and mental growth. They claim universal cross-cultural constancies in patterns of mental and psychological growth over the life span, which have repercussions for theories of moral development. Some life-span developmental psychologists claim universal patterns throughout the passages or stages of a life, even, following the lead of Erik Erikson, into old age and a final search for integrity.[24] Just as child psychologists pioneered the exploration of cross-cultural consistencies in early development, so life-span developmental psychologists think they discern cross-cultural constancies in the passages through the seasons of each individual life.

Whatever our estimate of each of these different approaches to human nature, it is significant that evidence from so many sources supports the existence of universal capacities, characteristics, and patterns of human development. While constancies of developing rationality and emotion have been discerned, perhaps the turn to a belief in innate, preprogrammed, cognitive capacities of human brains for rational thinking has been most influential in recent theories of moral development. Following psychology's cognitive revolution, the realization of the innately patterned power of the brain and intelligence had a bracing effect on those affirming the reality of moral reasoning.

Those who have been tempted to consign morality to the realm of illusion, like the psychoanalyst who confidently asserts "morality is dead," have a new problem.[25] When such true believers in deep unconscious forces proclaim that science has confirmed the demise of moral reasoning, they ignore scientific evidence of cognitive processes. While factors other than reason are important in moral development, the development of reasoning can never be underestimated. Some of the most important recent explorations of moral development have focused upon moral reasoning.

The Role of Reason in Moral Development

Making moral decisions of conscience is partially a form of problem solving, and intelligent reasoning counts. The psychological approach to moral development that most emphasizes cognitive and intellectual development was inspired by the work of the great cognitive psychologist Piaget and developed by the late Lawrence Kohlberg. This cognitive developmental approach has gathered many adherents, who have produced a great quantity of psychological research.[26] Within this group, there are many ongoing arguments and revisionist turns, but the basic approach is convincing in its appeal. The obvious question that emerges from any observation of human beings is, Why can most adults function more adequately than most children in moral decision making? And some adults do better than others. What makes the difference? If we want to encourage better moral functioning, what do we do? The claim of the cognitive developmental approach is that better moral reasoning and moral judgments are built upon reasoning ability tutored by social experience.

Obviously, intelligence and a certain level of rational competence are necessary to master a body of moral knowledge and traditional rules and principles with which each culture instructs its young. As children develop the mental capacities of memory, focused attention, and information processing, they can learn and remember the moral knowledge they are given. Learning the prescribed moral rules takes a certain amount of mental development, as well as time spent in informal learning or in formal, applied efforts.

The more complicated the system, the more time it takes simply to become familiar with the information and extent of knowledge. One thinks of students gradually mastering language and facts of world history, of yeshiva students studying traditional texts and law. A certain development of memory and the ability to think abstractly and handle concepts would be necessary in order to begin to master a complicated body of moral knowledge. But according to the cognitive developmental approach to moral development, simply having moral information or knowledge would never be enough to make adequate moral decisions.

The greatest strength of the cognitive developmental approach to moral development is the understanding that an individual does not learn to think by passively committing information to memory, but by actively manipulating and performing mental operations in order to solve new problems. In thinking through a problem, an individual has to be able to initiate, use, and appropriately apply mental strategies or operations. It is necessary to focus attention for extended periods of time and yet also to be mentally flexible enough to go backward and forward in time and imagine the problem from different perspectives. As was said earlier, being able to think is "the capacity to have vicarious subjective experience."

An ability to imagine the experiences of others is necessary in moral problem solving as well. To think at a high level, one has to be able to take the elements of puzzles apart and put them back together in meaningful, new wholes. If one cannot think flexibly then one cannot meet new contingencies in the environment with new solutions. Active use of mental structures and active mental operations ensure that there is a reason for what one is doing to solve the problem, not just random guessing made in hopes of a correct answer. As Lawrence Kohlberg and Anne Colby have recently written:

> The concept of structure implies that a consistent logic or form of reasoning can be abstracted from the content of an individual's responses to a variety of situations. It implies that moral development may be defined in terms of the qualitative reorganization of the individual's pattern of thought rather than in the learning of new content. Each new reorganization integrates within a broader perspective the insights that were achieved at lower stages.[27]

Important to the cognitive developmentalist approach is the conviction that progress in thinking and moral development must go through invariant stages. New operations are built upon mastery of previous capacities. These stages are necessarily the same for any individual. One can go through them more quickly, but they cannot be skipped. At the highest stages of abstract thinking, mental operations can be employed hypothetically, without touching, seeing, or actively manipulating the elements of a problem. One can imagine taking different perspectives on a problem; there is an ability to focus attention, shift attention at will, and remember and apply specific information and rules to integrate the pieces into an ordered, larger whole. A child with a photographic memory, or an idiot savant, could memorize all the moral rules and principles of a culture, but still not be able to use them to make an adequate moral judgment. Applying principles appropriately to a new question is a complex rational operation requiring judgments of when it is important to do which operation to get a solution.

Why in this system does an individual develop better moral judgments and move to higher and higher competences in taking different perspectives and employing different operations? What causes the development in moral development? Basically, it is the experiencing of conflict and puzzling discrepancies between one's own development and others, especially others with higher levels of moral development. In the cognitive approach, one develops morally by new engagements in social experiences that activate and then challenge one's old ways of moral decision making. Perceived discrepancies between one's own and others' points of view and different judgments stimulate the search for a better, higher, more adequate and inclusive level of reasoning. While there is some innate inner human impetus to prefer higher and better moral judgments, the process of development is initiated and founded upon social experience. Social give-and-take induces the individual to take the role and perspectives of others and so have more facets of a problem to be integrated in a solution.

As reasoning grows more competent, a person can hold more things in mind, compare them for logical inconsistencies, evaluate and reevaluate the application of rules and principles to specifics. The achievement of abstract reasoning brings an ability for hypothetical thinking and systematic testing of different options and solutions. Finally, a person who can assume a universal perspective by taking all pertinent role perspectives into account will reason at the highest levels of moral complexity. Kohlberg proposed his famous stage theories in which one moves from completely autistic, selfish amorality to a conventional morality of law and order, to the highest stages of complex role taking and considerations of universal values.

It takes a certain level of rational moral development and ability to assume another's point of view, even to interpret a situation one observes as morally problematic.[28] Cognitive developmentalists assess rational and moral maturity by the moral sensitivity and quality of the individual's interpretation of what is at stake in an observed situation. *Not seeing* a dilemma, or not noticing anything morally relevant in a morally problematic situation, is as indicative as other outward signs of moral immaturity or moral tone deafness.

When some moral problem is discerned, the way the self-self inner reasoning and dialogue proceeds provides the evidence for a qualitative assessment of moral development. Is there only a crude consideration, limited to what the individual self gains, only a goal of efficiency, or only some consideration of what will ensure external order and conformity to convention? On the other hand, in higher-stage moral thinking, there is a more subtle psychological inner dialogue that takes into account motives, different perspectives, different interests, different moral principles, and the long-term consequences for self and society.

I agree that in moral development there is a qualitative change in reasoning and more-inclusive and better strategies of mental operations. These procedures of moral thinking can develop as intelligence develops, and moral reasoning can be induced in others by the right kind of moral knowledge and provision of interpersonal experiences. Inducing subjective engagement and mental activity on the part of the one being educated is the key. Opportunities have to be given to master moral knowledge, but then there must be opportunity to actively engage in moral thinking.

High-quality inner dialogues within the stream of consciousness partly emerge from having experienced interpersonal dialogues with others— either personally or in other ways, such as through literature. Whether in structured schooling, in the family, among peers, in other group settings, or in worship, art, and literature, the quality of the moral dialogues attended to induces the repetition of an inner replay when one is "alone with one's self," as we ambiguously put it.[29] Vicariously experiencing how others actively reason together, meet moral conflicts, and solve moral problems morally prepares individuals to do it on their own.

In moral decision making, however, more goes on than active moral reasoning and problem solving. Why will one care about the different perspectives that one can rationally judge may be necessary for a just and moral solution? What will bring about the self-commitment to moral action at the end of the reasoning process? Those who support the cognitive approach seem to believe that the force of rationality alone will do all the work.[30] Others, including myself, think that other operations are necessary for moral development. The cognitive developmentalist approach to moral development is just one part of a more complex, more fully dimensioned story.

The Roles of Emotion, Early Experience, and Gender in Moral Development

Emotion and Moral Development

If we are not interested or do not care about finding the best solution, if we do not feel committed to being good, why persevere in moral reasoning? Emotional investment energizes the moral quest, and emotions initiate and shape moral deliberation. Emotions influence the thinking processes and are used to test final outcomes as well as the other way round. Emotions fused with ideas and moral scenarios and narratives are integral to moral knowledge, which constitutes the content of moral deliberation.

Both negative and positive emotions are important in the operations of conscience. Fear, guilt, anxiety, contempt, and shame become associated with certain forbidden behaviors. Even the thought of forbidden behavior can produce anxiety. The positive feeling gained from relief of anxiety upon doing the right thing and resisting the forbidden temptation reinforces socialized conduct. Negative emotions, like anger or contempt, produced by the behavior of others also play a part in moral decision making. But there is much more than these negative emotive factors to moral development.

New research on the role of empathy and the development of sympathy shows how important this innate human feeling is in moral development.[31] An infant is innately equipped to feel as others feel in instinctive empathetic reactions, which are almost a form of emotional contagion. Empathy is a direct experience of another's experience. As reason develops a better ability to interpret a situation, empathy can exist, but so can sympathy—a feeling for another who is recognized and cognitively known as a person different from the self. Certain kinds of discipline that a parent uses with a child can encourage and induce empathy and sympathy for those transgressed against.[32]

It may also be the case that the affective system develops in a semi-independent way and can actually sense things in a preconscious, nonverbal way. The old difference between knowing *how* to do something and consciously knowing *that* one is *doing* it becomes an issue in emotion's role in moral development. It may be that small children can act morally, or be taught moral habits, before full cognitive self-consciousness of what they are doing has been grasped, or fully articulated. In Norma Haan's work with small children, she has observed in four-year-olds surprising moral sensitivities to the wishes and needs of other children. They displayed abilities "to adjust their conduct and comments" so that "they showed an incidence of moral concern that was not radically different from that of the university students."[33] Such high levels of moral conduct would not be predicted in cognitive developmental approaches, which presume amoral selfishness or general moral incapacity until the later development of the prerequisite cognitive reasoning skills. Certain moral capacities may begin much earlier than supposed, although children cannot yet reason abstractly about what they do or why they do it.[34]

However, in the empathy research, it appears that with the development of higher reasoning and imaginative powers, with more-abstract thinking skills, a young person can compare her or his own fortunate state with the conditions of others who suffer. When persons can feel empathy and sympathy for the suffering of others, and realize their own good luck, through no act of merit, they can experience what has been called "existential guilt," "nonmoral guilt," or "survivor's guilt."[35] This emotional response to the unjust fate of individuals in the world can motivate altruism, and moral development. These feelings initiate acts of altruism, acts of reparation, and efforts to work for distributive justice to repair the unjust discrepancies of fate. The experience of emotion is a motivating force in initiating growth from one moral position, of autistic complacency, to another more-universal perspective.

Emotion makes one care enough to want to commit oneself to do something about the intellectual realizations that arise from cognitive conflicts and discrepancies. Emotions of interest in, and desire for, truth can make one stay open to dialogues, just as empathy facilitates taking the cognitive role of another; on the other hand selfish, fearful, defensive emotions, or a desire to dominate and control, can cut off a dialogue and curtail the new social experiences that might lead to further moral development. Once the "heart is hardened"—the self sets up emotional barricades to outside influence—the mind's eye can become blinded to new perspectives. Then all processes of growth can be suspended; nothing new can break through into the self-system.

Positive emotions in the primary affective system can often spur on self-transformations, overcoming stasis. Feelings of love, gratitude, admiration, and attachment to good persons create a desire to emulate and identify with those one loves. Attention is drawn to what one loves, so the effectiveness of the example, moral instruction, or moral discipline given by a beloved parent or admired mentor is magnified, while the messages of those in authority to whom one is hostile or indifferent are tuned out, ignored, or rejected because of their sources.

While fear, anxiety, and hate contract and paralyze the mind, positive emotions like joy and wonder induce the security, self-confidence, and playful freedom to take risks and think creatively. Love casts out fear and gives an individual the motivation to become more caring and attentive to moral perspectives—even moral perspectives that may involve greater efforts and sacrifice.

As the cognitive discrepancies between ourselves and others that emerge in moral dialogues challenge us to think anew, so emotional discrepancies between ourselves and others can nudge or even jolt us. If we differ from a beloved mentor, or an admired peer, in moral feelings, we can be stimulated to emulation, which can result in moral growth. Unfortunately, disillusionment or betrayal through the immoral behavior of those we love can have negative effects of moral regression.

The affective components of our social relationships become entwined with our moral thinking and moral worldviews.

More indirectly, other positive affective experiences may also have a stimulating role in our personal moral histories. A person can seek to grow morally and seek what the Shakers called "come up higher gifts" because of certain intense positive emotional experiences. Psychologists have called certain positive emotional states of altered consciousness "peak experiences."[36] These naturally occurring experiences of love, happiness, and trust in the reality of goodness in the world have been more noted in literature and religion, but given less attention in the psychology of moral development.

In literary criticism, such transforming moments have been named "epiphanies," following James Joyce. These near-mystical states of joyful oneness and affirmation of the goodness of the universe have also, naturally, played a large part in religious experience. Such intense, mystical moments are often described as confidence in "amazing grace," or "the heart burning within"; they are bouts of deep joy and basic trust in the reality of goodness. We can become transported into positive emotional states. As emotions, they obey the law of emotions and bestow a sense of energizing reality to the individual's moral quest. As acute emotions, they also fade quickly from consciousness, although not from memory.

Such near-ecstastic states have also been analyzed as quasi-pathological, either as regressions to infantile omnipotence and oceanic feelings, or as mild forms of a manic illness defending against depression. But summary dismissals of the emotional experiences of being "surprised by joy" are deficient. Poets and artists have always testified that such peak experiences are remembered as "emotion recollected in tranquillity," and serve as inspiration and validation of ongoing moral efforts to pursue the good, the true, the beautiful. The combination of the primary emotions of joy and surprise induces a sense of wonder that is fundamental to a quest for self-transformation. It is more sobering to consider whether sad and mysterious moments of nausea and emptiness, which like "tears idle tears" seem to rise "from the depth of some divine despair," have their negative moral effects.

In an important way, moral development and moral decision making are entwined with the positive and negative emotional course of individual developmental histories. Moral education, like all education, parenting, and psychotherapy, works most effectively through the positive emotions of love and admiration induced in the recipient. One must aspire before one can experience failure, loss, and guilt. Love and liking focus joyful interest and attention. One internalizes, identifies with, or desires to be like or conjoined with beloved parents, therapists, teachers, heroes, admired peers, and lovers. They become living models, embodying moral standards of worth. Good is personified, not just verbalized as a principle of beneficence.

Other persons can depress, discourage, and diminish our moral functioning by their betrayals and negative or cruel responses. It appears from many sad case histories that persons can also identify with their aggressors and tormentors. They internalize their abusers and then possess in their memories self-punitive critics and cruel inner dialogues; negative, morally despairing perspectives on self and the world can be assimilated. Fatalism, paralysis, and neurotic guilt are certainly not unknown; abused and cruelly treated children can display negative emotions toward self and others, which produce warped moral ideas and behavior.[37]

Early Experience and Moral Development

The challenge for those who take an integrated, holistic approach to moral development—giving full weight to moral agency of thought, feeling, and behavior—is to understand how reasoning and emotive factors interact in the developmental histories of the individual selves who become moral agents.[38] In order of appearance as influences, first there is an individual's genetic biological inheritance, then early nurturing. Our earliest beginnings interact with all the later environmental, socioemotional, cognitive experiences in the drama of conscience development.

The most unknown factor, and least investigated, is an understanding of how the self as free moral agent emerges and proceeds to select, attend, and assume ownership of all the different aspects and functioning of consciousness.[39] As investigators of the developing self as agent know, a child's sense of agency develops over time. From an early age, people actively struggle "by choice, against the constraints of their physical attributes, material conditions, limited abilities or current beliefs."[40]

The existence of a developing free self as agent means that all abused children do not automatically grow up to become child abusers; indeed, some children's ability to overcome dreadful beginnings has produced a category called "invulnerable children." On the other hand, well-nurtured children collapse in various ways—including moral failure. The external nurturing conditions, favorable or unfavorable, do not determine the whole story. As Socrates noted long ago, if loving and caring fathers of high virtue and wealth could not produce virtue in their sons through example and all the tutoring money could buy, something other than external influences must exist. In moral development, there must be a personal self-commitment to becoming good.

There are dimensions and components of the self that may be predisposed by nature and nurturing to develop in different degrees and patterns, but the individual self also has self-regulating power to exercise freedom and selection. Many, many microdecisions accumulate and build up memories and a pattern of predispositions and habits. But there are also factors that operate before a self-conscious deciding self can have evolved. At the very beginning of life, it seems clear that something like the genetic luck of the draw makes an all-important difference. Next the intrauterine environment of the developing organism also partially determines the basic equipment one starts with. Inherited temperament as well as inherited brain powers affect moral development.

Brain damage, disease, deprivation, and excessive abuse can mar a child's average, expectable environment and stifle or stunt development from the very beginning. There are critical periods when certain developments must take place or the damage is irreversible. Physically torture and tie up a child in a closet for years and even speech may never develop normally. But most children are reared within the normal range of the average, expectable environment. Within this average range of treatment, the genetic throw can still make a difference. The power of biological inheritance means that a variety of inherited differences plays a large part in developmental outcomes.[41] Inherited temperament can explain some of the variations in the success of an environment's conditioning and moral socialization.

If the positive emotions and negative emotions are independently based in different parts of the brain, individuals may inherit different predispositions for positive or negative emotional activation. Some children seem to inherit predispositions to shyness and timidity, or to a reflective cautious style.[42] Other children are more aggressive, extroverted, and impulsive. When children are observed in free-ranging, ethological style on the nursery-school playground as though they were small chimpanzees, it appears that some children already have social skills and abilities to get along and avoid conflicts while others do not.

Temperamental differences are revealed in the readiness or thresholds necessary for different stimuli to produce different emotions or social engagement. Highly negative, irritable, "difficult to rear" infants have been differentiated from babies with more positively toned, equable, and "easy to rear" temperaments. Some children will not be easily conditioned to avoid pain or to react with anxiety to danger or disapproval. Some observers have claimed that children's delinquency or conduct disorders are a result of inherited hyperactivity, aggressiveness, and temperamental insensitivities to socializing influence. Lacking a readiness to emotionally respond like other children do, it is harder for these children to learn the moral rules or develop moral responses and moral sensibilities. The more aggressive and active a child's innate temperament, the more it may interfere or conflict with the innate human propensity for empathy. It seems that from birth, some human beings will find it harder to be good.

To make it more complicated, each infant's inherited physiological and emotional temperament must interact with parental nurturing, expectations, and the social environment. Nurturing difficulties can arise from the misreading, misinterpreting, or mismatching of temperaments. As Daniel Stern, an infant researcher who studies the growth of the different levels of self, has shown, there are subtle microinteractions between infants and their parents and caretakers that can affect developmental outcomes.[43] Infants seem to be active participants in these transactions, but their part in the partnership can hardly as yet be the self-conscious strategy of a free moral agent.

Therefore, by the time a child can begin to be a self-conscious free moral agent, much has already taken place in a developmental process. Caretakers and a community culture have already taught, or neglected to transmit, or partially perverted through abuse the child's acquisitions of moral rules, moral outlooks, moral feelings, and moral habits of behavior. Selves come into full moral consciousness with personalities already having been partially formed by genes and earlier experiences, but these beginnings are lost behind the iron curtain imposed by amnesias in regard to one's infancy. When one looks at home movies of one's self as a baby, it becomes clear that a unique personality has already emerged—before any self-conscious awareness or self-direction that is accessible to present consciousness.

It is a universal human experience to come to mature self-consciousness and moral agency without memory or understanding of the past, or any conscious connection with the earlier conditions that have already shaped the rudiments of a personality never fully chosen. I think that this universal experience has produced ideas of karma, a fall from paradise, the existence of original sin, individual predestination, and reincarnation. Somehow, our developmental destinies and personal life courses are correctly perceived as having been given energy and force *before* we as free, conscious agents could direct them. Certainly it is an ancient lament that throughout life we remain somehow wounded and unable to freely do that which we would, or keep from doing that which we would not.

Skeptics about moral agency claim that children's inability to shape or choose their moral character in the face of internal and external pressures is the real human condition until death arrives as the final victory of fate over freedom. Those who agree with my perspective claim that in normal circumstances, moral self-consciousness, self-direction, and self-reorganizations, even of one's own difficult temperament, can start early and through repeated decisions gradually assume more and more control. Yes, it is important to emphasize the enormous influence of genes and early nurturing from caretakers, but at the same time, we must stress the reality of a human being's innately programmed ability to self-consciously and freely focus attention, and so make free choices. As more and more free acts are chosen, freedom and coherent character increase.

Reasoning, emotions, and behavior can be shaped by free, intentional acts. The preconscious and nonconscious encoding in long-term memory does begin from birth and is influenced by the earliest interpersonal experiences, but normal, nonimpaired individuals in average, expectable environments have freedom and flexibility to be the constructors of their own characters. According to Gordon Allport, activities that may have once been initiated by external pressures can later be freely appropriated for their intrinsic worth; these activities gain "functional autonomy."[44] Moral habits and moral thinking that may have been imposed by convention or conditioning can become appropriated and transformed into the free self-direction of conscience. The "musts" imposed from without can become my sense of "ought" in free generic moral self-guidance. In moral analysis, as in any other, it is a genetic fallacy to think that one has explained a present characteristic by tracing its historical beginnings.

If the human organism is always engaged in a dynamic process of becoming, it may be that the innate biological programs may have less and less influence after adolescence and the final maturing of the body and brain. If positive moral development takes place in the adult stages of life, it is even more freely initiated. Persons can also choose to stagnate, regress, and deteriorate. Life-span developmental progress toward moral integrity in old age is not automatic but emerges from self-conscious effort. One becomes more and more one's self only through free exercises of moral decision making.

However, it is difficult to correct overly deterministic or pessimistic views without falling into various forms of overoptimism or exaggeration.

Some theorists of moral development have overestimated the positive moral effects of good maternal nurturing while exaggerating the importance of female gender as a positive factor in moral decision making. In an effort to correct patriarchical bias and earlier Freudian orthodoxies, exaggerated claims are made. It is easy to see that the reigning Freudian picture of early development was skewed in regard to women and mothers in particular.

New interest in the birth of the unique self in different schools of psychology has produced a convergence of opinion: early infant experience and the earliest nurturing by the mothering one is much more important than Freud granted. As one psychoanalytic writer says, "Freud was not very interested in mothers."[45] Whether this was the result of his own repression or the male orientation of his culture, or both, his general lack of interest in mothering led him into all sorts of misreadings of both female development and the development of the self and morality. I agree with those who conclude that Freud's misreading of early moral experience was based on his underestimation of positive emotions, the self, and infant experiences with the mother. But one can go too far in the corrective effort.

One psychoanalytic observer, Eli Sagan, has written a book giving his revised version of moral development.[46] He still thinks the superego develops more or less as Freud envisioned, at around four years of age, but the earlier or pre-Oedipal infant's development of what he calls conscience is deemed much more important. Sagan contrasts conscience—defined simply as nurturing love—with the "corrupt superego" that results from later identification with the punitive socializers who enforce conformity to the cultural status quo. Conscience, or love, is an infallible guide, while the superego can lead to evil acts.

As Sagan says, in giving the core of his argument:

> In summary, the capacity to identify with both the nurturer and the victim is essential to both conscience and a healthy psyche. This conclusion never could have been reached by a psychoanalytic theory restricted to oedipal and post-oedipal life. The fundamental weakness in Freud's theory of morality and the superego is that it ignores the pre-oedipal life of the child.[47]

I would think the fundamental weakness of Sagan's argument to be his proclamation by fiat that the conscience is unconscious and, because formed by loving maternal nurture, automatically infallible. Like many psychoanalytic revisionists, he still maintains an underestimation of reasoning and rational moral judgements in morality. All inadequate moral action is blamed on the cruel conventional superego, while the more primeval positive conscience, acquired by identification with nurturing, is accorded infallibility and automatic trustworthiness.[48] But how in adulthood are the different sorts of inner guidance—superego or conscience—to be distinguished in the inner stream of consciousness? And why should we trust that conscience, equated here solely with a feeling of love, is infallible if we do not test it by moral reasoning?

Despite the flaws of Sagan's approach, we can appreciate his emphasis upon the importance of love, empathy, and idealization in moral development and his focus upon the importance of a strong sense of self developed by early nurturing. It is encouraging to see that the rehabilitation of emotions is making progress in psychoanalytic discussions of moral functioning. It is also important to emphasize that early experience and the development of the self sets the stage for moral action. But the picture of the earliest self and nurturing must include the intercorrelated development of programmed conscious reasoning and rational development that other infant researchers emphasize. Neither human emotions nor reasoning can be slighted in the growth of conscience. More importantly, both early preconscious experience and later freely chosen conscious reorganizations and self-directives are important.

Gender and Moral Development

A new interest in positive emotions of love and care, combined with a resurgence of interest in women and early nurturing, has also informed some feminist approaches to moral development. Unfortunately, here too some exaggerated claims have been made for the importance of gender and the automatic effects of early nurturing. The most famous exponent of the feminist critique of Kohlberg's over rationalist approach is found in Carol Gilligan's book *In a Different Voice*.[49] This was followed by another popular book called *Womens' Ways of Knowing*.[50] Then there appeared a veritable flood of articles and books devoted to the theme of women's distinctive moral ways of functioning.[51]

The major claim is made that men and women make moral decisions in different ways or in a different voice. Men are considered to be more linear, abstract reasoners in their advocacy of principled justice and rules. The cognitive developmental approach of Kohlberg and company has been considered to be biased in its masculine cast toward stages of increasingly abstract reasoning. By contrast, women are claimed to be more morally responsive than men to contexts, concerns of caring, interpersonal relationships, and emotional nuance. These gender differences in moral thinking and decision making are thought to emerge from differences in gender developments of the self both in early experience and later socialization.

The differences are said to arise because women, who, like men, initially identify with or internalize their mothers, never have to separate themselves from their primary caretaker in their road to gender identity; women in comparison to males, therefore, develop selves that are more interconnected to others, more fluid, and more oriented to the needs and responses of others.[52]

Men, in separating from the mother to take on a male identity, must repudiate or isolate the internalized, feminine mothering one. To achieve maleness, they must learn the disassociation, isolation, and repression of their early nurturing emotions. The result is a generalized repression of emotions that leads males to rationalistic abstract thinking that focuses upon abstract rules and principles like justice, rather than to a holistic morality of interpersonal responsiveness. Thus principled, abstract male moral reasoning oriented to justice contrasts with female caring and contextual thinking in preferred styles of moral decision making. Women, with their "women's ways of knowing," are thought to speak morally "in a different voice."

While these ideas of gender differences in moral reasoning are intuitively appealing, they do not seem to be borne out by empirical evidence. Study after study of moral judgment do not reveal any sex differences.[53] Men and women, girls and boys do not actually reason differently; women are as principled and justice oriented as men. Finally, the reliance upon gender as a major factor appears to be challenged by the fact that in other cultures such as African tribal groups, everyone—both men and women—has the supposedly feminine characteristics of communal, contextual, interpersonal approaches to morality.[54]

Other developments in infancy studies also cast doubt upon the way the male self and the female self are supposed to develop and identify with caretakers of one or another gender.[55] The neo-Freudian dynamics supposedly underlying female and male development in the proposed theories of gender differences have been seriously challenged by new emphases upon early cognitive development in the innately individuated self. The human organism seems genetically programmed to develop a complex self by cognitively processing information and experiencing emotional interpersonal experiences, but the infant may select and interact with its different caretakers in a more autonomous and varied way. Other characteristics in the caretaker or the child may be more influential than gender.

On another level of analysis, severe critiques of the Gilligan approach have been advanced that focus upon the implicit philosophical assumptions. Philosophically, the idea has been repudiated that justice and caring are in conflict, or somehow necessarily alternative modes of moral thinking. Many have noted that caring and justice are more realistically seen to be on a continuum of one dimension. Caring and love can be seen to include justice or fairness, but then go beyond them. Paul VI once said eloquently, "Justice is love's absolute minimum." Other philosophical critics see a much more nuanced moral situation than the purported two voices of the Gilligan approach.[56]

Class, race, age, and the power in any social system also make a difference in moral perspectives. Things always look different from the bottom than from the top. Moreover, out-groups with less power become the symbolic carriers of unowned characteristics that a dominant group projects.[57] Women, blacks, Native Americans, Jews, and Gypsies have all been given the same stereotypical characteristics of possessing more emotionality, less rationality, more global thinking, more impulsivity, more nurturance, and more intuition than dominant groups or races.

Most women have been relative outsiders and newcomers in the professional and public worlds of our culture. They may more often bring the view of the marginal person into the discussion; but men who are outsiders by class, race, or education can do the same. The moral resources of outsiders, whether women or men, can be invaluable. New insights and discoveries come from those who come into a system with a fresh eye and emotional reactions unhabituated by ideological blinders and routine.

On the other hand, when women are insiders and are given the same expectations and professional socialization as males, they develop and react in the same ways as their male colleagues. Privilege, education, and power produce their effects. Alas, it is a myth of female chauvinism that women, by their gender alone, could be counted upon to be more moral and caring leaders or administrators of any sort. We should think of Margaret Thatcher and other iron ladies when tempted toward exaggerated claims for the automatically nurturing moral influence of gender or maternal experience.

We must remember that those who describe and espouse the virtues of maternal thinking are describing the *thinking* that must take place in successful child rearing.[58] This thinking can be done by males or females. To nurture and rear offspring, a person must try simultaneously to ensure survival, encourage individual flourishing, and yet want to rear a socially acceptable child. The inner conflict between these goals and the reflection induced by the maternal or nurturing enterprise may produce a unique set of values. If women have more often developed maternal thinking, it is because of their self-conscious intellectual activity, not because of their female gender.

In the end, there is no automatic moral developmental process that can unfold magically because of gender, specific female experiences, or early experience with a nurturing female. A unique self must integrate experience and morally act in the service of moral ideals. An individual must avow and commit the whole self in moral decisions. Moral activity, allegiances, and character go beyond the limits of received gender and other social differences. Those who are truly "selved," to use Gerard Manley Hopkins's fine term, are whole persons whose unique, integrated personalities are too complex and differentiated to categorize by gender. What is morally important is who someone is as a whole person and how he or she has directed and shaped temperament, intelligence, moral knowledge, emotions, and experience.

Having come this far in our discussions of moral development, we can say that human nature is prepared and predisposed always and everywhere for the moral project. The next obvious question is how to nurture this development of conscience when so many things have to go on at once. There must be a development of a self who can freely and consciously integrate and evaluate one's whole processing of consciousness on the way to decisive moral commitments. But in order to make good moral decisions, one needs to develop specific capacities for reasoning, feeling, caring, imagining, and intuiting—plus the ability to reciprocally test all these functions. At the same time, the overarching ideals of goodness, rightness, and truth have to be felt as magnets attracting and exerting an overriding obligatory moral force.

Moral ideals will inevitably be mediated in the moral content and moral knowledge of a particular cultural tradition and community. Conscience and moral development are continuous, dynamic processes of great complexity. The moral nurturing of an individual conscience is an undertaking that cannot be done alone. Both emotional and rational development require relationships with other persons within the social bonds of a community.

Chapter 8

Nurturing Conscience

Individuals shape their own characters and create their moral careers by large and small moral decisions. We interpret our social worlds and select our own environments, as well as the other way around. Yet at the same time, no individual is self-created de novo, nor can anyone live a moral life alone. The self is always partially constituted by a history of interpersonal relationships within a specific community and culture. This sociality is particularly influential during the formative period of infancy and childhood when an individual learns a language and the culture's rules.

The problem of moral education and transmission of moral values worries those who see our society in the midst of serious moral decline and disintegration. If a community wishes to engender and nourish conscience and good moral decision making, what should be done?

The Foundations of Conscience and Moral
Decision Making

A sense of self and self-conscious agency is the necessary ground of conscience and all moral decision making. Therefore, all those things that further the development of a sense of self as conscious and responsible are important. Starting with the most basic of basics, psychological selves depend upon human brains and bodies in good working order. Unimpaired, noninjured, nondrugged, nonmalnourished brains and bodies are necessary for full self-consciousness and moral agency. The developing fetal brain produces 250,000 neurons a minute, all of which must migrate to their proper places to ensure normal functioning in life after birth.[1] Drug epidemics among pregnant women will have psychological and social repercussions in the next generation. If we would

further moral development of society's members, we can begin by pro-
tecting and ensuring healthy maternal and fetal development. The
health of children and their families must be a basic priority.

Still, more is required for moral development than a foundation of
satisfactory biological equipment. Children must also have adequate parenting in average, expectable child-rearing environments. We now know
enough about human development to know that the earliest experiences
of nurture and care affect the development of a self able to make moral
decisions later in life. I have argued for an innate species-specific human
nature in which self-conscious intellectual and emotional development is
genetically programmed to progress in certain patterned ways; but this
program depends upon a certain level of nurturance, emotional bonding,
and positive interpersonal experiences from caretakers.

A child must be protected from neglect and abuse, and be given
enough emotional care and intellectual stimulation to produce a minimal self that can be open to future social influence.[2] Today, social
pathology increasingly destroys the structure of family life, and we see
not only single mothers mired in poverty, but the "no-parent child"
who has been abandoned by a drug-addicted mother. Such breakdowns
of caretaking lead to an impaired development of selves. Family bonding is the most-fundamental moral socializing force known, but children in abusing and neglecting families must be protected from
irreversible harm in critical periods of psychological development. If
this means devising new protective measures such as mandatory treatment for abusers, more therapeutic surveillance by visiting nurses, or
the return of orphanages, the effort is worth it.

Individual behavioral controls that enable action and interaction
with the environment develop or fail to develop in infancy and early
childhood. Distortions of personality emerge from a failure to develop
a sense of self with appropriate self-controls. With tenuous self-
identities, one finds inappropriate regressions to magical thinking and
unmodulated infantile states of aggression or narcissistic entitlement.
Many observers of American culture are worried over the spread of
character disorders and flawed developments of the sense of self arising
from the increase of distorted nurturing in disorganized families.[3]

Psychological foundations of selfhood and self-agency are the crucial
prerequisites for the moral life. We cannot expect to see individual selves
who can integrate reasoning, intuition, imagination, and emotions on behalf of moral goods, when there is stunted mental and emotional development. Children must at least be able to think as self-conscious beings,
and have enough emotional attachment and love for themselves and their

caretakers to want to live, learn, and reach out to the world. If the first experiences of other people are disturbed and totally inadequate, these patterns can frustrate later efforts to persuade a child or adolescent to open up to other persons to correct the original bad start.

Self-esteem is necessary for the moral life. If one does not care for self, there is little reason to try to survive or flourish by seeking other goods. Seeking moral goodness and self-respect depends upon a deep attachment to one's own psychological being and social welfare. Love and goodwill toward others depend upon love and esteem for self. This truth is not recent news, nor the latest discovery of psychological research, or a sign of the triumph of a therapeutic point of view. In the eighteenth century, Bishop Butler understood that love of self and others "are so perfectly coincident, that the greatest satisfactions to ourselves depend upon our having benevolence in a due degree; and that self-love is one chief security of our right behaviour towards society."[4] He goes on to say that we cannot promote one without promoting the other, since human beings as social beings are made for both. Our modern gloss on this truth is to recognize how early treatment in infancy and childhood affects later self-consciousness and self-esteem.

Clearly any future efforts to nurture conscience in our society must ensure the physical, emotional, and intellectual well-being of babies. But babies are intimately connected to mothers, who are connected to fathers and their extended families, who in turn, through economics, employment, and the media, are connected to everyone and everything else in the country at large. Obviously, structural and political factors in the society affect the family and other intermediary institutions that stand between the state and the individual.

There are always implicit moral agendas given in the socioeconomic arrangements of class, race, sex, age, and neighborhood. Critical social theorists analyze the hidden agendas in the way a society apportions power and social resources.[5] Here, I emphasize the fact that covert, implicit social norms inculcate moral messages before anyone in a culture begins explicit moral socialization. Even if one has enough nurturing to have a sense of self, one's self-esteem can be damaged by meeting cultural prejudice, stigma, and messages about one's helplessness.

At the explicit ideological level, American society is dedicated to moral ideals of justice, fairness, and the moral equality of all. And for most Americans, the system works well enough in its rough fashion. There could never be a revolution in America, because the majority of Americans are not politically repressed or socially oppressed by flagrant, obvious, immoral abuses. Our moral crises are more subtle, the fruit of political freedom and affluence for the majority—if not for the unfortunate minorities born into poverty.

Despite being well fed, fairly treated, and affluent, many Americans sense our culture as morally disintegrating, mired in moral decadence and meaninglessness. It turns out that it is not enough to possess individualistic liberties, affluence, biologically good health, and unimpaired mental and psychological equipment.[6] The moral problem remains: how ought we to live? As free moral agents, we ask what moral choices are worth making, and what moral goods should be pursued.

Conscious Cultural Nurturing of Conscience

Different cultures and subcultures, indeed different families within the same community, produce variations upon the common theme of human moral development. As in the creation of each human face or each snowflake, there is an amazing interplay between general lawful patterns and specific conditions and contexts that produce uniqueness. I have emphasized the constancies and universality of individuals and of human cultures that produce commonalities of moral development, but cultures also vary within a range.

Within the innate programming of primary emotions, different societies may emphasize different emotions and different blends of feelings. These preferred patterns of emotions reflect different views of the meaning of the world of human experience. Languages are learned before the age of two, and as an infant's brain and vocal chords become committed to specific speech sounds, so a world of cultural meaning is conveyed. Each linguistic community gives a conceptual framework to its new members; as they learn the language, they learn the culture— including its moral rules.

Most cultures, like our own, recognize that human beings exist as individual, distinct self-conscious persons who can act in a world of ongoing, irreversible time. A core sense of self, self-agency, intersubjectivity and sociality, and symbolic self-concepts are undoubtedly universal to the human species, but may not be articulated in the same ways or with the same emphasis among cultures. In modern Western culture, the individual self as agent is symbolically validated with pronouns. When children can say "I" and "me," they display a symbolic conceptual sense of an individual self distinct from the environment and other persons.

Through verbal and symbolic conversations, the social world of meaning is constituted, conveyed, and continued. The dialogues and interchanges we hear from birth to old age convey social norms and moral judgments. Even "idle" gossip is not meaningless. Gossip conveys the social evaluations persons make about others; these conversations are the main means of constituting and reinforcing the moral standards by which a society lives.[7] Gossip among peers is a moral enforcer that is as potent as the law or physical coercion.

One eminent social scientist, Rom Harré, claims that the desire for respect and honor among one's fellows is the most important of all cultural universals.[8] This motivation for esteem is decidedly as important as biological and material survival needs. Always and everywhere in human groups, we see the desire for good reputation and social worth. As he notes:

> Even the apparently merely pleasurable activities, such as chatting and joking, are heavily loaded with expressive significance. The chatting is largely concerned with commentary upon the chatting and doings of others. . . . Of course life involves eating and drinking, but not "above all else." Above all else it involves honour and the respect of persons.[9]

Indeed, individuals in all cultures have been known to stop eating and drinking and waste away and die out of shame, humiliation, and loneliness. Our socially bonding, highly expressive species feeds upon approval and a sense of being recognized as worthwhile. Moral excellencies, as well as achievement, prowess, and talent, are central to the grading system.

Humans may universally desire esteem and honor, yet the virtues and values that bring the greatest honor vary in different cultures. What is considered most praiseworthy may deviate from one group to another and from one generation to another. A core of universal moral essentials may fluctuate because of the different weights given to which good things or virtues are most to be admired. Cultures are always changing, and traditions are in constant processes of renewal if they are going to survive.

Within our own Western Judeo-Christian culture descending intellectually from the Greeks, we can see different elaborations and moral ideals gaining ascendancy at different times and places. Some philosophers, like some anthropologists, have emphasized the incompatibility or discontinuity in these different ideals. Alasdair MacIntyre has been one of the foremost philosophical proponents of how different the varying dominant ideals of virtue in Western history have been.[10] MacIntyre claims that Homer and Aristotle would have been appalled by St. Paul, and that Jane Austen and Benjamin Franklin would have differences over the preeminent moral virtues.

This may well be true on one level, but there also would be many, many structural convergences and moral agreements across generations and epochs. MacIntyre, himself, recognizes a structural commonality in the different ideals of virtue.[11] All share the idea of a narrative unity of a person's life, and recognize the need for a person to experience mentored practice within a received moral tradition. An individual who would be virtuous must always and everywhere be a moral agent and take moral responsibility for the way his or her personal life story is being shaped. To be virtuous, one must also submit the autonomous and imperial self to the goods and values embodied in the community, honoring and valuing the traditional goods that exist beyond the self. One becomes virtuous by engaging in activity modeled upon mentors and then having these actions evaluated by the community. In a real sense, one builds moral intuition by effort and practice.

I also contend that there is a fair amount of agreement and commonality in the moral values of the Western tradition. At no time or place in the diverse configurations of different eras would cowardice, envy, murder, lying, false witness, promise breaking, and a host of other universally despised moral wrongdoings be condoned. There is a convergence in the content of morality as well as common structure. One cannot imagine, for instance, that Goebbels, Hitler, or Idi Amin would have been countenanced by Ben Franklin, Jane Austen, Homer, Aristotle, or St. Paul.

Whatever the epoch, the universal human need for honor and self-respect among one's group ensures that the larger community, like the family, will have morally socializing power. The moral inspiration induced by a cloud of witnesses has been known to all traditional societies. Thomas Jefferson, our own enlightenment sage, gave traditional mentoring advice to his nephew by morally advising him to "ask yourself how you would act were all the world looking at you, and act accordingly."[12] Jefferson wrote to the young man that rather than do an immoral act, he should "give up money, give up fame, give up science, give up earth itself and all it contains."[13] In other words, put moral self-esteem, moral reputation, and honor before all else. Of course, the effectiveness of this advice is predicated on the traditional assumption that we are free moral agents, with a high degree of self-esteem and emotional bonding to family, friends, and "all the world." Otherwise, we would not care what anyone thought, or want to live up to community ideals.

How should communities in our culture who possess morally socializing power operate? Ideally, the moral enterprise and the importance of the moral quest should be validated by the commitment of all the different institutions and admired persons a young person encounters. If there are no moral mentors, there will be no followers. The morally influential dialogues, conversations, and gossip of home and neighborhood devoted to moral evaluation should be reproduced in larger public arenas and forums. Fortunate children and families will have access to intact neighborhood institutions, such as churches, civic organizations, unions, youth groups, and so on, where moral discourse and moral evaluation of the day's events are still a part of life. The larger political arena and the media, despite trivialization and commercialization, can also be a source of moral discourse.

Each subcommunity or group is a mediating link between the larger culture and the individual. For children and youth however, there may be no place as influential as the explicitly educational institution of school. When a school takes up its moral responsibility for engendering and encouraging conscience development, what specific considerations should be addressed? Here too, there is the double challenge of conveying moral content and knowledge while encouraging structural processes in the group that encourage self-esteem, moral agency, and moral responsibility. The basic assumption that individuals are free moral agents must be reiterated constantly. The hidden curriculum of the school cannot be at odds with its overt efforts to encourage moral decision making in morally mature persons. Are persons treated with moral respect, be they students, teachers, staff, or administrators? Is the school community a just community, exemplifying and modeling the moral messages it would proclaim?[14]

The school's challenge of conveying moral knowledge can be met by a curriculum standard I call "maximum moral example." By this standard, no one leaving the educational system should be ignorant of the moral actions of the recognized moral exemplars of Western culture, or of the moral ideals and principles that motivated them in their various moral decisions resolving their conflicts of conscience. Yes, there should be formal training in moral principles and moral reasoning, but integrated with the study of real moral decisions. Moral examples can come from accounts of actual persons in history, from ancient times to the controversial present. But literary sources and Scriptures also provide a source of moral exemplars par excellence. The moral dilemmas of Antigone, Hamlet, and Huckleberry Finn are part of our store of moral knowledge.

If we take on the task of what I call the conscience curriculum, we end up endorsing a renewal of the study of the humanities—but the humanities with a moral agenda as well as historical and aesthetic concerns. We learn from our direct moral experiences in our families, neighborhoods, and schools, but individuals also expand moral awareness, moral sensibilities, and moral intuition, "through the indirect experiencing of the moral lives of real and fictional people," as philosopher Robert K. Fullinwider puts it.[15] As he wisely says, "A moral education is first and foremost an education in literature, history, drama and art."[16] A child, or an adult, must have actual cases and examples to fully appreciate deeper values, moral principles, and the complexities of moral decision making. Only by understanding the best of our moral tradition and conventions can we develop intuitively discriminating moral perceptions of present events, persons, and situations.

We can learn how to act from attending to the moral decision making of others. In literature, drama, and history, a person can confront at a distance the moral decisions of other moral agents—some heroic, others adequate, still others moral failures. A vicarious form of practicing and moral learning is accessible through the imagination. One gains an experience of cases that helps one classify and categorize moral challenges, at the same time one sees the outcomes of other decisions—good, bad and mediocre.

Reflecting on the moral decisions of others teaches us about moral failure, without our having to pay the price personally. In literature and dramas that portray the inner subjective life, we can see how others have been ignorant, weak, or subject to self-deception. We watch helplessly as Oedipus, Othello, and Lear let the moral flaw of arrogant pride prevail. We sorrowfully see Anna, Dorothea, and Millie drift on, unable to wake up from self-deception until it is too late. More wonderfully, we live vicariously with heroes and heroines who morally triumph over adversity; they inspire us with their example and strengthen our moral will to be good despite the cost. As a modern theologian has understood, "Fictions do not operate to help us escape reality, but to redescribe our human reality in such disclosive terms that we return to the 'everyday' reoriented to life's real—if forgotten or sometimes never even imagined—possibilities."[17] If Jane Eyre overcame temptation in her struggle of conscience, then so can I.

Stories created by the imagination and actual historical events move and shape our moral lives. Every culture has known the power of stories to pass on the traditional wisdom and morally educate the young. There is "a power of enchantment" and empathetic emotional engagement in parable and story.[18] Mind and heart, reason and emotion are simultaneously stimulated to respond to a narrative. The moral images in a narrative are more emotionally compelling, more real, more vivid, more concrete and contextual than a set of abstracted principles and rules. Stories don't simply impart information; they demonstrate and recreate experience through imagery and form.

There has been a resurgence of interest in narrative thinking in literature, in the fields of cognitive science, philosophy, theology, psychoanalysis, family systems theory, and moral psychology.[19] Our brains may be preset to function in a narrative mode of thinking, as well as through conceptual abstractions and categories. The narrative mode of thinking helps us cope with life in linear time, where episode follows episode in a causal chain of acts and consequences. Narrative thinking also helps us cope with other persons whose motivations and plans we must understand. Stories prepare us to read the motivations, intentions, and plans of those we encounter.

Persons are inevitably following various scripts and playing parts in the many narratives and dramas of social interaction—and one must understand their intended narrative lines in order to navigate. Stories further social skills because "the story mode requires imagination, an understanding of human intention, and an appreciation of the particulars of time and place."[20] These are the same qualities we need for making moral decisions. The listeners to stories learn implicitly and explicitly a great deal about moral contexts, moral goods, and moral choices. Since each moral agent or self is constructing a life story and moral career, the story of moral choices instructs mind and heart at the same time. Moral reasoning is partly constituted of imagined scenarios envisioning what is at stake in any choice. When we empathetically enter into moral stories, we are helping to create our future thoughts and feelings.

Great spiritual masters of the past understood the power of narrative and created parables and teaching stories. As the listeners to a story become engaged and transported into the story, they become emotionally and empathetically hooked, only to suddenly find that the story demands a moral response from those who have ears to hear. The story leads to new intentions and new actions. Traditional masters of morality have also always known the importance of responsive action and conduct in the moral education of conscience.

Personal actions change a self and the environment; the effects of change then produce consequences for moral actors.[21] Moral conduct, or moral failure to act, influences one's view of one's self and one's moral capacities. Those who emphasize virtuous practice as the way to virtue and character formation have always recognized the power arising from sustained, repeated action. Good conduct produces different thoughts and feelings and strengthens the force of past action patterns. Great moral stories portray the importance of active moral responses to crises.

Efforts to provide moral education without stories or emotional attachments to admired models is doomed to failure. It takes a desire to do good, avoid evil, and seek what is true before moral instruction can make a difference. Love of other persons makes one listen and appropriate the moral desires and standards of the mentor. Moral emotions make morality appear "real." If one concentrates only on teaching words, one gets only words in return, with only an outward verbal conformity to moral standards. The intrinsic satisfactions and empowerment of moral reasoning and problem solving will not be operative unless persons care enough to become engaged. Integration of moral reasoning, moral emotions, and moral action are necessary.

Moral development becomes more complex when self-conscious reasoning initiates moral critiques of the received moralities of one's community. Often it is the great teaching story or the example of a great moral hero that opens one's heart and mind in a new and revolutionary way of moral thinking. Many of the emotional peak experiences that undergird new moral quests for the good are induced by the personal response to a magnanimous human feat. Reason assents to a new moral vision.

But moral reasoning, emotion, and willingness to act can also be withheld or rejected. No matter how adequate the moral environment and moral community, individuals can resist or refuse to be influenced. In thinking about moral development and moral education, we also have to recognize the hard truth of a human being's freedom to choose to grow, or to rebel. No one can be coerced into moral freedom, and no system of moral education can guarantee to produce a morally developed person. A family, a community, a school, a church, a society can set the stage, produce moral mentors, and tell the traditional great stories, but the individual must still choose to say yes or no. Communities can prepare environments where it is easy to be good, but each person must create a uniquely self-authored story.

Moral Commitments and Change

A morally developed person must create her or his own moral narrative, and so cannot remain uncommitted to some worldview or specific moral beliefs about the good. All moral stories cannot be accepted as equally valid. Choices will be made, commitments entered into, and fidelity displayed despite stress and struggle. An integrated, morally mature person may be flexible, open-minded, loving, caring, and tolerant of others, but must still be firmly directed toward a personally owned vision.

The necessity for decision and steadfast commitment brings to the fore a most delicate and difficult moral challenge for individuals and for communities. In nurturing conscience and moral decision making, how do we confront the problem of moral fallibility and moral insufficiencies, even among the most sincere and good moral exemplars, or in excellent moral traditions? We have firsthand experience that individual and collective moral understandings can change and develop, but at the same time, we fully acknowledge the need for loyalty, steadfastness, and fidelity to moral commitments and moral decisions. How can we be humble seekers of the true and the good, always open to our limitations and the possibility of apprehending new moral truths, and yet firmly stand by past moral decisions? We as individuals and communities wish to be faithful to traditional moral understandings, but cannot give up the moral inquiry or moral critiques impelled by visions of a transcendent good.

The problem is also exemplified in making promises. Promises are acts in which we as free moral agents bind ourselves to produce acts in the future. Hannah Arendt called a promise "a sacrament of the will," and it is a visible sign manifesting the invisible but real capacity to freely direct personal action in future time. Complete moral fatalists could not make promises with any conviction, because they could not believe themselves free to exert the moral agency it takes to carry out a promised act.

The giving of a sincere promise reveals a belief in the capacity of a person to control future motivations and acts and so shape one's future personal identity. The self who promises is confident that the moral obligation undertaken in the present can be met by the future self— next week, next month, or from now until death do us part. The promising act avows that one can exercise enough self-control and self-mastery that personal identity and present intentions will continue to exist. The specific commitment is built on the assumption that there can be a coherent integration of character and will, not only in the presently existing self, but over time as well.

This promising sense of stable identity and moral character most often is grounded on past experiences of making things happen as we said we would. Those who have carried through on past self-binding, self-creating projects have moral confidence in their ability to control the inner self and their own external environments. Of course, it is easier to have had such moral experiences and assurances when a person lives in a stable community where most people honor their moral commitments.

Giving and keeping promises is a key example of moral action because it can only be accomplished by free moral agents who possess powers of foresight, decision, speech, and self-direction. We are the only "promising primates," and the ability to make promises is a mark of our humanness; it makes possible extended social bonding and organization.[22] When young persons are loathe to make promises or moral commitments, it often signals a lack of trust in the stability of self-identity, along with doubts over one's control of self and the environment. The reluctance to make promises can be as alarming as the more overt cultural deterioration that occurs when promises are broken regularly and mutual trust breaks down.

There are other moral difficulties involved in making and fulfilling moral commitments or promises—difficulties that do not arise from timidity or lack of moral will.[23] Knowing that we are subject to moral failures through ignorance, human limitations, weakness, and self-deceit, we must always be open to self-correction and amendment. We have made mistakes before, changed our minds before, and grown into what we can now see is a fuller moral understanding of some matters. Underlying any specific moral decision or promise is the more fundamental commitment to an ongoing quest for the good and right, which must imply a willingness to change.

Moreover, many moral decisions of conscience must be made without full knowledge of all possible pertinent facts or complete, overwhelming conviction. Many would agree with the philosopher C. D. Broad, who claims that we are obligated to morally decide an issue or dilemma if we have only a preponderance of moral belief that it is the better decision. We have a duty to act when we are probably convinced that some "alternative is more right or less wrong than any of the others which are open."[24] This course, which makes sense when one must morally decide, means that some specific moral decision or moral commitment may be made despite the knowledge of many countervailing arguments and emotions. If one has not been absolutely, overwhelmingly convinced at the moment of moral decision, there is the possibility that as one gains further experience and knowledge and deliberates more fully, a new and different moral decision may emerge as more compelling. Would not this realization forbid promises in most situations?

Morally changing one's mind and heart presents the dilemma of being both faithful to past commitments and promises and yet being open to newer understandings of truth and moral duty. One can only justify moral changes on serious moral grounds. We should not change simply because our nonmoral interests or desires have changed. This course would justify a self with no coherence or integration, a person who can happily move from one identity to another—a protean, ever-changing self, who would let new personal interests displace past moral commitments. Such inconsistent chameleons are rightly despised as having no character or backbone; they are not trustworthy. The lack of consistency, integrity, or fidelity to promises breaks social bonds.

The situation is different when a new and seriously compelling moral understanding of what ought to be done is the cause of the change from the commitments or promises of the past. The person's moral integrity is preserved because the person's past core commitment to moral truth, to the good, and to conscientious decision making has not changed. The fundamental moral vision and sense of compelling moral obligation remain intact. Our practice of morally deciding by activating and integrating all one's capacities with mutual testing and tutoring remains the same. But living in time, with limited knowledge and capacities, may mean that new moral knowledge, new reasoning, and new emotions now impel us to new and different moral obligations that override earlier decisions or commitments. Our whole past self-identities have not been repudiated, but we have undertaken what we now see as a morally more-worthy course, a developmental change for the better. Our present moral commitments seem more inclusive, more comprehensive, and morally better decisions than our earlier ones.

Persons of good conscience do not change their commitments lightly. Rigid fanatics will never open themselves to change; morally indifferent persons will reverse commitments without a qualm. But the morally mature person will struggle and suffer, in order not to fall into self-deception or fail to be true to one's moral standards. The struggle is compounded when a change will mean going against one's traditional moral community, or braving the potent disapproval of those whose esteem matters. The binding forces of social groups are strong and make nonconformity psychologically arduous.

In this challenge of intense group pressures, there is a resource that springs from human imagination and the telling of stories. In learning the stories of great moral exemplars in history or literature, a person is given access to alternative moral communities that give moral support in a crisis. Indeed, many moral exemplars had to endure conflict and moral persecution; remembering them gives courage. William James described this process:

> When for motives of honor and conscience I brave the condemna-
> tion of my own family, club, and "set"; when as a Protestant, I turn

Catholic; as a Catholic, freethinker; as a "regular" practitioner, "hom-
eopathe," or what not, I am always inwardly strengthened in my
course and steeled against the loss of my actual social self by the
thought of other and better possible social judges than those whose
verdict goes against me now.[25]

For James, the moral course of development is both individual and
social, rational and emotional, for "the emotion that beckons me on" is
the pursuit of the "ideal social self . . . the true, the intimate, the ultimate, the permanent me which I seek."[26] Social bonds are always a part
of us, but we can seek the best community possible as our idealized
moral compatriots. Moral development of conscience can be concep-
tualized as a wholehearted, reasoned progress through a better and
better series of communities, with more admired moral exemplars and
social judges. The individual may be a social self, but also an "I" who
as a free agent can become more and more discriminating in the selection of ideal moral witnesses among whom the self seeks moral confirmation and honor. We are social creatures, we flourish in communities,
but with imagination and reason our conscience is not confined to the
present condition.

Summing Up

We have discussed conscience and moral decision making in a way
that takes full account of the subjective, conscious processing of the person making a decision about the good and right thing to do. We have
articulated a broad understanding of conscience as a self-conscious activity
of a person who is thinking, feeling, imagining, and willing action on
behalf of moral standards of worth. Personal moral decision making does
not differ when directed to self, to others, or to larger questions of moral
belief—or by its orientation to the past, present, or future. We morally
commit ourselves in acts of conscience when we morally decide what we
ought to have done, what we ought to do, what others ought to do, and
what things ought to be believed and effected.

Before making our moral decisions, we may seek information, use
different rational strategies of ethical analysis, imagine various moral
scenarios, and seek moral counsel from others. Producing an ethical
analysis of a problem is different from the moral committing of self in
decision. The self-committed moral acts of free moral agents differ from

moral descriptions, moral analyses, and moral critiques, and moral decisions differ from other kinds of decisions we make devoted to questions of efficiency, taste, etiquette, legality, and preference.

The self who decides is made up of many dimensions and experiences many variations in consciousness and self-consciousness. The
psychological complexity of the self makes different kinds of self-
consciousness possible but also complicates the process of the core
self's moral agency. As biological human organisms dependent upon
genetic heritage and environmental contingencies, we can be only partially free and only partially self-conscious.

There are systems of rational, emotional, and physical functioning
in the human organism that operate outside the level of conscious
awareness or personal control. Intuitions and emotions spontaneously
emerge in consciousness. These characteristics of spontaneous subjective consciousness can be neutral, negative or positive in influence.

I am convinced that the value of human reason to apprehend moral
truth and reality has been validated many times over and that the scientific quest for knowledge is another manifestation of the effectiveness
of human rationality. Rational problem solving and decision making
appear to be strategically much the same, whether focused upon questions of reality and truth in science, in politics, or in morality. It also
appears evident that human reasoning is a subjective, personal activity
of complex, multidimensioned beings with many levels and kinds of
information processing going on simultaneously.

Reasoning, human intuition, emotions, and social communications
are integral to the scientific and moral quest for personal conviction.
Knowing this, we should also beware of overanalytic rationalist methods of moral decision making, which fail to take into account the subjective person's moral resources of nonconscious mental and emotional
signals. Emotional commitment, care, and desire are never irrelevant in
morality.

Moral failure and continuing moral development are also realities
that are personal and subjective in origin. The inner complexity and
different dimensions of the self can be both an asset and a source for
self-deception. Moral education and an effort to encourage progress
toward the freedom, coherence, and committed integrity of the good
person is a many-faceted enterprise. Today, the different approaches to
moral development need to be unified in a more-adequate holistic model. A conscience curriculum needs to simultaneously engender moral
emotions, teach moral reasoning, and convey moral knowledge. Moral
education can fail by slighting either the need for critical thinking or

the need for personal motivations emerging from empathy, caring, and emotional attachments to a vision of the good. It is difficult to give full weight to everything needed for the successful growth and development of conscience. Many factors operate in the moral enterprise: moral freedom and human limits, active directed thinking and spontaneous preconscious operations, reason and emotion, the individual self and the constitutive community.

In the final analysis, each person runs the course and authors a morality play. Moral communities partially shape self-conscious selves, who become free moral agents selecting and creating a moral world. With large and small moral decisions of conscience, we strengthen, or alternately erode and destroy, moral consciousness—in ourselves, in our families, and in our fellow sojourners. We can usually recognize extremes of moral evil, moral weakness, or moral heroism. In the middle range, we can usually distinguish better moral decisions from those that are worse. Unfortunately, we cannot have infallible, guaranteed moral assessments of the human mind and heart—including our own. The morally wise grow humble and careful, albeit steadfast and firm. The moral quest continues to attract and compel humankind. Conscience holds its own.

Notes

In an interdisciplinary enterprise devoted to the exhaustively explored topics of conscience and morality, I could not begin to give comprehensive documentation. In these notes, I have selected the most accessible, least technical sources on the topics at hand. The citations are more or less cumulative so that discussions in later chapters are built upon sources in earlier chapters. I have tried to keep to bare essentials, with a minimum of repetition.

Introduction

1. Reported in *Time*, 5 March 1990, 5.
2. Richard Powers, *Three Farmers on the Way to a Dance* (New York: McGraw Hill Paperback Edition, 1987), 98.
3. For a pessimistic account see Alan Bloom, *The Closing of the American Mind* (New York: Simon and Shuster, 1987), 227–40.
4. Natan Sharansky, *Fear No Evil* (New York: Random House, 1988); Nien Cheng, *Life and Death in Shanghai* (New York: Grove Press, 1986).
5. Sidney Callahan, "Value Choices in Abortion," in *Abortion: Understanding Differences*, ed. Sidney Callahan and Daniel Callahan (New York: Plenum Press, 1984), 285–301; Sidney Callahan, "The Role of Emotion in Ethical Decisionmaking," *Hastings Center Report* (June/July 1988): 9–14; Sidney Callahan, "The Ethical Challenge of the New Reproductive Technology," in *Medical Ethics: A Guide for Health Professionals*, ed. John F. Monagle and David C. Thomasma (Rockville, MD: Aspen Publishers, 1988), 26–37.
6. This phrase by Clifford Geertz is discussed along with its implications for interdisciplinary work between the humanities and social sciences in Jonathan Z. Smith, "'Religion' and 'Religious Studies': No Difference at All," *Soundings: An Interdisciplinary Journal*, vol. LXXI, no. 2–3, (Summer/Fall 1988): 231–44.
7. "Thick description" is another provocative phrase by Clifford Geertz that describes a form of interpretative social science—Clifford Geertz, "From the Native's Point of View: On the Nature of Anthropological Understanding," in *Interpretative Social Science: A Reader*, ed. Paul Rabinow and William M. Sullivan (Berkeley: Univ. of California Press, 1979), 225–41. Cf. on interpretative social science David Braybrooke, *Philosophy of Social Science* (Englewood Cliffs, NJ: Prentice-Hall, 1987), 1–20.
8. C. S. Lewis, "The Way," in *The Abolition of Man* (New York: Macmillan, [1947] 1978), 39–53; see also Mortimer J. Adler, *Six Great Ideas: Truth. Goodness. Beauty. Liberty. Equality. Justice* (New York: Macmillan, 1981).
9. The philosopher Paul Churchland considers folk psychology hopelessly primitive and deeply confused and predicts that it will go the way of a belief in witches: "The concepts of folk psychology—belief, desire, fear, sensation, pain, joy, and so on await a similar fate. . . . And when neuroscience has matured to the point where the poverty of our current conceptions is apparent to everyone, and the superiority

of the new framework is established, we shall then be able to set about reconceiving our internal states and activities, within a truly adequate conceptual framework at last"—Paul Churchland, *Matter and Consciousness: A Contemporary Introduction to the Philosophy of Mind*, rev. ed. (Cambridge, MA: The MIT Press, 1988), 44–45.

10. Quoted by Patricia Smith Churchland, *Neurophilosophy: Toward a Unified Science of the Mind-Brain* (Cambridge, MA: The MIT Press, 1988), 265.

11. Edwin Schur, *The Awareness Trap: Self Absorption Instead of Social Change* (New York: Quadrangle, 1976); see also Christopher Lasch, *The Culture of Narcissism: American Life in An Age of Diminishing Expectations* (New York: Warner Books, 1979).

12. For these critiques of the culture, see Phillip Rief, *The Triumph of the Therapeutic: Uses of Faith After Freud* (New York: Harper & Row, 1968); Richard Sennet, *The Fall of Public Man* (New York: Knopf, 1977).

Chapter 1.   What Is Conscience and How Does It Operate?

1. *The Random House Dictionary of the English Language*, 2d ed. unabridged, s.v. "conscience."

2. Tod S. Sloan, *Deciding: Self Deception in Life Choices* (New York: Methuen, 1987), 58. Sloan is adopting the phenomenology of deciding given by Paul Ricoeur, *Freedom and Nature: The Voluntary and the Involuntary*, trans. E. V. Kohan (Evanston, IL: Northwestern Univ. Press, 1950).

3. For a history of the concept of conscience, see Eric D'Arcy, *Conscience and its Right to Freedom* (London: Sheed and Ward, 1961); the discussion of legislative versus antecedent conscience can be found on pages 4–5. Other discussions of the historical development of the concept of conscience can be found in Joseph V. Dolan, S.J., "Conscience in the Catholic Theological Tradition," in *Conscience: Its Freedom and Limitations*, ed. William C. Bier, S.J. (New York: Fordham Univ. Press, 1971). In the Bier collection, there are other helpful papers; see in particular David Little, "A View of Conscience Within the Protestant Theological Tradition," 20–28. Other useful collections of papers on conscience can be found in C. Ellis Nelson, ed., *Conscience: Theological and Psychological Perspectives* (New York: Newman Press, 1973) and John Donnelly and Leonard Lyons, eds., *Conscience* (Staten Island, NY: Alba House, 1973).

4. Iris Murdoch gives an example of a moral change of mind about the past in Iris Murdoch, "The Idea of Perfection," *The Sovereignty of Good* (London: Routledge & Kegan Paul, 1970, Ark Edition 1985), 1–45.

5. Many theorists would disagree with this; see John Kleinig, "Always Let Your Conscience Be Your Guide?" *Interchange* vol. I, no. 2 (1967): 107–24. Kleinig holds that "our own conscience is limited in its application to my own actions where it is the registration of inconsistency between my moral beliefs and seriously contemplated actions or action already performed." In other words, conscience is only judicial and personal. However, it is interesting to note that a definition of conscience in a legal dictionary includes, besides the personal moral sense, the activity of conscience "in a wider sense, denoting a similar application of the standards of morality to the acts of others"—Henry Campbell Black, *Black's Law Dictionary: Definitions of the Terms and Phrases of American and English Jurisprudence, Ancient and Modern*, abridged 5th ed. (St. Paul, MN: West Publishing, 1983), 159. As William Frankena says in his *Ethics*, we are moral agents, but "we also want to make judgments about what others should do . . . we are also spectators, advisers, instructors, judges, and critics." William R. Frankena, *Ethics* 2nd ed. (Englewood Cliffs, New Jersey: Prentice Hall, 1973), 12.

6. Louis Fischer, ed., *The Essential Gandhi: His Life, Work, and Ideas–An Anthology* (New York: Random House, 1962), 199.

7. See Rom Harré, "Social Foundations of Mind," in *Personal Being: A Theory for Individual Psychology*, Cambridge, MA: Harvard Univ. Press, 1984), 20–33; for an approach

to story and literature, see also Paul C. Vitz, "The Uses of Stories in Moral Development: New Psychological Reasons for an Old Education Method," *American Psychologist* vol. 45, no. 6 1990, 709–20.

8. Sloan, *Deciding*, 52–61.

9. For a recent accessible summary of the tradition of informing and forming conscience, see Richard M. Gula, S.S., "The Formation of Conscience," in *Reason Informed by Faith: Foundations of Catholic Morality* (Mahwah, NJ: Paulist Press, 1989),
136–51.

10. Gula, *Reason Informed by Faith*, 123–35. Gula follows closely the tripartite view of
conscience given by Timothy E. O'Connell, "Conscience," in *Principles for a Catholic
Morality* (San Francisco: Harper & Row, 1978), 83–97.

11. See the discussion of heart imagery for conscience in Paul Lehmann, *Ethics in a
Christian Context* (New York: Harper & Row, 1963), 352–57; see also Walter Conn's
discussion, development, and critique of heart imagery for conscience in Walter E.
Conn, *Conscience: Development and Self-Transcendence* (Birmingham, AL: Religious
Education Press, 1981), 15–18, 215.

12. Jerome Kagan, *The Nature of the Child* (New York: Basic Books, 1984), 119.

13. Quoted by John Kleinig, "Conscience Be Your Guide?" 115.

14. James Joyce, *Portrait of the Artist as a Young Man* (New York: Penguin, 1964).

15. George Herbert, "Conscience," in *The Country Parson, The Temple*, ed. John N. Wall,
Jr. (New York: Paulist Press, 1981), 225–26.

16. Murdoch, *Sovereignty of Good*, 31.

17. For a comprehensive statement of the most recent cognitive behaviorist model, see
Albert Bandura, "Human Agency in Social Cognitive Theory," *American Psychologist*,
vol. 44, no. 9 (September 1989): 1175–84.

18. See a recent comprehensive statement of the traditional Freudian view in Eli Sagan,
"The Psychoanalytic Theory of Morality—A Critique," in *Freud, Women, and Morality: The Psychology of Good and Evil* (New York: Basic Books, 1988), 69–156; Sagan
wishes to revise the psychoanalytic view of conscience and the superego. Cf. a
nonpsychoanalytic theological distinction between conscience and superego in Gula,
Reason Informed by Faith, 123–30.

19. Jacques Monod as quoted in Freeman Dyson, "The argument from design," in *From
Creation to Chaos: Classic Writings in Science*, ed. Bernard Dixon (Oxford: Basil
Blackwell, 1989), 51.

20. Dyson, "Argument from design," 51.

21. Dyson, "Argument from design," 51. When Dyson writes that "mind is already inherent in every electron and the processes of human consciousness differ only in
degree but not in kind from the processes of choice between quantum states which
we call 'chance' when they are made by electrons," he is stating views that are
daringly developed by Danah Zohar, *The Quantum Self: Human Nature and Consciousness Defined by the New Physics* (New York: William Morrow, 1990).

22. George Wald, in an extract from his article in *Proceedings of the National Academy of
Sciences, 1964*, in Dixon, *From Creation to Chaos*, 275.

23. For a discussion of the way scientific realism and moral realism can be related, see
Richard N. Boyd, "How to Be a Moral Realist," in *Essays on Moral Realism*, ed.
Geoffrey Sayre-McCord (Ithaca, NY: Cornell Univ. Press, 1988), 181–228; see also in
the same volume of essays, Geoffrey Sayre-McCord, "Introduction, The Many Moral
Realisms," 1–23.

24. Norman K. Denzin, *On Understanding Emotion* (San Francisco: Jossey-Bass, 1984),
233. As Denzin adds, "The emotionally divided self does not feel self-respect. He
has not subjected himself, freely and rationally to himself in the face of something
outside himself," 234.

25. Murdoch, *Sovereignty of Good*.

26. Murdoch, *Sovereignty of Good*, 41. "Goodness and beauty are not to be contrasted, but are largely part of the same structure."
27. See for example John Welwood, "Exploring Mind: Form, Emptiness, and Beyond," in *The Meeting of the Ways: Explorations in East/West Psychology*, ed. John Welwood (New York: Schocken Books, 1979), 29–39.
28. Emile Durkheim, *Moral Education: A Study in the Theory & Application of the Sociology of Education* (New York: The Free Press, 1973), 98.
29. As Iris Murdoch has put it, "The ordinary person does not, unless corrupted by philosophy, believe that he creates values by his choices. He thinks that some things really are better than others and that he is capable of getting it wrong. We are not usually in doubt about the direction in which Good lies." *Sovereignty of Good*, 97.
30. D'Arcy, *Conscience and its Right to Freedom*, 8–12.
31. D'Arcy, *Conscience and its Right to Freedom*, 8–12. See also Kleinig, "Conscience Be Your Guide?" 116. A discussion of conscience, its biblical foundation and theological analysis, can be found in *New Catholic Encyclopedia*, s.v. "conscience" (New York: McGraw-Hill, 1967).
32. *New Catholic Encyclopedia*.
33. See the discussion of these biblical verses in O'Connell, *Principles*, 20–23.
34. Rom. 10:10.
35. Joseph Butler, *Sermons* (Charlottesville, VA: Facsimile Reprint, Ibis Publishing, 1986), 42.
36. See notes 3,9,10,11; see also John Donnelly, "Conscience and Religious Morality," in Donnelly and Lyons, *Conscience*, 159–73; and also Richard J. Regan, S.J., "Conscience in the Documents of Vatican II," in Bier, *Conscience: Its Freedom and Limitations*, 29–36.
37. For an example of the philosophical analysis of conscience, see C. D. Broad, "Conscience and Conscientious Action," in Donnelly and Lyons, *Conscience*, 5–23.

Chapter 2.   Who Has a Conscience?
The Self and Self-Consciousness

1. Natan Sharansky, *Fear No Evil* (New York: Random House, 1988), 8.
2. Willard Trask, comp. and trans., *Joan of Arc: Self-Portrait* (New York: Collier Books, 1961), 121.
3. See B. F. Skinner's attack on autonomous, free moral self-determination when he says, "Personal exemption from a complete determination is revoked as a scientific analysis progresses, particularly in accounting for the behavior of the individual"— *Beyond Freedom & Dignity* (New York: Bantam Book, 1972), 18. Cf. Richard Restak, "Is Free Will a Fraud," in *Taking Sides: Clashing Views on Controversial Psychological Issues* 5th ed., ed. Joseph Rubinstein and Brent Slife (Guilford, CT: Dushkin Publishing Group, 1988), 40–43.
4. See Charles Taylor, "Self-Interpreting Animals," *Human Agency and Language: Philosophical Papers* I (Cambridge: Cambridge Univ. Press, 1985), 45–76.
5. Roger Penrose doubts that computers can ever equal human thinking, since it takes human consciousness to make innovative judgments; Roger Penrose, *The Emperor's New Mind: Concerning Computers, Minds and the Laws of Physics* (New York: Oxford Univ. Press, 1989). For a playful array of essays and fictions devoted to the problems of consciousness and artificial intelligence, see Douglas R. Hofstadter and Daniel C. Dennett, comps. and eds., *The Mind's I: Fantasies and Reflections on Self and Soul* (New York: Basic Books, 1981).
6. See Thomas Nagel, "What Is It Like To Be a Bat?" in Hofstadter and Dennett, *The Mind's I*, 391–403.

7. The idea of "limit-language" and "limit-experience" is discussed by David Tracy, "The Search for Adequate Criteria," *Blessed Rage for Order: The New Pluralism in Theology* (San Francisco: Harper & Row, 1988), 64–86.

8. For a succinct psychological analysis of the necessary characteristics of conscience, see Jane Loevinger, "The Phenomena of Conscience," in *Ego Development: Conceptions and Theories* (San Francisco: Jossey-Bass, 1976), 397–99. Cf. the philosophical account of Taylor, "The Concept of a Person," *Human Agency*, 97–114; for a traditional moral theological summary, see Timothy E. O'Connell, "For one can only be morally responsible when one has knowledge and freedom, when one is truly in control of the events that transpire," *Principles for a Catholic Morality* (San Francisco: Harper & Row, 1978), 47ff.

9. See Elaine Scarry, "As in dying and death, so in serious pain the claims of the body utterly nullify the claims of the world," *The Body in Pain: The Making and Unmaking of the World* (New York: Oxford Univ. Press, 1985), 33.

10. William James long ago pointed out the multiple and yet unified character of the self; see William James, "The Consciousness of Self," in *The Principles of Psychology* vol. I (New York: Dover Publications, 1950 [1890]), 291–401. The idea of multiple selves has been taken further by modern psychologists so influenced by behaviorism that they question the unity of the self even in normal persons; see Benzion Canowitz and Ellen J. Langer, "Self-Protection and Self-Inception," in *Self-Deception and Self-Understanding: New Essays in Philosophy and Psychology*, ed. Mike W. Martin (Lawrence: Univ. of Kansas Press, 1985), 117–35. Cf. Anthony G. Greenwald, "Is Anyone in Charge? Personalysis Versus the Principle of Personal Unity," in *Psychological Perspectives on the Self*, vol. 1, ed. Jerry Suls (Hillsdale, NJ: Lawrence Erlbaum Associates, 1982), 151–81.

11. Oliver Sacks, *The Man Who Mistook His Wife for a Hat: And Other Clinical Tales* (New York: Harper & Row, 1985), 114.

12. See Leo Katz, "Those Who Know Not What They Do," *Bad Acts and Guilty Minds: Conundrums of the Criminal Law* (Chicago: Univ. of Chicago Press, 1987), 113–22.

13. C. D. Broad, "Conscience and Conscientious Action," in *Conscience*, ed. John Donnelly and Leonard Lyons (Staten Island, NY: Alba House, 1973), 8.

14. Broad, "Conscience and Conscientious Action," 8.

15. Broad, "Conscience and Conscientious Action," 8.

16. See O'Connell, *Principles for a Catholic Morality*, 64; Richard M. Gula, S.S., *Reason Informed By Faith: Foundations of Catholic Morality* (New York: Paulist Press, 1989), 78–81.

17. See Charles Taylor, "What Is Human Agency?" in *The Self: Psychological and Philosophical Issues*, ed. Theodore Mischel (Totowa, NJ: Rowman and Littlefield, 1977), 103–35.

18. Taylor, "What Is Human Agency?" 103–35.

19. William T. Powers, "A Systems Approach to Consciousness," *The Psychobiology of Consciousness*, ed. Julian M. Davidson and Richard J. Davidson (New York: Plenum Press, 1980), 236.

20. See Karl H. Pribram, "The Cognitive Revolution and Mind/Brain Issues," *American Psychologist*, vol. 41, no. 5 (May 1986): 507–20; see also R. W. Sperry, "Psychology's Mentalist Paradigm and the Religion/Science Tension," *American Psychologist*, vol. 43, no. 8 (August 1988): 607–13.

21. Sperry, "Psychology's Mentalist Paradigm," 609.

22. Michael Ignatieff, "Modern Dying," *The New Republic*, 26 Dec. 1988, 29.

23. See Richard R. Bootzin and Joan Ross Acocella, "Abnormal Behavior: Yesterday and Today," *Abnormal Psychology: Current Perspectives*, 5th ed. (New York: Random House, 1988), 1–22.

24. Sacks, *Man Who Mistook*, and *Awakenings* (New York: E. P. Dutton, 1983).

25. Sperry, "Psychology's Mentalist Paradigm," 609.

26. Sperry, "Psychology's Mentalist Paradigm," 609.
27. E. Roy John, "A Model of Consciousness," in *Consciousness and Self-Regulation Advances in Research*, vol. 1, ed. Gary E. Schwartz and David Shapiro (New York: Plenum Press, 1976), 1–50.
28. John, "Model of Consciousness," 1.
29. John, "Model of Consciousness," 2. Cf. the Gestalt psychology's principles of organization summarized by Edna Heidbreder, "Gestalt Psychology," *Seven Psychologies* (New York: Appleton-Century-Crofts, 1961), 228–275.
30. John, "Model of Consciousness," 3–8.
31. John F. Kihlstrom, "Conscious, Subconscious, Unconscious: A Cognitive Perspective," in *The Unconscious Reconsidered*, ed. Kenneth S. Bowers and Donald Meichenbaum (New York: John Wiley & Sons, 1984), 149–211.
32. See Kenneth S. Pope and Jerome L. Singer, "The Waking Stream of Consciousness," in Davidson and Davidson, *Psychobiology of Consciousness*, 169–91.
33. John, "Model of Consciousness," 6.
34. John, "Model of Consciousness," 6.
35. Danah Zohar, *The Quantum Self: Human Nature and Consciousness Defined by the New Physics* (New York: William Morrow, 1990).
36. See R. Nisbett and T. D. Wilson, "Telling More Than We Can Know: Verbal reports on mental processes," *Psychological Review*, no. 84 (1977): 231–59; see also L. Ross, "The intuitive psychologist and his shortcomings: Distortions in the attribution process," in *Advances in Experimental Social Psychology*, vol. 10, ed. Leonard Berkowitz (New York: Academic Press, 1977).
37. For a recent instance of this ongoing debate in psychology, see the affirmative claims of G. S. Howard and C. G. Conway, "Can There Be An Empirical Science of Volitional Control?" *American Psychologist*, no. 41 (1986): 1241–51; some replies, challenges, and negative comments are in Comment Section, *American Psychologist* (November 1987): 1029–34.
38. Many behaviorists, as already noted, keep their allegiance to the environmental determinist approach of B. F. Skinner; for instance, in the debate described in the previous note, see the reply to Howard and Conway by Steven C. Hayes, "Contextrual Determinants of 'Volitional Action': A Reply to Howard and Conway," *American Psychologist* (November 1987): 1029–30.
39. See Silvan S. Tomkins, *Affect, Imagery and Consciousness*, vol. 1 (New York: Springer Verlag, 1962).
40. A. R. Luria, "The Human Brain and Conscious Activity," in *Consciousness and Self-Regulation: Advances in Research and Theory*, vol. 2, ed. Gary E. Schwartz and David Shapiro (New York: Plenum Press, 1978), 5.
41. Nicholas Humphrey, "The social function of intellect," in *From Creation to Chaos: Classic Writings in Science*, ed. Bernard Dixon (Oxford: Basil Blackwell, 1989), 93–105. Cf. Richard Davidson's more inward cognitive version of the purposes of the evolution of consciousness in which it serves to "transform and restructure information as well as information-processing structures themselves," and "to facilitate access to particular subprograms or structures (subroutines) by other subprograms or structures," making humans more cognitively flexible—Richard Davidson, "Consciousness and Information Processing: A Biocognitive Perspective," in Davidson and Davidson, *Psychobiology of Consciousness*, 24–25.
42. This interrelated systems approach to the human being is based upon that given by the psychologist Carroll E. Izard, "Emotion-cognition relationships and human development," in *Emotions, Cognition and Behavior*, ed. Carroll E. Izard, Jerome Kagan, and Robert B. Zajonc. (Cambridge: Cambridge Univ. Press, 1984), 17–37.
43. In addition to references to John's model and Kilstrohm's work that have already been cited, see Colin Martindale, *Cognition and Consciousness* (Homewood, IL: The

Dorsey Press, 1981); the question of nonconscious mental operations will be discussed in the next chapter on reason and intuition.

44. See Michael S. Gazzaniga, "Organization of the Human Brain," *Science*, vol. 245, 1 Sept. 1989, 947–52; the modular models of the brain do not necessarily imply that self-consciousness will not be unified, according to Daniel N. Robinson, "Cerebral Plurality and the Unity of Self," *American Psychologist*, vol. 37, no. 8: 904–10.

45. See John R. Anderson, "Memory and Learning," in *Cognitive Psychology and Its Implications* (San Francisco: W. H. Freeman, 1980), 163–254. See also Henry L. Roediger III, "Implicit Memory: Retention Without Remembering," September, 1990, *American Psychologist*, vol. 45, no. 9, 1043–1056.

46. Laboratory tests and other ways of assessing mental functioning can be found in Bootzin and Acocella, "Diagnosis and Assessment," in *Abnormal Psychology*, 135–66.

47. See B. F. Skinner, *Science and Human Behavior* (New York: Macmillan, 1953); see also Willard F. Day, who says, "What is the Self? To a behaviorist, there is no such thing"—Willard F. Day, Jr., "On the Behavioral Analysis of Self-Deception and Self-Development," in Mischel, *The Self*, 248.

48. For a representative sampling of the huge array of research on the self, excluding psychoanalytic thinkers, see the collection of articles in Morris Rosenberg and Howard B. Kaplan, eds., *Social Psychology of the Self-Concept* (Arlington Heights, IL: Harlan Davidson, 1982); see also the papers in Suls, *Psychological Perspectives*. Cf. the continuing interest and debate in psychology over the importance of self-concepts in Philip Cushman, "Why the Self Is Empty: Toward a Historically Situated Psychology," *American Psychologist*, vol. 45, no. 5: 599–611.

49. See Hazel Markus and Keith Sentis, "The Self in Social Information Processing," in Suls, *Psychological Perspectives*, 41–70; see also Anthony G. Greenwald, "Is Anyone In Charge?" in Suls, *Psychological Perspectives*, 151–81.

50. The research problems involved in studying the self as dynamic agent and the self as conceptual object are discussed in William Damon and Daniel Hart, "Understanding the self-as-subject," in *Self-Understanding in Childhood and Adolescence* (Cambridge: Cambridge Univ. Press, 1988), 123–38; for a classic statement of the theoretical and methodological problems, see Chad Gordon, "Self-Conceptions: Configurations of Content," in *The Self in Social Interaction*, vol. 1, ed. Chad Gordon and Kenneth J. Gergen (New York: John Wiley & Sons, 1968), 115–36. Cf. the research described in Kay Deaux and Lawrence S. Wrightsman, "The Self," in *Social Psychology* (Pacific Grove, CA: Brooks/Cole, 1988), 61–91.

51. James, *Principles*, vol. I, 291–401.

52. Gordon Allport, "The Proprium," in *Becoming* (New Haven: Yale Univ. Press, 1955), 41–57.

53. George Herbert Mead, "The Genesis of the Self," in Gordon and Gergen, *Self in Social Interaction*, 51–59; see also Edward E. Jones and Thane S. Pittman, "Toward a General Theory of Strategic Self-Presentation," in Suls, *Psychological Perspectives*, 231–62.

54. See Erving Goffman, *The Presentation of Self in Everyday Life* (New York: Overlook Press, 1959).

55. See Daniel Stern, *The Interpersonal World of the Infant* (New York: Basic Books, 1984).

56. See a summary of the social psychological research on nonverbal channels of communication, "Communication," Deaux and Wrightsman, "The Self," 128–57; other sophisticated psychoanalytic research of unconscious dynamics is described and discussed in Sidney J. Blatt and Howard Lerner, "Investigations in The Psychoanalytic Theory of Object Relations and Object Representations," in *Empirical Studies of Psychoanalytical Theories*, vol. 1, ed. Joseph Masling (Hillsdale, NJ: Lawrence Erlbaum Associates, 1983), 189–249. Experimental infant studies also employ ingenious new research techniques.

57. James, *Principles*, vol. I, 224–90.
58. See Pope and Singer, "Waking Stream," 169–91. Cf. Mihaly Csikszentmihalyi, "The Anatomy of Consciousness," in *Flow: The Psychology of Optimal Experience* (New York: Harper & Row, 1990), 23–42.
59. See James, *Principles*, vol. I, 258; see also Csikszentmihalyi, "The Conditions of Flow," in *Flow*, 71–93; for a philosophical analysis of how freedom of attention relates to freedom of the will, see Harry G. Frankfurt, "Freedom of the Will and the Concept of a Person," in *What Is a Person?* ed. Michael F. Goodman (Clifton, NJ: Humana Press, 1988), 127–44.
60. See Pope and Singer, "Waking Stream," 185–88; for the idea of enacted emotions, see Roy Shafer, "Defining Emotion as Action," in *A New Language for Psychoanalysis* (New Haven: Yale Univ. Press, 1976), 271–93.
61. See Howard Margolis, *Patterns, Thinking, and Cognition: A Theory of Judgement* (Chicago: Univ. of Chicago Press, 1987), 80; for a psychological concept of "mindlessness," see Ellen Langer, Arthur Blank, and Benzion Chanowitz, "The Mindlessness of Ostensibly Thoughtful Action: The Role of Placebic Information in Interpersonal Interaction," *Journal of Personality and Social Psychology* 36(1978): 635–42.
62. Pope and Singer, "Waking Stream," 175.
63. Allport, *Becoming*, 36–56; William Damon and Daniel Hart, "Introduction," in *Self-Understanding in Childhood and Adolescence* (Cambridge: Cambridge Univ. Press, 1988), 1–19.
64. See E. Diener, "Deindividuation, self-awareness, and disinhibition," *Journal of Personality and Social Psychology* 37 (1979): 1160–71.
65. Charles T. Tart, "A Systems Approach to Altered States of Consciousness," in Davidson and Davidson, *Psychobiology of Consciousness*, 243–69.
66. See Serge-Christophe Kolm, "The Buddhist theory of 'no-self,'" in *The Multiple Self*, ed. Jon Elster (Cambridge: Cambridge Univ. Press, 1986), 233–65; see also Derek Parfit, *Reasons and Persons* (Oxford: Oxford Univ. Press, 1984).
67. See Allport, *Becoming*; Carl R. Rogers, *On Becoming A Person* (Boston: Houghton Mifflin, Sentry Edition, 1970); Abraham H. Maslow, *Motivation and Personality* (New York: Harper & Row, 1954).
68. Besides the references just given, see Albert Bandura, "The Self and Mechanisms of Agency," Suls, *Psychological Perspectives*, 3–39; see also Joseph F. Rychlak, "Free Will: Doing Otherwise, All Circumstances Remaining the Same," in *Taking Sides: Clashing Views on Controversial Psychological Issues*, 5th ed., ed. Joseph Rubinstein and Brent Slife (Guilford, CT: Dushkin Publishing Group, 1988), 44–50.
69. James, *Principles*, vol. II, 561–62.
70. For a succinct overview of the literature and developments in psychoanalysis, see Leo Rangell, M.D., "The Self in Psychoanalytic Theory," *Journal of the American Psychoanalytic Association*, vol. 30, no. 4 (1982): 863–91. Cf. in the same issue, Ernst A. Ticho, Ph.D., "The Alternate Schools and the Self," 849–62. Cf. Jane Loevinger's description of the early developments in psychoanalysis, *Ego Development*, 314–95.
71. C. G. Jung, *The Undiscovered Self*, 1st ed. (Boston: Little Brown, 1958).
72. James, *Principles*, vol. I, 310–13; see Gordon, "Self-Conceptions," 115–36; see also Morris Rosenberg, "Psychological Selectivity in Self-Esteem Formation," in *Attitude, Ego-Involvement and Change*, ed. Carolyn W. Sherif and Muzafer Sherif (New York: John Wiley and Sons, 1967).
73. Kurt Lewin, *Principles of Topological Psychology* (New York: McGraw Hill, 1936).
74. See Morris Rosenberg, *Conceiving the Self* (New York: Basic Books, 1979); see also Howard B. Kaplan, "Prevalence of the Self-Esteem Motive," in Rosenberg and Kaplan, *Social Psychology of the Self-Concept*, 139–51.
75. Hazel Markus, "Self-Schemata and Processing Information about the Self," *Journal of Personality and Social Psychology* 35 (1977): 63–78.

76. Rogers, *On Becoming A Person*.

77. See Prescott Lecky, *Self-Consistency: A Theory of Personality* (New York: The Island Press, 1945); see also Erik Erikson, "The Life Cycle: Epigenesis of Identity" in *Identity: Youth and Crisis* (New York: W. W. Norton, 1968), 91–135; for a subtle philosophical discussion of the need for integral life plans and achieved selfhood in different cultural systems, see Charles Taylor, "The Self in Moral Space," in *Sources of the Self: The Making of the Modern Identity* (Cambridge: Harvard Univ. Press, 1989), 25–52.

Chapter 3.   Reason and Intuition

1. See Howard Gardner, *The Mind's New Science: A History of the Cognitive Revolution* (New York: Basic Books, 1987); see also Owen J. Flanagan, Jr., *The Science of the Mind* (Cambridge, MA: The MIT Press, 1984).

2. For a summary of the range of "thinking" see Colin Martindale, *Cognition and Consciousness* (Homewood, IL: The Dorsey Press, 1981); see also Kenneth S. Pope and Jerome Singer, "Regulation of the Stream of Consciousness: Toward a Theory of Ongoing Thought," in *Consciousness and Self-Regulation: Advances in Research and Theory*, vol. 2, ed. Gary E. Schwartz and David Shapiro, (New York: Plenum Press, 1978).

3. See Ulric Neisser, "Theories of Perception," in *Cognition and Reality: Principles and Implications of Cognitive Psychology* (New York: W. H. Freeman, 1976), 13–33; John R. Anderson, "Perception and Attention," in *Cognitive Psychology and Its Implications* (San Francisco: W. H. Freeman, 1980), 21–59.

4. See Jerome Kagan, *The Nature of the Child* (New York: Basic Books, 1984). Cf. Jean Piaget, *The Psychology of Intelligence* (London: Routledge & Kegan Paul, 1950).

5. See Richard E. Mayer, *Thinking, Problem Solving, Cognition* (New York: W. H. Freeman, 1983).

6. See Percy H. Hill et al., *Making Decisions: A Multidisciplinary Introduction*, Foreward by Jean Mayer (New York: Univ. Press of America, 1986). *Making Decisions* grew out of an interdisciplinary team-taught course at Tufts University and includes chapters on ethical, statistical, medical, political, interpersonal, and economic decisions written by Tufts faculty from different disciplines. For another example see David C. Hoaglin et al., *Data For Decisions. Information Strategies for Policy-Makers* (New York: University Press, 1982).

7. The philosopher Hugo Bedau has a chapter on ethical decision making in Hill et al., *Making Decisions*, 27–55. Cf. Howard Brody, *Ethical Decisions in Medicine* (Boston: Little, Brown, 1976) in which Brody gives decision-tree diagrams for various forms of ethical decision making.

8. See Churchland, "AI Again: Parallel Distributed Processing," *Matter and Consciousness: A Contemporary Introduction to the Philosophy of Mind*, Revised Edition (Cambridge, Massachusetts: MIT Press, 1988), 156–65. Cf. Patricia Smith Churchland, "Parallel Models of Neuronal Computation," in *Neurophilosophy: Toward a Unified Science of the Mind-Brain* (Cambridge, MA: The MIT Press, 1988), 458–74.

9. See Roger Penrose, "Parallel computers and the 'oneness' of consciousness," in *The Emperor's New Mind: Concerning Computers, Minds, and The Laws of Physics* (New York: Oxford Univ. Press, 1989), 398–99.

10. See Mayer, "Beginnings," in *Thinking*, 5.

11. The usual linear flowchart approach can be seen in Hill, "The Decision-Making Process," *Making Decisions*, 21–26, fig. 3–1, 22; Another more dynamic model and flowchart can be found in Irving L. Janis and Leon Mann, *Decision Making: A Psychological Analysis of Conflict, Choice and Commitment* (New York: The Free Press, 1977).

12. See Martindale, "Types of Thinking," in *Cognition and Consciousness*, 296–300. Cf. Mihaly Csikszentmihalyi, "Attention and the Holistic Approach to Behavior," in *The*

Stream of Consciousness: Scientific Investigations into the Flow of Human Experience, ed. Kenneth S. Pope and Jerome L. Singer (New York: Plenum Press, 1978), 335–58.

13. See the definition of intelligence given by Douglas R. Hofstadter, *Godel, Escher, Bach: An Eternal Golden Braid* (New York: Basic Books, 1979).

14. See Mayer, "Expert-Novice Differences," in *Thinking,* 320–23. In a more colloquial way, Robert M. Pirsig expresses it after talking of the discoveries of the mathematician Poincare: "As Poincare pointed out, there *must* be a subliminal choice of what facts we observe. The difference between a good mechanic and a bad one, like the difference between a good mathematician and a bad one, is precisely this ability to *select* the good facts from the bad ones on the basis of quality"—Robert M. Pirsig, *Zen and the Art of Motorcycle Maintenance* (New York: Bantam Books, 1974), 275.

15. See Pirsig, *Zen,* 282–320.

16. See Alasdair MacIntyre, *Whose Justice? Which Rationality?* (Notre Dame, IN: Univ. of Notre Dame Press, 1988).

17. A traditional statement of these criteria can be found in Abraham Kaplan, "Validation of Theories," in *The Conduct of Inquiry: Methodology for Behavioral Science* (New York: Harper & Row, 1963), 311–22.

18. Thomas Kuhn, *The Structure of Scientific Revolutions,* 2d ed. (Chicago: Univ. of Chicago Press, 1970).

19. Stephen G. Brush, "Prediction and Theory Evaluation: The Case of Light Bending," *Science,* 1 Dec. 1989, 1124–29.

20. Clifford Geertz, "From the Native's Point of View: On the Nature of Anthropological Understanding," in *Interpretative Social Science: A Reader,* ed. Paul Rabinow and William M. Sullivan (Berkeley: Univ. of California Press, 1979).

21. Geertz describes the "hermeneutic circles" involved in understanding which are more completely discussed in Hans-Gorg Gadamer, *Truth and Method,* 2d rev. ed. (New York: Crossroad, 1989).

22. John Henry Newman, *A Grammar of Assent* (Garden City, NY: Doubleday, 1955 [1870]), 254.

23. David Braybrooke, "Uses and Abuses of Quantities," *Philosophy of Social Science* (Englewood Cliffs, NJ: Prentice-Hall, 1987), 35–36.

24. Roger Penrose claims that "somehow, consciousness is needed in order to handle situations where we have to form new judgements, and where the rules have not been laid down beforehand." If an answer is already resolved with rules and an algorithm provided, then it can be programmed, computerized, and operate unconsciously—Penrose, *Emperor's New Mind,* 411.

25. William R. Freudenburg, "'Human Error' in Estimation Techniques," in "Perceived Risk, Real Risk: Social Science and the Art of Probabilistic Risk Assessment," *Science,* 7 Oct. 1988, 45–47.

26. Robert J. Sternberg, "Human Intelligence: The Model Is the Message," *Science,* 6 Dec. 1985, 1111–18.

27. Sternberg, "Human Intelligence," 1111.

28. Howard Gardner, *Frames of Mind: The Theory of Multiple Intelligences* (New York: Basic Books, 1985).

29. See William R. Freudenburg, "Perceived Risk," 44–49.

30. Michael Polanyi, "The Art of Knowing: Probability," *Personal Knowledge: Towards a Post-Critical Philosophy* (Chicago: Univ. of Chicago Press, 1962), 18–32.

31. Richard E. Nisbett et al., "Teaching Reasoning," *Science,* 30 Oct. 1987, 625–31; Richard J. Sternberg, "How Can We Teach Intelligence?" in *Taking Sides: Clashing Views on Controversial Psychological Issues,* 5th ed., ed. Joseph Runinstein and Brent Slife (Guilford, CT: Dushkin Publishing Group, 1988), 176–86.

32. See Richard R. Bootzin and Joan Ross Acocella, *Abnormal Psychology: Current Perspectives,* 5th ed. (New York: Random House, 1988; see also the criteria of mental disor-

ders set forth in *Diagnostic and Statistical Manual of Mental Disorders (DSM III-R)*, 3d ed., rev. (Washington, DC: American Psychiatric Association, 1987).

33. The importance of voluntary focusing of attention in mental health, optimal functioning, and pathology is pointed out by Csikszentmihalyi, "Attention and the Holistic Approach," 335–58. Cognitive therapies focus on correcting both the content and processes of thinking. Cf. Albert Ellis and Russell Grieger, eds., *Handbook of Rational-Emotive Therapy* (New York: Springer, 1977) and Aaron T. Beck, *Cognitive Therapy and the Emotional Disorders* (New York: International Universities Press, 1976).

34. For descriptions of primary thinking, see Martindale, "States of Consciousness," in *Cognition and Consciousness*, 311–38. Cf. Tony Bastick, "Primary Processing Thinking," in *Intuition: How we think and act* (New York: John Wiley & Sons, 1982), 143–50; John C. Nemiah, "The Unconscious and Psychopathology," in Bowers and Meichenbaum, *Unconscious Reconsidered*, 49–87.

35. John F. Kihlstrom, "The Cognitive Unconscious," *Science*, 18 Sept. 1987, 1445–52; Kenneth S. Bowers, "On Being Unconsciously Influenced and Informed," in Bowers and Meichenbaum, *Unconscious Reconsidered*, 227–72.

36. Jean Piaget, "The Affective Unconscious and the Cognitive Unconscious," *Journal of the American Psychoanalytic Association*, Volume 21, no. 2 (1973): 249–61.

37. Bowers, "Being Unconsciously Influenced," 256.

38. For a comprehensive discussion of the research on human error, biased thinking, and irrationality coexisting with human reasonableness, see Gardner, "How Rational a Being?" in *Mind's New Science*, 360–80. Cf. with Donald Meichenbaum and J. Barnard Gilmore's excellent summary of the influence of unconscious cognitive schema and structures on functioning, "The Nature of Unconscious Processes: A Cognitive-Behavioral Perspective," in Bowers and Meichenbaum, *Unconscious Reconsidered*, 273–98. Another account of how abstract logical thinking and robust practical human reasoning overlap but are not always identical can be found in Howard Margolis, "Knowledge, Belief, Logic," *Patterns, Thinking, and Cognition: A Theory of Judgment* (Chicago: Univ. of Chicago Press, 1987), 87–111.

39. Amelie Oksenberg Rorty, "Self-deception, akrasia and irrationality," in *The Multiple Self*, ed. Jon Elster (Cambridge: Cambridge Univ. Press, 1985), 115–16, 131.

40. Kihlstrom, "Cognitive Unconscious," 1445–52; Daniel N. Robinson, "Psychobiology and the Unconscious," in Bowers and Meichenbaum, *Unconscious Reconsidered*, 212–26.

41. Ernest R. Hilgard, "Neodissociation Theory of Multiple Cognitive Control Systems," in Schwartz and Shapiro, *Consciousness and Self-Regulation*, vol. 2, 137–71. Cf. Kihlstrom's discussion of dissociation in "Conscious, Subconscious, Unconscious," 170–97.

42. Kenneth S. Pope and Jerome L. Singer, "The Waking Stream of Consciousness," in *The Psychobiology of Consciousness*, ed. Julian M. Davidson and Richard J. Davidson (New York: Plenum Press, 1980), 169–91.

43. Richard J. Davidson, "Consciousness and Information Processing: A Biocognitive Perspective," in Davidson and Davidson, *Psychobiology of Consciousness*, 11–46.

44. See Kilstrom, "Cognitive Unconscious," 1445–52; Pawel Lewicki, "Internal Processing Algorithms," *Nonconscious Social Information Processing* (New York: Academic Press, 1986), 28–37. Cf. a popular presentation of the model of nonconscious processing in Daniel Goleman, "The Intelligent Filter," in *Vital Lies, Simple Truths: The Psychology of Self-Deception* (New York: Simon and Schuster, 1985), 61–66. Another intriguing new hypothesis by psychoanalytic researchers is that the unconscious mind makes therapeutic plans to lift repression when it judges the psychotherapist to be trusted: "The control hypothesis postulates that because patients bring forth repressed material only after they have unconsciously overcome their worry about the consequences, they will not feel especially anxious as they become aware of the

material"—Joseph Weiss, "Unconscious Mental Functioning," *Scientific American*, March 1990, 105.

45. Goleman, *Vital Lies*, 61–66. Cf. also note 44.

46. Mardi J. Horowitz, "Psychological Response to Serious Life Events," in *The Denial of Stress*, ed. Shlomo Breznitz (New York: International Universities Press, 1983), 129–66.

47. See Roger Penrose, "Inspiration, insight, and originality," *Emperor's New Mind*, 418–23.

48. Penrose, *Emperor's New Mind*, 419.

49. Margolis, *Patterns*, 78–85.

50. Stephen G. Brush, "Light Bending," 1124–29. Cf. Polyani on "Commitment," *Personal Knowledge*, 299–324.

51. Reported in Brush, "Light Bending," 1125.

52. Brush, "Light Bending," 1125.

53. See Polyani, "Elegance and Beauty," *Personal Knowledge*, 145–50. Cf. Penrose, "A beautiful idea has a much greater chance of being a correct idea than an ugly one," *Emperor's New Mind*, 421. Cf. James Gleick's discussions with the mathematician Mitchell Feigenbaum, "Universality," in *Chaos: Making A New Science* (New York: Viking, 1987), 157–87.

54. See Julian Jaynes, *The Origin of Consciousness in the Breakdown of the Bicameral Mind* (Boston: Houghton Mifflin Company, 1977).

55. Daniel Kahneman and Amos Tversky, "Choices, Values and Frames," *American Psychologist*, vol. 39, no. 4, (April 1984): 341–50; see also a summary and discussion of the research on bias and error attribution in Kay Deauz and Lawrence S. Wrightsman, "Social Knowledge," in *Social Psychology* (Pacific Grove, CA: Brooks/Cole, 1988), 93–125.

56. "Illusions of control," are nonveridical perceptions that a person can affect or control environmental outcomes—Ellen J. Langer, "The Illusion of Control," *Journal of Personality and Social Psychology*, 32, 311–328.

57. See Elizabeth F. Loftus, *Eyewitness Testimony* (Cambridge: Harvard Univ. Press, 1979). Cf. the discussion on self-generated hallucinations.

58. As discussed in the previous chapter on the self, a dynamic inner seeking for the good and full self-realization is a tenet of humanistic and self psychologists, as typified in Gordon Allport's *Becoming* (New Haven: Yale Univ. Press, 1955) and in a philosopher such as Iris Murdoch, who speaks of "that endless aspiration to perfection which is characteristic of moral activity," in "The Idea of Perfection," in *The Sovereignty of Good* (London: Ark Paperbacks, 1985 [1970]), 31.

59. Donald Meichenbaum and J. Barnard Gilmore attempt to bridge the gaps that separate the behavioral and psychodynamic approaches to therapeutic listening to the unconscious stream of thinking in "Nature of Unconscious Processes," 273–298. Cf. Paul Wachtel, *Psychoanalysis and Behavior Therapy: Toward an Integration* (New York: Basic Books, 1977).

60. See Eugene T. Gendlin, *Focusing*, 2d ed. (New York: Bantam Books, 1978, 1979) for a self-activated technique of creating intuitions by questioning and penetrating a person's defenses and distractions.

61. Gendlin, "Receiving," in *Focusing*, 60–61.

62. Those trying to instill both creative and critical thinking in educational curriculums have articulated this need in textbooks, see for instance, Carole Wade and Carol Tavris "Thinking Critically and Creatively," *Psychology*, 2d ed. (New York: Harper & Row, 1990).

63. See Churchland, "The Problem of Self-Consciousness: A Contemporary View," in *Matter and Consciousness*, 73–75. Cf. with other behaviorist social psychologists who deny the privileged position of introspection—D. J. Bem, "Self-perception theory," in *Advances in Experimental Social Psychology*, vol. 6, ed. Leonard Berkowitz (New York: Academic Press, 1972).

64. Bastick, *Intuition*, 127–33.

65. The idea of the need for combining positive results from intuitive thinking and critical thinking in order to have convinced knowledge is an old truth; it is given a new twist in a matrix describing various other permutations, and combinations of intuition and critical thinking, labeled "doubt," "paradox," "belief," and "uncertainty," in Margolis, *Patterns*, 97–101.

Chapter 4.   Emotions and Moral Decision Making

1. Gordon Allport, "The Proprium," in *Becoming* (New Haven: Yale Univ. Press, 1955), 41–56; see also Carroll E. Izard, *Human Emotions* (New York: Plenum Press, 1977) and Joseph J. Campos and Karen Caplovitz Barrett, "Toward a new understanding of emotions and their development," in *Emotions, Cognition and Behavior*, ed. Carroll E. Izard, Jerome Kagan, and Robert B. Zajonc (Cambridge: Cambridge Univ. Press, 1984), 229–63.

2. See Robin May Schott, *Cognition and Eros: A Critique of the Kantian Paradigm* (Boston: Beacon Press, 1988); see also Robert C. Solomon, *The Passions* (New York: Anchor Books, 1977).

3. Schott, *Cognition and Eros*, 40–41.

4. Quoted by Aileen Kelly in *The New Republic*, 23 April 1984, 30.

5. Milan Kundera, "An Introduction to a Variation," *New York Times*, 6 Jan. 1986.

6. Kundera, "Introduction."

7. Quoted by Joel Feinberg, "Sentiment and Sentimentality in Practical Ethics" (Presidential address delivered before American Philosophical Association, Sacramento, CA, 26 March, 1982).

8. Ignatius Loyola, "First Way Of Making A Good And Correct Choice Of A Way of Life," in *The Spiritual Exercises of St. Ignatius*, trans. Louis J. Puhl, S.J. (Chicago: Loyola Univ. Press, 1951), 75.

9. Loyola, "First Way," 76.

10. Quoted by Schott, *Cognition and Eros*, 106.

11. Schott, *Cognition and Eros*, 106.

12. H. Tristram Engelhardt, Jr., *The Foundations of Bioethics* (New York: Oxford Univ. Press), 10.

13. James Rachels, *The End of Life: Euthanasia and Morality* (Oxford: Oxford Univ. Press, 1986), 149.

14. Feinberg, "Sentiment"; see also Joel Feinberg, "The Mistreatment of Dead Bodies: The Moral Trap of Sentimentality," in *Hastings Center Report* 15 (February 1985): 31–37.

15. Feinberg, "Sentiment."

16. The phrase "hot cognition" is another way of expressing what has been called emotion's "Law of Concern: Emotions arise in response to events that are important to the individual's goals, motives or concern"—Nico H. Frijda, "The Laws of Emotion," *American Psychologist*, vol. 43, no. 5:351.

17. Izard, *Human Emotions*.

18. Robert Plutchik, *Emotion: A Psychoevolutionary Synthesis* (New York: Harper and Row, 1980).

19. Silvan S. Tomkins, "Affect Theory," in *Approaches To Emotion*, ed. Klaus R. Scherer and Paul Ekman (Hillsdale, NJ: Lawrence Erlbaum Associates, 1984), 163–95; see also Izard, *Human Emotions*.

20. See Richard R. Bootzin and Joan Ross Acocella, "The Emotional Disorders," *Abnormal Psychology: Current Perspectives*, 5th ed. (New York: Random House, 1988), 167–255.

21. Paul Ekman discusses the panhuman commonalities discovered in cross-cultural research in Paul Ekman, "Expression and the Nature of Emotion," in Scherer and Ekman, *Approaches to Emotion*, 319–43; see also Robert I. Levy, "The Emotions in Comparative Perspective," in Scherer and Ekman, *Approaches to Emotion*, 397–412.

22. Ekman; see also Tomkins, "Affect Theory"; Izard, *Human Emotions;* and Plutchik, *Emotions.*

23. Paul Ekman "Cross-cultural studies of facial expression," in *Darwin and facial expression: A century of research in review,* ed. Paul Ekman (New York: Academic Press, 1973).

24. Colwyn Trevarthen, "Emotions in Infancy: Regulators of Contact and Relationships with Persons," in Scherer and Ekman, *Approaches to Emotion,* 129–57; see also Daniel N. Stern, "Affect Attunement," in *The Interpersonal World of the Infant: A View from Psychoanalysis and Developmental Psychology* (New York: Basic Books, 1985), 138–61, and Edward Z. Tronick, "Emotions and Emotional Communication in Infants," *American Psychologist,* vol. 44, no. 2 (February 1989): 112–9.

25. In addition to the sources already cited, see Ross Buck, *The Communication of Emotion* (New York: The Guilford Press, 1984); see also Ellen Berscheid, "Attraction and Emotion in Interpersonal Relations," in *Affect and Cognition: The Seventeenth Annual Carnegie Symposium on Cognition,* ed. Margaret Sydnor Clark and Susan T. Fiske (Hillsdale, NJ: Lawrence Erlbaum, 1982), 37–54.

26. Izard, *Human Emotions.*

27. Plutchik, *Emotion;* see also Nico H. Frijda, "Theory of emotion," *The Emotions: Studies in Emotion & Social Interaction* (Cambridge: Cambridge Univ. Press, 1986), 453–79.

28. Izard, *Human Emotions;* see also Campos and Barrett, "Toward a New Understanding."

29. Plutchik, *Emotion.*

30. An approach different from the perspective of the researchers cited previously stresses the cognitive, social constructionist elements of emotions; emotions are held to be cognitive systems of rules of behavior. These emphases can be found in James R. Averill, "Emotions and Anxiety: Sociocultural, Biological and Psychological Determinants," in *Explaining Emotion,* ed. Amelie O. Rorty (Berkeley: Univ. of California Press, 1980), 37–72; for other social construction approaches, see Rom Harré, "An Outline of the Social Constructionist Viewpoint," in *The Social Construction of Emotions,* ed. Rom Harré (Oxford: Basil Blackwell, 1986), 2–14.

31. See Ekman, and Levy, in *Approaches to Emotion.*

32. See an example of social construction theory and ethnopsychology in Catherine A. Lutz, *Unnatural Emotions: Everyday Sentiments on a Micronesian Atoll & Their Challenge to Western Theory* (Chicago: Univ. of Chicago Press, 1988).

33. Robert N. Emde, "The Affective Core" (Paper presented at the Second World Congress of Infant Psychiatry, Cannes, France, March 1983), 1.

34. See Norman K. Denzin, "Emotionality, then, reveals the self to itself in a way that no other line of action can. Emotionality awakens inner feelings and thoughts. It enlivens the person's own presence before himself," *On Understanding Emotion* (San Francisco: Jossey-Bass, 1984), 273.

35. Frijda, "Laws of Emotion," 349–58.

36. Frijda, "Laws of Emotion," 355.

37. See Oliver Sacks, *The Man Who Mistook His Wife for a Hat; And Other Clinical Tales* (New York: Harper & Row, 1985).

38. R. B. Zajonc, "Feeling and Thinking: Preferences Need No Inferences," *American Psychologist,* vol. 35, no. 2: 154; Zajonc has continued to hold that initial affective responses can precede the cognitive contributions to subjective experiences of emotion, at least in primitive responses; see R. B. Zajonc, "The Interaction of Affect and Cognition," in Scherer and Ekman, *Approaches to Emotion,* 239–46.

39. See Richard S. Lazarus, "Thoughts on the Relations Between Emotion and Cognition," in Scherer and Ekman, *Approaches to Emotion,* 247–57; if cognition is not defined as unitary, or including only conscious thinking, the question of the complex interactions and even fusion of cognition and various levels and types of emotions

becomes feasible; see Howard Leventhal, "A Perceptual Motor Theory of Emotion," in Scherer and Ekman, *Approaches to Emotion*, 271–91; as Leventhal says, "Emotion is elicited by cognition and emotion activates cognition," 281.

40. Leventhal, "Perceptual Motor Theory," 289; see also, from a psychoanalytic perspective, Willard Gaylin, *Feelings: Our Vital Signs* (New York: Harper & Row, 1979).

41. Gordon H. Bower and Paul R. Cohen, "Emotional Influences in Memory and Thinking: Data and Theory," in *Affect and Cognition*, 291–332.

42. For a summary and discussion of this extensive research, see Stephen G. Gilligan and Gordon H. Bower, "Cognitive consequences of emotional arousal," in Izard, Kagan, and Zajonc, *Emotions, Cognition and Behavior*, 547–88; see also Donald Meichenbaum and J. Barnard Gilmore, "The Nature of Unconscious Processes: A Cognitive-Behavioral Perspective," in *The Unconscious Reconsidered*, ed. Kenneth S. Bowers and Donald Meichenbaum (New York: John Wiley & Sons, 1984), 273–98.

43. See also Carroll E. Izard on the interaction of cognition and emotion in "Emotion-cognition relationships and human development," in Izard, Kagan, and Zajonc, *Emotions, Cognition and Behavior*, 17–37.

44. Michael Lewis and Linda Michalson, *Children's Emotions and Moods* (New York: Plenum Press, 1983), 88.

45. Joseph DeRivera, "Development and the Full Range of Emotional Experience," *Emotion in Adult Development*, ed. Carol Zander Malatesta and Carroll E. Izard (Beverly Hills, CA: Sage Publications, 1984), 45–63.

46. H. M. Cleckley, *The Mask of Sanity* (St. Louis: Mosby, 1976).

47. See a discussion of the criteria necessary for differentiation of mental disorder from voluntary criminal behavior in Bootzin and Acocella, "Antisocial Personality Disorder," in *Abnormal Psychology*, 266–71.

48. Roy Schafer, *A New Language for Psychoanalysis* (New Haven: Yale Univ. Press, 1976), 195.

49. Silvano Arieti and Jules Bemporad, *Severe and Mild Depression: The Psychotherapeutic Approach* (New York: Basic Books, 1978), 17.

50. See Mihaly Csikszentmihalyi, "Attention and the Holistic Approach to Behavior," *The Stream of Consciousness: Scientific Investigations into the Flow of Human Experience*, ed. Kenneth S. Pope and Jerome L. Singer (New York: Plenum Press, 1978), 335–58; see also Mardi J. Horowitz, "Psychological Response to Serious Life Events," *The Denial of Stress*, ed. Shlomo Breznitz (New York: International Universities Press, 1983), 129–66.

51. Schafer, *A New Language*, 298; see also Gail S. Reed, "Any affect may defend against another," "Rules of Clinical Understanding in Classical Psychoanalysis and in Self Psychology: A Comparison," *Journal of the American Psychoanalytic Association*, vol. 35 (1987): 421–44.

52. Campos and Barrett, "Toward a new understanding," 242–44.

53. For psychological versions of control and regulation see Leventhal, "The control of emotion," in Scherer and Ekman, *Approaches to Emotion*, 285–88; Schafer, *A New Language*, 294–300; Meichenbaum and Gilmore, "Nature of Unconscious Processes," 273–98. Philosophical discussions of directing emotions can be found in Robert C. Solomon, "Emotions and Choice," in *What Is An Emotion: Classic Readings in Philosophical Psychology*, ed. Cheshire Calhoun and Robert C. Solomon (Oxford: Oxford Univ. Press, 1984), 305–26.

54. John Sabini and Maury Silver, "Emotions, responsibility, and character," in *Responsibility, Character, and the Emotions: New Essays in Moral Psychology*, ed. Ferdinand Schoeman (Cambridge: Cambridge Univ. Press, 1987), 165–75.

55. For a popular treatment of an array of different physiological and cognitive methods for stress reduction, see Ronald G. Nathan, Thomas E. Staats, and Paul J. Rosch, *The Doctors' Guide to Instant Stress Relief* (New York: G. P. Putnam's Sons, 1987).

56. See Aaron T. Beck, *Cognitive Therapy and the Emotional Disorders* (New York: International Universities Press, 1976), and Albert Ellis and Russell Griegeer, *Handbook of Rational-Emotive Therapy* (New York: Springer, 1977); for a discussion of emotional change processes in psychotherapy, see Leslie S. Greenberg and Jeremy D. Safran, "Emotion in Psychotherapy," *American Psychologist*, vol. 44, no. 1 (January 1989): 19–29.

57. Walter Mischel, Yuichi Shoda, and Monica L. Rodriguez, "Delay of Gratification in Children," *Science*, May 1989, 933–38.

58. "As in Lefortovo [prison], I returned to my memory journeys, recalling all the best and most precious times of my life. Now however, the goal was different—to feel that I was continuing that life, that I had no other way, that this was the life of a free man. . . ." Natan Sharansky, *Fear No Evil* (New York: Random House, 1988), 259.

Chapter 5.   Making Moral Decisions

1. Edmond Cahn, *The Moral Decision: Right and Wrong in the Light of American Law* (Bloomington: Indiana Univ. Press, 1981 [1955]), 64.

2. Cahn, *Moral Decision*, 64.

3. Charles I. Larmore, *Patterns of Moral Complexity* (Cambridge: Cambridge Univ. Press, 1987), 15; Larmore goes on to show the difficulties of moral judgment in a world in which it is difficult to reconcile different moral obligations, but he too as a philosopher is less interested in the psychological process of deciding and judging.

4. In the chapter on reasoning, I have discussed the vast array of literature in different disciplines on decision making, which often has not taken into account the need for a conscious human subject; as Daniel Kahneman and Amos Tversky point out, "Making decisions is like speaking prose—people do it all the time, knowingly or unknowingly. It is hardly surprising then that the topic of decision making is shared by many disciplines, from mathematics and statistics, through economics and political science to sociology and psychology"—Daniel Kahneman and Amos Tversky, "Choices, Values, and Frames," *American Psychologist*, vol. 39, no. 4 (April 1984): 341.

5. See Tod S. Sloan, *Deciding: Self-Deception in Life Choices* (New York: Methuen, 1987).

6. See Paul C. Vitz's discussion of narrative thought and moral development, Paul C. Vitz, "The Uses of Stories in Moral Development: New Psychological Reasons for an Old Education Method," *American Psychologist*, vol. 45, no. 6: 709–20.

7. Gordon W. Allport, *Becoming* (New Haven: Yale Univ. Press, 1955), 51.

8. Kazuo Ishiguro, *The Remains of The Day* (New York: Alfred A. Knopf, 1989), 243.

9. William James, *The Principles of Psychology*, vol. I (New York: Dover Publications, 1950 [1890]), 288.

10. Viktor E. Frankl, *Man's Search for Meaning: An Introduction to Logotherapy* (New York: Pocket Books, 1963), 104.

11. Kenneth S. Pope and Jerome L. Singer, "The Waking Stream of Consciousness," in *The Psychobiology of Consciousness*, ed. Julian M. Davidson and Richard J. Davidson (New York: Plenum Press, 1980), 176.

12. Iris Murdoch, *The Sovereignty of Good* (London: Ark Paperbacks, 1985), 37.

13. I have discussed intuition and the nonconscious mind's relation to directed thinking in chapter 3 on reason and intuition.

14. Kahneman and Tversky in their study of choices have shown how difficult, risky choices are decided by "the effects of mental accounting," and "framing effects"—Kahneman and Tversky, "Choices, Values, and Frames," 349; moral choosing and difficult decision making will be even more affected by inner moral accounting and existing moral frames within the person.

15. Paul Churchland, *Matter and Consciousness: A Contemporary Introduction to the Philosophy of Mind*, rev. ed. (Cambridge MA: The MIT Press, 1988), 160.

16. Ignatius Loyola, *The Spiritual Exercises of St. Ignatius,* trans. Louis J. Puhl, S.J. (Chicago: Loyola Univ. Press, 1951), 149.

17. As George C. Rosenwald has said, "When approaching difficult choices, we are handicapped by our misconceptions of what a decision involves. Traditional psychological approaches to decision theory, far from enlightening us about this matter, tend to abet our rationalistic illusions"—Forward to Sloan, *Deciding,* xii; or as Tod Sloan avers in *Deciding,* "The psychology of decision making, perhaps because it takes the term psychology in too limited a fashion, cuts off aspects of the deciding process which make it human," 70.

18. James, *Principles,* vol. II, 534.

19. The problems of lack of integration and weakness of will are discussed in the next chapter on moral failure.

20. R. M. Hare, *Moral Thinking: Its Levels, Method, and Point* (Oxford: Clarendon Press, 1981), 52.

21. See Percy H. Hill, "The Decision-Making Process," in *Making Decisions: A Multidisciplinary Introduction,* ed. Percy H. Hill et al. (New York: Univ. Press of America, 1986), 21–26.

22. See Alasdair MacIntyre, "All the traditions with which we have been concerned agree in according a certain authority to logic both in their theory and in their practice," *Whose Justice: Which Rationality?* (Notre Dame, IN: Univ. of Notre Dame Press, 1988), 351.

23. Thomas Kuhn, *The Structure of Scientific Revolutions,* 2d ed. (Chicago: Univ. of Chicago Press, 1970).

24. Michael Stocker, "Intellectual Desire, Emotion and Action," *Explaining Emotions,* ed. Amelie Oksenberg Rorty (Berkeley: Univ. of California Press, 1980), 325.

25. See Arlie Hochschild, *The Managed Heart: Commercialization of Human Feeling* (Berkeley: Univ. of California Press, 1983).

26. Joseph Butler, *Fifteen Sermons* (New York: Robert Carter & Brothers, Facsimile Reprint, 1986).

27. Nico H. Frijda, "The Laws of Emotion," *American Psychologist,* vol. 43, no. 5: 353–54.

28. Martin L. Hoffman, "Interaction of affect and cognition in empathy," in *Emotions, Cognition and Behavior,* ed. Carroll E. Izard, Jerome Kagan, and Robert B. Zajonc (Cambridge: Cambridge Univ. Press, 1984), 103–31.

29. Robert B. Zajonc, "Attitudinal effects of mere exposure," *Journal of Personality and Social Psychology Monographs,* 9 (1968): 1–28.

30. Carroll E. Izard, *Human Emotions* (New York: Plenum Press, 1977), 94–95. Intimacy, passion, and commitment are seen as the core of love in Robert J. Sternberg, "A triangular theory of love," *Psychological Review* 93, 119–135; see also Willard Gaylin, M.D., *Rediscovering Love* (New York: Viking, 1986).

31. Kenneth Clark, *Moments of Vision* (New York: Harper & Row, 1982).

32. Iris Murdoch, *Sovereignty of Good,* 56.

33. Mary Midgley, "The Flight from Blame," *Philosophy* 62 (1987): 171–91.

34. Midgley, "Flight from Blame."

35. Grant Gillett, "Euthanasia, letting die and the pause," *Journal of Medical Ethics* 14 (1988): 61–68.

36. Jonathan Bennett, "The conscience of Huckleberry Finn," *Philosophy* 49 (1974): 123–34.

37. Bennett, "Huckleberry Finn."

38. Bennett, "Huckleberry Finn."

39. This idea of the best, most avowedly worthy emotions seems to be similar to Hume's idea of a ruling or "master passion," as described by Annette Baier, "Master Passions," in Rorty, *Explaining Emotions,* 403–23.

40. One model of the psychological dimensions of conviction are described as "ego preoccupation, cognitive elaboration and emotional commitment"—Robert P. Abelson, "Conviction," *American Psychologist*, vol. 43, no. 4 (April 1988): 267–75.

41. Obviously, I follow here an approach that holds that in morality, as in science, human reasoning can discern moral realities. See Richard N. Boyd, "How to Be a Moral Realist," *Essays on Moral Realism*, ed. Geoffrey Sayre-McCord (Ithaca, NY: Cornell Univ. Press, 1988), 181–228.

42. See James F. Childress, "If a person autonomously chooses to yield first order decisionmaking to a professional or to a religious institution, that person has exercised what may be called second-order autonomy," "The Place of Autonomy in Bioethics," in *Hasting Center Report*, vol. 20, no. 1, (January/February 1990): 13; see also D. O. Thomas, "I wish to argue that conscience requires that we do what we ultimately think we ought to do, and that it may be consistent with conscience to defer to the judgment of another," "Obedience to Conscience," *Conscience*, ed. John Donnelly and Leonard Lyons (Staten Island: Alba House, 1973), 184.

43. Gilbert Meilaender, "Virtue in Contemporary Religious Thought," *Virtue-Public and Private* (Grand Rapids, MI: William B. Eerdmans Publishing, 1986), 29; see also Alasdair MacIntyre, "The Virtues, the Unity of a Human Life and the Concept of a Tradition," in *After Virtue* (Notre Dame, IN: Univ. of Notre Dame Press, 1981), 190–209.

Chapter 6.   Moral Failure and Self-Deception

1. See Peter L. Berger and Thomas Luckmann, *The Social Construction of Reality* (New York: Anchor Books, 1967); see also Howard Kaminsky, "Moral Development in a Historical Perspective," in *Morality, Moral Behavior, and Moral Development*, ed. William M. Kurtines and Jacob L. Gewirtz (New York: John Wiley & Sons, 1984), 400–413.

2. See Amelie Oksenberg Rorty, "Agent Regret," in *Explaining Emotions*, ed. Amelie Oksenberg Rorty (Berkeley: Univ. of California Press, 1980), 489–506; see also Herbert Morris, "Nonmoral Guilt," in *Responsibility, Character, and the Emotions: New Essays in Moral Psychology*, ed. Ferdinand Schoeman (Cambridge: Cambridge Univ. Press, 1987), 220–40.

3. Mary Midgley, "The Problem of Natural Evil," in *Wickedness: A Philosophical Essay* (London: Routledge & Kegan Paul, 1985), 1–16. For a psychological explanation of the dependence of evil on good, see Harry Stack Sullivan, "The Malevolent Transformation," in *The Interpersonal Theory of Psychiatry* (New York: W. W. Norton, 1953), 213–16.

4. Robert Jay Lifton, "The Quest for Transcendence," in *The Nazi Doctors: Medical Killing and the Psychology of Genocide* (New York: Basic Books, 1986), 473–75.

5. Harry G. Frankfurt describes a human being without moral self-evaluation as "a wanton,"—"Freedom of the will and the concept of a Person," in *What Is a Person?* ed. Michael F. Goodman (Clifton, NJ: Humana Press, 1988), 133. Cf. M. Scott Peck, M.D., *People of the Lie: The Hope for Healing Human Evil* (New York: Simon & Schuster, 1983), 76–77.

6. Literature, drama, and Scriptures abound with depictions of moral failure and evil in all its forms, from the serpent in the garden to Iago, to modern novels and short stories; for a psychological treatment of encounters with evil in America see Peck, *People of the Lie*, 85–149; another penetrating psychological analysis of evil as ordinary can be found in John Sabini and Maury Silver, "On Destroying the Innocent with a Clear Conscience: A Sociopsychology of the Holocaust," in *Moralities of Everyday Life* (Oxford: Oxford Univ. Press, 1982), 55–87.

7. I will not repeat my earlier arguments for free will and notes from previous chapters on the self; but see Paul Ricoeur: "Evil has the meaning of evil because it is the work of freedom. Freedom has the meaning of freedom because it is capable of evil: I both recognize and declare myself to be the author of evil"—"Guilt, Ethics And

Religion," in *Moral Evil Under Challenge*, ed. Johannes B. Metz (New York: Herder and Herder, 1970), 17; see also Midgley, *Wickedness*, 70–72. Cf. Abigail L. Rosenthal, "Thinking Like a Nazi," in *A Good Look at Evil* (Philadelphia: Temple Univ. Press, 1987), 209–20.

8. Amelie Oksenberg Rorty, "Self deception, Akrasia and Irrationality," in *The Multiple Self*, ed. Jon Elster (Cambridge: Cambridge Univ. Press, 1985), 115–31; See also Donal Davidson's definition of weakness of will in Donald Davidson, "Deception and Division," in Elster, *Multiple Self*, 80–81.

9. For a psychological exploration of excuses, see C. R. Snyder, Raymond L. Higgins, and Rita J. Stucky, *Excuses: Masquerades in Search of Grace* (New York: Wiley, 1983).

10. G. A. Marlatt and J. R. Gordon, *Relapse Prevention: Maintenance Strategies In Addictive Behavior Change* (New York: Guilford Press, 1985).

11. Lifton, "Numbing and Derealization," in *Nazi Doctors*, 442–47.

12. R. D. Laing, *The Divided Self* (Baltimore: Penguin, 1973).

13. Lifton, "Doubling: The Faustian Bargain," in *Nazi Doctors*, 418–30.

14. E. R. Guthrie, *The Psychology of Learning* (New York: Harper & Row, 1938).

15. I have discussed the unity of the many-dimensioned self and the quest for integration and identity in chapter 2; see also Leon Festinger, *The Theory of Cognitive Dissonance* (Stanford CA: Stanford Univ. Press, 1957).

16. For a comprehensive philosophical discussion of the various forms of self-deception, see Mike W. Martin, *Self-Deception and Morality* (Lawrence: Univ. Press of Kansas, 1986); see also Herbert Fingarette, *Self-Deception* (Atlantic Highlands, NJ: Humanities Press, 1969); for a psychological approach, see Daniel Goleman, *Vital Lies, Simple Truths: The Psychology of Self-Deception* (New York: Simon and Schuster, 1985) and Harold A. Sackeim, "Self-Deception, Self-Esteem, and Depression: The Adaptive Value of Lying to Oneself," in *Empirical Studies of Psychoanalytical Theories*, vol. 1, ed. Joseph Masling (Hillsdale, NJ: Lawrence Erlbaum Associates, 1983), 101–57.

17. Erving Goffman, *Strategic Interaction* (New York: Ballantine, 1969).

18. Martin, *Self-Deception*, 6–30.

19. Martin, *Self-Deception*, 38.

20. Joseph Butler, *Fifteen Sermons* (New York: Robert Carter & Brothers, Facsimile Reprint, 1986), 122.

21. See Goleman, *Vital Lies*, 106–16.

22. Goleman, *Vital Lies*, 22.

23. Roy Shafer, "The Pursuit of Failure and the Idealization of Unhappiness," *American Psychologist*, vol. 39, no. 4 (April 1984): 398–405.

24. I have taken up the functioning of the mind in more detail in chapter 3; see Ulric Neisser, "Theories of Perception," in *Cognition and Reality: Principles and Implications of Cognitive Psychology* (New York: W. H. Freeman, 1976), 13–33.

25. Goleman, *Vital Lies*, 61–66.

26. Research on human error, biased thinking, and irrationality is discussed in Howard Gardner, "How Rational a Being?" in *The Mind's New Science: A History of the Cognitive Revolution* (New York: Basic Books, 1987), 360–80.

27. I have treated these psychological issues of self-consciousness, emotion, and thinking in previous chapters; see also David Pears, "The goals and strategies of self-deception," in Elster, *Multiple Self*, 59–77.

28. See Anna Freud, *The Ego and the Mechanisms of Defense* (New York: International Universities Press, 1966); a reinterpretation can be seen in Roy Shafer, "Danger Situations," *The Analytic Attitude* (New York: Basic Books, 1983), 96–112; see also a reinterpretation of psychological defense in Sackeim, "Self-Deception, Self-Esteem," 101–56. An interesting philosophical analysis of self-deceptive emotions can be seen in Ronald De Sousa, "Self-Deceptive Emotions," in Rorty, *Explaining Emotions*, 293–97.

29. See Paul Ekman, *Telling Lies* (New York: Berkley Books, 1985).

30. See Roy Shafer's discussion of self-deception in relation to resistance, "The Idea of Resistance," in *A New Language for Psychoanalysis* (New Haven: Yale Univ. Press, 1976), 213–63; for Shafer's account of the process, see Shafer, *Analytic Attitude*, 66–81.

31. See Erving Goffman, "On Face-Work: An Analysis of Ritual Elements in Social Interaction," in *Interpersonal Dynamics: Essays and Readings on Human Interaction*, ed. Warren G. Bennis, Edgar H. Schein, Fred I. Steele, and David E. Berlew (Homewood, IL: The Dorsey Press, 1968), 226–49.

32. Goffman, "On Face-Work."

33. See J. C. Flugel, "Overcoming and Evading the Super-Ego," *Man, Morals and Society: A Psycho-analytical Study* (New York: International Universities Press, 1945), 189–214.

34. See Jon Elster's description of the issue, "Introduction," in Elster, *Multiple Self*, 1–34.

35. Butler, *Sermons*, 117.

36. See Shelley Duval and Robert A. Wicklund, *A Theory of Objective Self-awareness* (New York: Academic Press, 1972); see also Milton Rokeach, *The Open and Closed Mind: Investigations Into The Nature of Belief Systems and Personality Systems* (New York: Basic Books, 1960). Cf. Eric Hoffer, *The True Believer* (New York: Harper, 1951).

37. See Goleman, *Vital Lies*, 241–43; see also Sackheim, "The Adaptive Value of Lying to Oneself," in "Self-Deception, Self-Esteem"; see also Martin, *Self-Deception*, 109–37.

38. See Ernest Becker, *The Denial of Death* (New York: Free Press, 1975).

39. A. Rosenblatt, J. Greenberg, et al., "Evidence for Terror Management Theory I: The Effects of Mortality Salience on Reactions to Those Who Violate or Uphold Cultural Values," in *Journal of Personality and Social Psychology*, 57 (November, 1989) 681–90.

40. Becker, *Denial of Death*; Cf. Daniel Callahan's analysis of a "science of limits," *The Tyranny of Survival: And Other Pathologies of Civilized Life* (New York: Macmillan Publishing, 1973), 249–62.

41. See Kenneth S. Pope and Jerome L. Singer on "Current Concerns, Unfinished business, and Unresolved stress" in "The Waking Stream of Consciousness," in *The Psychobiology of Consciousness*, ed. Julian M. Davidson and Richard J. Davidson (New York: Plenum Press, 1980), 178–79; see also Mardi Horowitz, "Psychological Response to Serious Life Events," in *The Denial of Stress*, ed. Shlomo Breznitz (New York: International Universities Press, 1983).

42. Goleman, *Vital Lies*.

43. M. Scott Peck, *The Road Less Travelled: A New Psychology of Love, Traditional Values and Spiritual Growth* (New York: Simon and Schuster, 1978), 44.

44. See Alan Donagan, "The Corruption of Consciousness," *The Theory of Morality* (Chicago: Univ. of Chicago Press, 1977), 138–42.

45. A summary of the psychoanalytic approach can be found in James Gilligan, "Beyond Morality: Psychoanalytic Reflections on Shame, Guilt, and Love," in *Moral Development And Behavior: Theory, Research, and Social Issues*, ed. Thomas Lickona (New York: Holt, Rinehart and Winston, 1976), 144–56; a general psychological approach to shame and guilt can be found in Carroll E. Izard, "Shame and Shyness," "Guilt, Conscience and Morality," in *Human Emotions* (New York: Plenum Press, 1977), 385–452; a philosophical treatment can be found in Gabriele Taylor, *Pride, Shame and Guilt: Emotions of Self-Assessment* (Oxford: Clarendon Press, 1985).

46. William James, *Principles of Psychology*, vol. 1 (New York: Dover Publications, 1950), 314–15.

47. See Gordon Allport, *Becoming* (New Haven: Yale Univ. Press, 1955), 85.

48. See Sharon S. Brehm and Jack W. Brehm, *Psychological Reactance: A Theory of Freedom and Control* (New York: Academic Press, 1981).

49. Sidney M. Jourard, *The Transparent Self: Self Disclosure and Well-Being* (Princeton, NJ: D. van Nostrand, 1964).

50. See Harry Frankfurt, "Identification and Wholeheartedness," in Schoeman, *Responsibility, Character,* 27–45.

51. Role-playing is analyzed in psychology in the development of altruism; see Martin Hoffman, "Empathy, Role Taking, Guilt, and Development of Altruistic Motives," in Likona, *Moral Development,* 124–43. Cf. the role of imagination in religious ethics as discussed in Phillip S. Keane, S.S., *Christian Ethics & Imagination* (New York: Paulist Press, 1984).

52. Ignatius Loyola, "Second Way of Making A Correct and Good Choice of a Way of Life," in *The Spiritual Exercises of St. Ignatius,* trans. Louis J. Puhl, S.J. (Chicago: Loyola Univ. Press, 1951), 76–77.

53. Loyola, "Second Way"; see also Viktor E. Frankl, "A Logodrama," in *Man's Search for Meaning: An Introduction to Logotherapy* (New York: Pocket Books, 1959, 1963), 184–86.

54. Butler, *Sermons,* 121.

Chapter 7. Moral Development:
The Birth and Growth of Conscience

1. Alexander Rosenberg, *Philosophy of Social Science* (Boulder, CO: Westview Press, 1988), 45.

2. James Rest takes up some of the problems of measuring moral development in James Rest, "New Approaches in the Assessment of Moral Judgment," in *Moral Development and Behavior: Theory, Research and Social Issues,* ed. Thomas Lickona (New York: Holt, Rinehart and Winston, 1976), 198–218; see also Norma Haan, Eliane Aerts, and Bruce A. B. Cooper, "Assessing Morality," in *On Moral Grounds: The Search for Practical Morality* (New York: New York Univ. Press, 1985), 92–103.

3. For the foundation of the cognitive developmental approach, see Jean Piaget, *The Moral Judgement of the Child* (New York: Harcourt Brace, 1932); for the major cognitive developmental theorist's statement, see Lawrence Kohlberg, "Moral Stages and Moralization: The Cognitive-Developmental Approach," in Lickona, *Moral Development,* 31–53. Cf. the more stringently cognitivist approach of Michael Scriven, "Cognitive Moral Education," *Moral Education . . . It Comes With The Territory,* ed. David Purpel and Kevin Ryan (Berkeley CA: A Phi Delta Kappa Publication, 1976), 313–29.

4. See Justin Aronfreed, *Conduct and Conscience: The Socialization of Internalized Control Over Behavior* (New York: Academic Press, 1968); see also Justin Aronfreed, "Moral Development from the Standpoint of a General Psychological Theory," in Lickona, *Moral Development,* 54–69. Another summary of the learning-behavioral point of view on moral development can be found in Robert M. Liebert, "What Develops in Moral Development?" in *Morality, Moral Behavior, and Moral Development,* ed. William M. Kurtines and Jacob L. Gewirtz (New York: John Wiley & Sons, 1984), 177–92.

5. Martin L. Hoffman, "Empathy, its development and prosocial implications," Nebraska Symposium on Motivation, vol. 25, ed. C. B. Keasey (Lincoln: Univ. of Nebraska Press, 1978), 169–218; see also Haan, Aerts, and Cooper, *On Moral Grounds;* Cf. Robert Coles, *The Moral Life of Children* (New York: Atlantic Monthly Press, 1986).

6. James Gilligan, "Beyond Morality: Psychoanalytic Reflections on Shame, Guilt, and Love," in Lickona, *Moral Development,* 144–58; other examples can be found, such as Peter Blos, "Character Formation in Adolescence," in *The Psychoanalytic Study of the Child* 23 (New York: International Universities Press, 1968), 245–63. It should also be remembered that the popular works of Erik Erikson and Bruno Bettelheim on development of values are mainstreaming a modified Freudian theory; see Erik H. Erikson, *Insight and Responsibility* (New York: W. W. Norton, 1964); see, for instance,

Bruno Bettelheim, *The Uses of Enchantment: The Meaning and Importance of Fairy Tales* (New York: Alfred A. Knopf, 1977).

7. Many such approaches are based upon the work of John W. Whiting and Irving L. Child, *Child Training and Personality: A Cross-cultural Study* (New Haven: Yale Univ. Press, 1953); for a summary of this approach, see James Garbarino and Urie Bronfenbrenner, "The Socialization of Moral Judgement and Behavior in Cross-Cultural Perspective," in Lickona, *Moral Development*, 70–83; for a more general approach, see Barbara Rogoff and Gilda Morelli, "Perspectives on Children's Development From Cultural Psychology," *American Psychologist*, vol. 44, no. 2, (February 1989): 343–48.

8. In chapter 2, I have addressed the question of the unity and integration of the self; the controversy over whether traits exist across situations is a subset of these arguments; for a discussion in the context of the moral development debate, see John C. Gibbs and Steven V. Schnell, "Moral Development 'Versus' Socialization, A Critique," *American Psychologist*, vol. 40, no. 10 (October 1985): 1071–80.

9. See Walter Mischel and Harriet N. Mischel, "A Cognitive Social-Learning Approach to Morality and Self-Regulation," in Lickona, *Moral Development*, 84–107.

10. The case for panhuman and innate reasoning and emotional developments is discussed in chapters 2 and 3; the universality of the self, albeit with cultural variations, can be seen in Vytautas Kavolis, "On the Self-Person Differentiation: Universal Categories of Civilization and Their Diverse Contents," in *Designs of Selfhood*, ed. Vytautas Kavolis (Cranbury, NJ: Associated Univ. Presses, 1984), 132–53. Cf. Drew Westen who recognizes the universal use of "I" and "me" in all languages, but stresses the different boundaries the self can have in different cultures, *Self & Society: Narcissism, Collectivism, and Development of Morals* (Cambridge: Cambridge Univ. Press, 1985), 251–54.

11. Jerome Kagan, *The Nature of the Child* (New York: Basic Books, 1984), 152.

12. Carroll E. Izard, "Perhaps all of the emotions play some part, directly or indirectly, in the development of conscience and morality," *Human Emotion* (New York: Plenum Press, 1977), 421.

13. Kagan, *Nature of the Child*, 119.

14. James R. Rest et al., "Different Cultures, Sexes, and Religions," in James R. Rest, *Moral Development: Advances in Research and Theory* (New York: Praeger, 1986), 110.

15. Rest et al., "Different Cultures," 91.

16. Rest et al., "Different Cultures." See also Uwe P. Gielen, "Some Themes in the Ethos of Traditional Buddhist Ladakh," *Acta Biologica Montana* 5:235–46.

17. Howard Gardner, *Frames of Mind: The Theory of Multiple Intelligences* (New York: Basic Books, 1983).

18. Gardner, *Frames*, 59–70.

19. Gardner, *Frames*, 239.

20. Gardner, *Frames*.

21. See E. O. Wilson, *On Human Nature* (Cambridge: Harvard Univ. Press, 1978). For a description and critique of sociobiology and its claims on morality, see Owen J. Flanagan, Jr., "Minds, Genes, and Morals: The Case of E. O. Wilson's Sociobiology," *The Science of the Mind* (Cambridge, MA: The MIT Press, 1984), 249–90.

22. Wilson, *On Human Nature*; see also Robert L. Trivers, "The Evolution of Reciprocal Altruism," *Quarterly Review of Biology* 46: 35–57.

23. A summary of the Jungian and transpersonal views of consciousness can be seen in Ken Wilber, "Psychologica Perennis: The Spectrum of Consciousness," in *The Meeting of the Ways: Explorations in East/West Psychology*, ed. John Welwood (New York: Schocken Books, 1979), 7–28.

24. See Erik H. Erikson, *Childhood and Society*, 2d ed. (New York: Norton, 1963); see also P.B. Galtes, H. W. Reese, and L. Lipsitt, "Lifespan Developmental Psychology," *An-*

nual Review of Psychology 31:65–110. See also Daniel Levinson, "A Conception of Adult Development," *American Psychologist* 41 (1986): 3–13.

25. Gilligan, "Beyond Morality," 144.

26. See note 3; see also Lawrence Kohlberg's later formulation, Anne Colby and Lawrence Kohlberg, "Invariant Sequence and Internal Consistency in Moral Judgment Stages," in Kurtines and Gewirtz, *Morality*, 41–51.

27. Colby and Kohlberg, "Invariant Sequence," 41.

28. James R. Rest, in his four component model of moral action—interpreting of a situation, figuring out what one ought to do, choosing among moral and nonmoral values, and executing or implementing what one intends—puts first the need "to interpret the situation in terms of how one's actions affect the welfare of others"— James R. Rest, "The Major Components of Morality," in Kurtines and Gewirtz, *Morality*, 27.

29. For a statement of the constituent and activating force of internal dialogue, see Rom Harré, "The Self in Monodrama," in *The Self: Psychological and Philosophical Issues*, ed. Theodore Mischel (Totowa, NJ: Rowman and Littlefield, 1977); for further development of Harré's ideas on personal psychology, see Rom Harré, *Personal Being: A Theory for Individual Psychology* (Cambridge: Harvard Univ. Press, 1984).

30. In Kohlberg's last published reflections on his highest stage of moral reasoning, he emphasizes that the moral point of view implies a respect for persons that includes both justice and active benevolent attitudes toward others. See Lawrence Kohlberg, Dwight R. Boyd, and Charles Levine, "The Return of Stage 6: Its Principle and Moral Point of View," in *The Moral Domain: Essays in the Ongoing Discussion between Philosophy and the Social Sciences*, ed. Thomas E. Wren (Cambridge, MA: The MIT Press, 1990).

31. Martin L. Hoffman, "Empathy, Its Limitations, and Its Role in a Comprehensive Moral Theory," in Kurtines and Gewirtz, *Morality*, 283–302.

32. Herbert D. Saltzstein, "Social Influence and Moral Development: A Perspective on the Role of Parents and Peers," in Lickona, *Moral Development*, 253–65.

33. Haan, Aerts, and Cooper, *On Moral Grounds*.

34. Haan, Aerts, and Cooper, *On Moral Grounds*, 300.

35. Martin Hoffman discusses "existential guilt," in "Empathy, Role Taking, Guilt and Development of Altruistic Motives," in Lickona, *Moral Development*, 124–43; for a philosophical discussion of these same issues, see Herbert Morris, "Nonmoral guilt," in *Responsibility, Character, and the Emotions: New Essays in Moral Psychology*, ed. Ferdinand Schoeman (Cambridge: Cambridge Univ. Press, 1987), 220–40.

36. Abraham Maslow, *The Farther Reaches of Human Nature* (New York: Viking, 1971); see also Mihaly Csikszentmihalyi, "Towards a Psychology of Optimal Experience," in *Review of Personality and Social Psychology*, vol 2., ed. L. Wheeler (Beverly Hills, CA: Sage, 1982).

37. Alice Miller, *For Your Own Good: Hidden Cruelty in Childrearing and the Roots of Violence* (New York: Farrar, Straus and Giroux, 1984).

38. Many theorists of moral development, outside the psychoanalytic Eriksonian tradition, have seen moral identity as embedded in the general development of self identity, and the self's interpretation of self; for instance, see Robert Hogan and Catherine Busch, "Moral Action as Autointerpretation," in Kurtines and Gewirtz, *Morality*, 227–40; see also Augusto Blasi, "Moral Identity: Its Role in Moral Functioning," in Kurtines and Gewirtz, *Morality*, 128–39.

39. See William Damon and Daniel Hart, *Self-Understanding in Childhood and Adolescence* (Cambridge: Cambridge Univ. Press, 1988).

40. Damon and Hart, *Self-Understanding*, 132.

41. Genetic factors have been seen in moral socialization, as for instance in Hans J. Eysenck, "The Biology of Morality," in Lickona, *Moral Development*, 108–23; another

approach is exemplified by Sarnoff A. Mednick, William F. Gabrielli, Jr., and Barry Hutchings, "Genetic Influences in Criminal Convictions: Evidence from an Adoption Cohort," *Science*, vol.224 (25 May 1984): 891–94. A psychological overview can be found in Robert Plomin, "Environment and Genes: Determinants of Behavior," *American Psychologist*, vol. 44, no.2 (February 1989): 105–11. A biological anthropologist has also tackled the difficult, tangled, complex issues of nature-nurture interactions in Melvin Konner, *The Tangled Wing: Biological Constraints on The Human Spirit* (New York: Harper & Row, 1982).

42. Jerome Kagan sums up his decades of research on temperament and child development in Kagan, *Nature of the Child*.

43. Daniel N. Stern, *The Interpersonal World of The Infant* (New York: Basic Books, 1985).

44. Gordon Allport, *Becoming* (New Haven: Yale Univ. Press, 1955), 68–74.

45. Roy Shafer, "Resisting Maternal Authority," *A New Language for Psychoanalysis* (New Haven: Yale Univ. Press, 1976), 245–54.

46. Eli Sagan, *Freud, Women, and Morality: The Psychology of Good and Evil* (New York: Basic Books, 1988).

47. Sagan, *Freud, Women*, 160.

48. Sagan, *Freud, Women*, 185.

49. See Carol Gilligan, *In a Different Voice: Psychological Theory and Women's Development* (Cambridge: Harvard Univ. Press, 1982).

50. Mary Field Belenky et al., *Women's Ways of Knowing: The Development of Self, Voice and Mind* (New York: Basic Books, 1986).

51. A summary of feminist arguments for a different psychological style of functioning can be found in Catherine Keller, *From A Broken Web: Separation, Sexism, and Self* (Boston: Beacon Press, 1986); see also a galaxy of articles accompanied by a feminist-oriented "Selected Bibliography On Western Philosophical Conceptions of Reason, Rationality and Gender," compiled by Karen J. Warren and found in *American Philosophical Association Newsletter on Feminism and Philosophy*, ed. Nancy Tuana, no. 88 (2 March 1989): 53–58.

52. These arguments are defended by Keller, who, along with many feminists, follows the revised psychoanalytic model proposed by Nancy Chodorow, *The Reproduction of Mothering: Psychoanalysis and the Sociology of Gender* (Berkeley: Univ. of California Press, 1978).

53. Rest, *Moral Development*, 111–18; for a discussion of how popular beliefs in a different feminine morality can continue despite the evidence, see Martha T. Mednick, "On the Politics of Psychological Constructs: Stop the Bandwagon, I Want to Get Off," *American Psychologist*, vol. 44, no.8 (August 1989): 1118–23.

54. Sandra Harding, "The Curious Coincidence of Feminine and African Moralities: Challenges for Feminist Theory," *Women and Moral Theory*, ed. Eva Feder Kittay and Diana T. Meyers (Totowa, NJ.: Rowman & Littlefield, 1987), 296–315.

55. Stern, *Interpersonal World of the Infant*; for an overview of the complex, goal-organized activities of infants, see Edward Z. Tronick, "Emotions and Emotional Communication in Infants," *American Psychologist*, vol. 44, no.2 (February 1989): 112–19.

56. See for instance Owen Flanagan and Kathryn Jackson, "Justice, Care, and Gender: The Kohlberg-Gilligan Debate Revisited," *Ethics* (April 1987): 622–37. See also Susan Moller Okin, "Reason and Feeling in Thinking about Justice," *Ethics* 99 (January 1989): 229–49.

57. Jean Baker Miller, *Toward a New Psychology for Women* (Boston: Beacon Press, 1973).

58. Sara Ruddick, "Maternal Thinking," *Mothering: Essays in Feminist Theory*, ed. Joyce Trebilcot (Totowa, NJ: Rowman & Allanheld, 1984), 213–30.

Chapter 8.   Nurturing Conscience

1. Bryan Kolb, "Brain Development, Plasticity, and Behavior," *American Psychologist* (September 1989): 1204.
2. Christopher Lasch, *The Minimal Self: Psychic Survival in Troubled Times* (New York: W. W. Norton, 1984).
3. See Alan E. Kazdin, "Developmental Psychopathology: Current Research, Issues and Directions," *American Psychologist*, vol. 44, no. 2 (February 1989): 180–87; in this special issue of *American Psychologist* devoted to children and their development, see G. R. Patterson, Barbara D. DeBaryshe, and Elizabeth Ramsey, "A Developmental Perspective on Antisocial Behavior," 329–35, for an analysis of how ineffective parenting sets the stage for later failures and deviant behaviors.
4. Joseph Butler, *Fifteen Sermons* (New York: Robert Carter & Brothers, Facsimile Reprint, 1986), 29.
5. For a description of critical social science's approach to society's hidden agendas and resistance to change in the power structure, see David Braybrooke, *Philosophy of Social Science* (Englewood Cliffs, NJ: Prentice-Hall, 1987), 68–91.
6. See a perceptive discussion by psychologist Paul L. Wachtel, *The Poverty of Affluence: A Psychological Analysis of Life in the Consumer Society* (New York: Free Press, 1983).
7. "Gossip, then, is a means of social control in that it allows individuals to express, articulate and commit themselves to a moral position in the act of talking about someone publicly. Thus it is a way we come to know what our own evaluations really are"—p.105 in John Sabini and Maury Silver, "A Plea for Gossip," in *Moralities of Everyday Life* (Oxford: Oxford Univ. Press, 1982), 89–106.
8. Rom Harré, *Social Being: A Theory for Social Psychology* (Totowa, NJ: Littlefield, Adams, 1980).
9. Harré, *Social Being*, 31,33.
10. Alasdair MacIntyre, *After Virtue* (Notre Dame, IN: Univ. of Notre Dame Press, 1981).
11. MacIntyre, *After Virtue*, 190–209.
12. Quoted in Bertram Wyatt-Brown, *Southern Honor: Ethics and Behavior in the Old South* (Oxford: Oxford Univ. Press, 1982), 99.
13. Wyatt-Brown, *Southern Honor*.
14. For a discussion of the hidden or unstudied curriculum in moral education, see Lawrence Kohlberg, "The Moral Atmosphere of the School," in *Moral Education . . . It Comes With The Territory*, ed. David Purpel and Kevin Ryan (Berkeley, CA: McCutchan, 1976), 196–220; see also Seymour B. Sarason, *The Culture of the School and the Problem of Change* (Boston: Allyn and Bacon, 1971); another perceptive study of how the moral education of children is influenced by the community, the teachers, and the schools can be found in Betty A. Sichel, *Moral Education: Character, Community, and Ideals* (Philadelphia: Temple Univ. Press, 1988).
15. Robert K. Fullinwider, "Moral Conventions and Moral Lessons," *Social Theory and Practice: An International and Interdisciplinary Journal of Social Philosophy*, vol. 15, no. 3 (Fall 1989): 324.
16. Fullinwider, "Moral Conventions."
17. David Tracy, *Blessed Rage for Order: The New Pluralism in Theology* (San Francisco: Harper & Row, 1988), 207.
18. See Paul C. Vitz, "The Uses of Stories in Moral Development: New Psychological Reasons for an Old Education Method," *American Psychologist*, vol. 45, no. 6: 709–20.
19. See Theodore R. Sarbin, "The Narrative as Root Metaphor for Psychology," in *Narrative Psychology: The Storied Nature of Human Conduct*, ed. T. R. Sarbin (New York:

Praeger, 1986). A collection of papers discussing the importance of narrative in theology and ethics can be found in Stanley Hauerwas and L. Gregory Jones, *Why Narrative?: Readings in Narrative Theology* (Grand Rapids, MI: William B. Eerdmans, 1989); see in particular Stanley Hauerwas and David Burrell, "From System to Story: An Alternative Pattern for Rationality in Ethics," 158–90.

20. See Vitz, "Uses of Stories"; see also Gordon H. Bower and Daniel G. Morrow, "Mental Models in Narrative Comprehension," *Science,* vol. 247: 44–48; also pertinent is Jean Matter Mandler, *Stories, Scripts, and Scenes: Aspects of Schema Theory* (Hillsdale, NJ.: Lawrence Erlbaum, 1984).

21. Iris Murdoch speaks of how "an overt action can release psychic energies which can be released in no other way. We often receive an unforeseen reward for a fumbling half-hearted act: a place for the idea of grace," Iris Murdoch, *The Sovereignty of Good* (London: Routledge & Kegan Paul, 1970, Ark Edition 1985), 43.

22. Peter J. Wilson, *Man: The Promising Primate: The Conditions of Human Evolution* (New Haven: Yale Univ. Press, 1980). .

23. Margaret A. Farley, *Personal Commitments: Making, Keeping, Breaking* (San Francisco: Harper & Row, 1985).

24. C. D. Broad, "Conscience and Conscientious Action," *Conscience,* ed. John Donnelly and Leonard Lyons (Staten Island, NY: Alba House, 1973), 22.

25. William James, *The Principles of Psychology,* vol. I (New York: Dover Publications, 1950), 315.

26. James, *Principles.*

Index